own Church. E. the Abby Church. F. the Tower. G. St Marys Chappel.   E. Kirkall scul:
Monks Lodgings. N. the Almery.

GLASTONBURY ABBEY

The Holy House
at the head of the Moors Adventurous

GLASTONBURY ABBEY

*The Holy House
at the head of
the Moors Adventurous*

James P. Carley

St. Martin's Press, New York

For Aelred and for Ralegh

© James P. Carley 1988

All rights reserved. For information, write:
Scholarly and Reference Division,
St. Martin's Press, Inc., 175 Fifth Avenue, New York, NY 10010

First published in the United States of America in 1988

Printed in GREAT BRITAIN

ISBN 0-312-02116-X

Library of Congress Cataloging-in-Publication Data
Carley, James P.
  Glastonbury Abbey : the holy house at the head of the moors
adventurous / James P. Carley.
    p.   cm.
  Includes index.
  ISBN 0-312-02116-X
  1. Glastonbury Abbey – History. 2. Glastonbury (Somerset) – Church
history. 3. Glastonbury (Somerset) – Antiquities. 4. England –
Antiquities. I. Title.
DA690.G45C37   1988
942.3'83–dc19   88-10196
                            CIP

Printed and bound in Great Britain by
The Camelot Press PLC, Southampton

Contents

Modern well cover at Chalice Well. Designed by F. Bligh Bond in the form of a vesica piscis. Bond believed that this mystical symbol was the basis for a hidden pattern underlying the design of Glastonbury Abbey.

PREFACE

One of the best known of children's fables concerns the emperor's new clothes. As the story is usually related, a slick charlatan persuades the gullible emperor that for a substantial fee he can create the most beautiful outfit imaginable for him, the fabric of which is magical and invisible to anyone unfit for the position he holds. After much palaver and elaborate preparation on the part of the soi-disant tailor the emperor sallies forth to show the costume to his people, who in turn unite in expressing the most effusive admiration for the garb. Suddenly the illusion is broken, however, by the shrill voice of a little child who points out that the emperor has nothing on.

The moral of this tale seems relatively obvious: the emperor is punished for his naive vanity and ostentatious pride, the fawning obsequiousness of the crowd is ridiculed and the young child, of course, emerges as a hero. As I begin to write a history of Glastonbury Abbey – a monastery which has itself been called a forgery factory by sober nineteenth-century historians and which has been harshly dealt with in another children's tale, the one in which Jack Horner's plum is nothing less than the deed to one of the abbey estates – I should like to propose an alternative reading of the fable of the emperor's new clothes. Do clothes have to exist in the nominalist sense to be real? The emperor saw garments which gave him delight and which no doubt warmed him too. What more can one ask from clothing? How do we know, moreover, that his courtiers did not also share in his pleasure and thus see the 'real' clothes? Perhaps the child, rather than being heroically honest, was needlessly destructive, reducing what John Cowper Powys has called the essential human 'life illusion' to a pathetic sham. Does his success in destruction make his judgement admirable, or even correct? Myself, I hope the wretched child was severely punished for interference and insubordination.

If that same little nuisance were to accompany his parents to Glastonbury today he would certainly know what to say and would query the fuss which the place seems to generate. From a purely rational point of view, Glastonbury is nothing more

The Holy Grail.
*Alabaster statue by
Katherine E. Maltwood.*

than a small and not particularly beautiful town, parts of which have an attractive view over moors which sometimes in misty weather can eerily resemble lakes. The architectural features of the town are undistinguished and not many medieval buildings still stand. The Tor, the most unusual feature in the landscape, is distinctive, but not geographically unparalleled in the region. The surviving monastic ruins are few, and it is hard to imagine that one of the largest and most ornate churches in England once stood on the site. And, *pace* William Blake, the trip from the Holy Land would have been a long one in the first century, one which even flooded moors and navigable rivers would not have made especially practicable.

One of the perpetual miracles of Glastonbury is that more people do not react like our imaginary child; on the contrary, many visitors, young or old, pious or sceptical, consider it among the holiest sites in Britain, perhaps even one of the chief sacred places in the world. 'There are only about a dozen reservoirs of world magic on the whole surface of the globe,' says the hero of John Cowper Powys' *A Glastonbury Romance*, 'Jerusalem ... Rome ... Mecca ... Lhassa – and of these Glastonbury has the largest residue of unused power. Generations of mankind, aeons of past races, have – by their concentrated will – made Glastonbury miraculous.' In spite of its lack of surface appeal, then, Glastonbury emanates to a remarkable degree a sense of mystery and power; there is an overwhelming *genius loci*, so much greater than mere physical circumstances would warrant. And because there is no longer any real, or at least tangible physical correlative on which to pin the transcendent atmosphere which Glastonbury generates, mysteries tend to be invented, the numinous demystified and made specific by an appeal to hidden structures anciently imposed on the landscape. The formless, in other words, is made formal. And to return to my initial fable: it seems to me that those who can trace Joseph of Arimathea's footsteps on Wearyall Hill or detect the Holy Blood in the reddish tinge of the water flowing from Chalice Well are the fortunate ones; they are the emperors of the Glastonbury kingdom.

Every pilgrim worthy of his scrip, too, returns from Glastonbury with his own small miracle, his own private myth of the place. Let me give some personal examples, the witnesses to which range from the gullible believer to the hardened agnostic. When I made my first visit to Glastonbury in 1969 I had come from Victoria, B.C., Canada, where I had just spent a rather heady time at the Maltwood Museum, cataloguing the Glastonbury/Zodiac papers contained in Katherine E. Maltwood's ancient Bible box.[1] The papers had been wrapped in a black velvet case which was heavily sealed and the following note attached:

> Discovery of the Signs of the Zodiac in Somerset, England, laid out on the ground near Glastonbury. This collection of maps and books must be kept safe. It will be of the greatest value someday. If anything is taken out of the black case, it must be put back, because the collection is complete as it is.

Glastonbury for me, therefore, represented what Tibet did for some of my more exotic friends. The last stages of my pilgrimage, from London onwards, were made by thumb. Just past Heathrow I was picked up by a pleasant motorist of about my own age who lived in Bath. It was already early evening when we got to Bath and he generously volunteered to drive me the rest of the way. When we arrived at Glastonbury I thanked him profusely and got out of the car. Just as I set foot on the High Street the clouds opened and the evening sun shone forth in three lines of light, the shape of the unutterable name of God and the mystical reconciling symbol at the centre of Mrs Maltwood's zodiac. Immediately afterwards, as I stared in delighted wonder, an ancient woman threw her arms around me and greeted me as Bors. As I tried to correct her in my most prim manner she interrupted and assured me that Bors was my real name, that I was one of King Arthur's knights, re-incarnated (most peculiarly, it seemed to me) as a quite ordinary young man from Victoria, that most provincial of Canadian towns. Needless to say, I was hooked and have never looked back.

My second story concerns the Holy Thorn. Recently I had dinner with an eminent Cambridge don, one whose own roots, however, lie in New England. Talk turned to my work on Glastonbury and my friend related the following tale with utmost seriousness. She first came to England when she was in her early twenties and went to visit Glastonbury because her church at home was dedicated to St Joseph of Arimathea. When she saw the Holy Thorn in the Abbey grounds she remembered that her vicar had often wished to have a shoot. There was nobody around and so she fetched out her Swiss Army knife, got to work and soon returned to her hotel room with a fine healthy cutting. This she wrapped carefully in tissue

Christmas Stamps, 1986. Stamp depicting Glastonbury Thorn.

[1] During the course of preparing illustrations for a re-issue of Sebastian Evans' translation of the medieval French romance *Perlesvaus* – itself often associated with Glastonbury/Avalon – Mrs Maltwood observed a variety of strange configurations in the landscape and came to the conclusion that these represented the remains of a giant zodiac, centred at Butleigh. In her scheme Wearyall Hill, for example, forms Pisces and the Tor constitutes Aquarius in the shape of a giant Phoenix.

and stowed safely in her suitcase. Next morning, when she opened the bag, it was gone and she could find no trace. Not a superstitious person or given to flights of fancy, my friend swears to the truth of the episode, which has made a lasting impression on her.

In 1984 my wife and I came to Glastonbury on the last weekend of June and took part in the annual Anglican pilgrimage. A friend accompanied us: she was almost 85 at the time and is a woman whose life has been devoted to pragmatic enterprises, one for whom religion has no appeal. As we walked around the site in the late afternoon after the other pilgrims had left, our friend became more and more tired and dazed by the sun. Just to the south west of the ruins she stopped, caught her breath and spontaneously announced 'this is a holy place', the first time, I am sure, that such language ever passed her lips. Not long afterwards I related the story to Dom Aelred Watkin, the titular abbot of Glastonbury, who asked me where we had been standing at the time. When I told him he said in the most matter-of-fact manner, 'Oh yes, near St Dunstan's Chapel. It often takes them that way.'

In spite of my fascination with the topic, however, the book which I have written is not about the modern Avalon of the heart which so many pilgrims have discovered. Nor have I dealt with the literary and musical festivals which took place earlier in this century and which might well have led to the creation of an English Bayreuth or Oberammergau; their mood is thoroughly evoked in *A Glastonbury Romance* and their history has been chronicled by Geoffrey Ashe in his *Avalonian Quest*. My own scholarly career began with a master's thesis on Joseph of Arimathea which was followed by a Ph.D. dissertation on John of Glastonbury's *Cronica sive Antiquitates Glastoniensis Ecclesie*. In his preface, written over five hundred years ago when the fortunes of Glastonbury Abbey were at a zenith and when the future seemed to stretch forward in an unbroken continuity until the Day of Judgement, John outlined his method and goals: 'I have collected materials for this work from diverse books, from legends of the saints as well as from other writings in ancient books, for it is easier to find things quickly which have been rearranged in one small book than to search in many different ones.' In spite of all the vagaries of time and fortune my basic criteria are the same as his.

Much has been written over the centuries about Glastonbury from radically different perspectives: the historical, the literary, the ecclesiastical, the occult. In my account I have aimed at providing some sort of synthesis. Often, too, I have paraphrased the medieval texts rather than attempting to impose my own critical judgements. My scholarly expertise is as a medievalist, it is true, but my passion is for the stories themselves. Elsewhere I have placed Glastonbury in a wider historiographical context: here I am trying to recreate its history as the monks themselves imagined it. The sources for this book are many and the main references are listed at the appropriate spots; the notes are by no means comprehensive, nevertheless, and for a more scholarly apparatus I refer the interested reader to my edition of John of Glastonbury's chronicle. For my basic historical framework I rely most heavily on three texts: William of Malmesbury's *The Early History of Glastonbury*, written in the late-1120s; Adam of Damerham's *History of Glastonbury*, c.1290; and John of Glastonbury's *The Chronicle of Glastonbury*, probably composed shortly after 1340. William, a monk of Malmesbury Abbey, was invited by the Glastonbury community to inspect the archives and to compose a history of the monastery. He analysed his sources carefully and put together a comprehensive account from earliest times up to the post Conquest era. His use of charter material was masterful and his judgements concerning historical matters sound. Over 150 years later Adam of Damerham, himself a Glastonbury monk, provided a supplement to William in which he gave, among other things, a dramatic account of the ongoing Glastonbury disputes with Wells and of Edward I's royal visit to Glastonbury in 1278, when Arthur's bones were deposited in a place of great honour in front of the High Altar. The third important Glastonbury chronicler is the monk John, whom I have tentatively identified as John Seen, a man well known at Oxford and elsewhere as an authoritative historical writer.[2] John recapitulated and revised material in William and Adam and also continued the account up to 1342. Fortunately, too, one of the later manuscripts of his chronicle contains a further summary by the monk William Wyche up to the year 1493.[3]

Glastonbury has dominated my thinking and my professional career for my whole adult life. Jessie Weston's book, *From Ritual to Romance*, first started me on my quest and I continue to consider it one of the most exciting books about the Grail. Since I left Victoria and the Maltwood Museum I have spent time in Zurich and have learned much from Marie-Louise von Franz and the perspectives she developed in her

---

[2] See my 'An Identification of John of Glastonbury and a New Dating of His Chronicle', *Mediaeval Studies* 40 (1978), 478–83. It should be noted, however, that no less an authority than Antonia Gransden disputes my dating and holds firmly to the traditional date of 1400.

[3] Printed by Thomas Hearne in his edition of *Johannis ... Glastoniensis, Chronica sive Historia de Rebus Glastoniensibus*, 2 vols. (Oxford, 1726), 1. 272–83.

psychological studies of the Grail legend.[4] Mary Williams opened up the world of Welsh romances to me and guided me in the direction of the academic groves. As a Ph.D. student I profited from the supervision of George Rigg, whose own book *A Glastonbury Miscellany of the Fifteenth Century* provided the model of erudition and careful research which I have since tried to emulate. Geoffrey Ashe's *The Quest for Arthur's Britain* showed me the value of the interdisciplinary approach. Dom Aelred Watkin has been a source both of information and creative thinking, a guide and a friend. I have been most fortunate to know C. A. Ralegh Radford and to have spent instructive and enjoyable days examining the site with him; he has also advised me on all matters archaeological, on which he is an unparalleled authority. Robert Dunning, Hazel Hudson and Frances Neale have made it possible for me, not a native of the region, to deal with the twelve hides and problems of historical topography. Without their aid there would have been many geographical blunders. Neill Bonham provided me with information about antiquarian sketches of the ruins and Chris Black helped me find local authorities on specific details. Lisa Goldberg worked with me on the compilation of the index and checked various other items. Richard Barber suggested that I write this book. He has encouraged me at every stage and has given guidance both on minor and major issues. My mentor for many years has been Valerie M. Lagorio, a fine and imaginative Arthurian scholar, one whose articles on the evolution of the Joseph of Arimathea legend must be regarded as definitive. More importantly, Professor Lagorio has taught me by her own example that ordinary life and scholarship cannot be divided from one another and put into separate compartments.

When Michael Lapidge, that most rigorous of scholars, kindly went over a draft of my text he ironically added a subtitle in red – *A Fabulous History* – and pointed out, in particular, that any consecutive narrative history of the early abbots is based on wishful thinking, since no authoritative list exists for the pre-conquest period. There is almost no hard evidence, moreover, to substantiate the accounts found in my chapter on Glastonbury saints. In this sense, then, *Glastonbury Abbey* can be labelled fabulous rather than factual. It is also fabulous, however, because like all fables the Glastonbury stories contain grains of profound truth even if they are inaccurate historically; they are exemplary tales, ones which portray a past as it should have been. Finally, the early history

---

[4] See Emma Jung and Marie-Louise von Franz, *The Grail Legends*, trans. Andrea Dykes (London, 1972).

of Glastonbury is fabulous in the colloquial use of the word: it is a gripping narrative, full of excitement and drama.

Many people have read sections of my manuscript at varying stages of completeness and have given me advice: Lesley Abrams, Geoffrey Ashe, Paul Ashdown, Pamela Blanpied, David Dumville, Robert Dunning, Ann Hutchison, Michael Lapidge, Ralegh Radford, Philip Rahtz, Aelred Watkin, and Charles Wood. This book has, I know, many lacunae, but the time has come for such a book even in imperfect form. The gaps and errors arise from my own limitations; many of the virtues come from the experts with whom I have been privileged to consult.

Butleigh, Somerset
August 15, 1987

A reconstruction of the Glastonbury Lake Village. Drawn by R. Walker.

INTRODUCTION

Although Glastonbury Abbey forms the principal focus of this book, the monastery did not, and could not, exist in a vacuum. Nor in absolute terms has its rise and fall represented more than a small fragment of the span of human habitation of the region. At various points in prehistory, depending on the relative current levels of sea and land, the Bristol Channel must have been much more extensive than it is now and the central part of Somerset would have been covered by sea and swamp. Even so, as the archaeologists are discovering, the area seems to have supported human communities in prehistoric times, and great concentrations of important neolithic finds come from the Levels.

Archaeologists have found a variety of fragments from very ancient times, but the most significant discovery is the so-called Sweet Track linking the slopes of the Polden Hills with the island of Westhay. This is an ingenious raised plank walkway of over 1,500 metres into the swamp whose elaborateness indicates a permanent community with complex skills and significant manpower available. The number of artefacts dropped beside the Sweet Track – pottery vessels, tools, knives, arrowheads and so forth – suggest that once built it was also well used. The Sweet Track is the oldest trackway discovered so far, dating back to 4,000 B.C., but it is not unique: many similar structures dating from 3,000 B.C. to 700 B.C. – such as the Abbot's Way between Burtle and Westhay – have turned up in the bogs. What all these remains indicate is that the marshlands were being regularly used by our prehistoric ancestors, who themselves were living on higher ground.[1]

As the Somerset Levels evolved from estuary to swamp to raised bog, so too did the human habitations establish themselves on the emerging hills and islands. By the third or second

---

[1] An exciting book on the topic of prehistory in the Somerset Levels has recently been written by Bryony and John Coles, who have excavated in the area for over twenty years: *Sweet Track to Glastonbury. The Somerset Levels in Prehistory* (Frome and London, 1986).

century B.C. each region seems to have been dominated by a single hillfort, which acted as a central place in terms of defence, markets and administration. In other words a distinct territoriality had developed. Around Glastonbury itself there are also two examples of the second kind of Iron Age community, that is the raised island surrounded and protected by water: these are the Glastonbury Lake Village and the settlement at Meare. At the former there were probably about five to seven groups of houses as well as sheds and barns; a palisade encircled the whole settlement, which would never have had a population of over 100 people. Much of the food for the community would have come from farming, but the inhabitants also gathered wild plants, such as elder, black-berries and apple. The bogs were used as hunting areas and there would have been an abundance of fish in the surrounding pools. The Lake Villagers thatched their buildings with reed, made baskets from withies and used coppiced hazel for fencing and walls. They were skilled craftsmen in bronze, iron and glass, as their beautiful mirrors, bracelets, rings and brooches in the late Celtic style make obvious. The Meare Village, on the other hand, seems to have been a seasonal site and was probably occupied only during annual summer gatherings from all around the region for trade and barter.

Some scholars, perhaps the most distinguished of whom is Margaret Deanesly, have speculated that Christianity could have been brought independently of the Roman occupation to some of the La Tène Celts lodged in the hill- and island-settlements. Deanesly pointed out that even before Julius Caesar raided Britain in 55 and 54 B.C. there was a Mediterranean trade route by way of the Severn mouth. The chief port in this system could have been at Glastonbury, situated at the head of the Old Rhyne. Glastonbury was, moreover, a focal point of the trackways linking the Midlands, Wiltshire and Somerset, and near to important lead and tin workings. Glastonbury would, then, be a natural location for the dissemination of Christianity when it first arrived from the Mediterranean area. Deanesly noted, moreover, that

> it is strange that early medieval tradition in Britain should have asserted that the church of Glastonbury was the oldest in the land, when the men who made the tradition were without any predilection for a western origin, without the evidence of Glastonbury's economic and cultural importance available to modern archaeologists, and without the pointer that Glaston-bury and the Severn mouth were indeed the places where a trade-borne Christianity was likely to have arrived in the second or even the first century.[2]

[2] *The Pre-Conquest Church in England* (London, 1961), pp. 13–14. In a thesis

No subsequent archaeological evidence, alas, has turned up either to support or confute Deanesly's speculations, which must therefore remain entirely hypothetical.

Nowadays, many archaeologists suggest that the major colonization of Britain by the Romans beginning around A.D. 43 was not as disruptive an influence as historians once thought.[3] In Somerset the economic cycle of the Iron Age villages probably carried on in an uninterrupted pattern even after the appearance of the Fosse Way and the concerted exploitation of the silver and tin mines in the Mendips. The local Romano-British villas appear to have been the focus for farming activity which included some draining of the marshlands. The social organization, moreover, seems to have been based on old-fashioned kinship patterns. Bath is the most enduring local creation of the invaders; because of its curative waters a great temple of Sulis-Minerva was erected and visitors came from all parts of the Empire.[4]

After the eventual Roman withdrawal, the Britons appear to have returned to pre-Roman patterns of civilization. At this time various hillforts, the most famous of which is South Cadbury – popularly associated with King Arthur – were reoccupied. In the fifth and sixth centuries, one can speculate, Somerset was populated by a people

> much influenced by memories of Roman times, and continually conscious of its physical residues in decaying towns, villas, temples, and roads. Their language was Celtic, with probably a decreasing use of Latin and especially of written forms. Surviving place-names may be of pre-Roman origin, but may equally have been introduced into the area by Celtic-speaking people from Wales, the south west, or Ireland, possibly displacing some Roman names.[5]

It is in this period that the story of Glastonbury Abbey begins to move slightly out of the mists of legend and into the realm of (almost) verifiable fact.

completed shortly before Deanesly's book was published, E. E. Barker made a number of similar points, observing that 'William of Malmesbury's conclusion that missionaries may have reached the region in apostolic times remains as valid to-day as it was in the twelfth century. The commanding position of Glastonbury Tor and the largely marshy character of the land between it and the sea make it a likely choice as a landing-place, settlement and headquarters for early missionaries, who may have come by the ancient and well-known sea route from the Iberian Peninsula to the Bristol Channel.'

[3] In *Christianity in Roman Britain to AD 500* (London, 1981) Charles Thomas has argued that the most likely date for the (very scattered) introduction of Roman Christianity into Britain is around A.D. 200.

[4] At Glastonbury itself the main monastic site, as well as Beckery Chapel and the Tor, yielded some Roman-period finds, although those at Beckery were no more than might turn up in any field. It is at least possible, nevertheless, that a Roman settlement determined the choice of site for a Christian community – as was the case at Wells.

[5] Philip Rahtz, 'The Dark Ages 400–700 AD', in Michael Aston and Ian Burrow, eds., *The Archaeology of Somerset* (Taunton, 1982), p. 101.

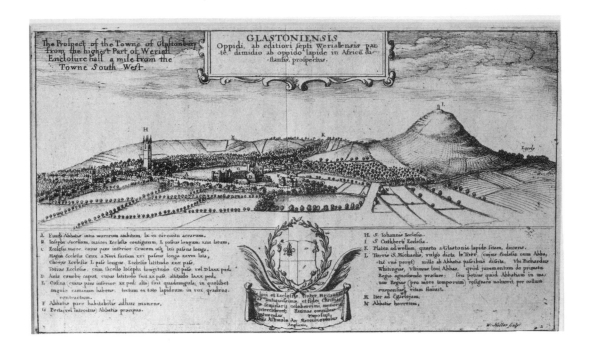

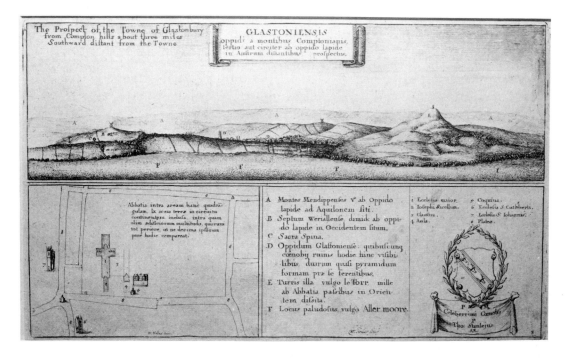

Wenceslaus Hollar's engravings of Glastonbury as it was c.1670. Based on Dugdale.

TABLE OF DATES[1]

Date	Abbot	Building	Other
A.D. 63			Joseph of Arimathea's supposed mission to Glastonbury
c.166			Alleged visit to Glastonbury by Phagan and Deruvian
433	St Patrick is said to have arrived		
449			Traditional date of coming of Angles, Saxons and Jutes to Britain
472	St Benignus is supposedly made abbot		
488			St Brigit's alleged arrival
495			Cerdic's arrival in Wessex, according to the *Anglo-Saxon Chronicle*
c.540			Traditional date for Gildas' *De excidio Britanniae*
c.542			Geoffrey of Monmouth's date for death of King Arthur
c.563			St Columba settles on Iona, founding abbey
			St David's alleged visit to Glastonbury
597			St Augustine's mission to Kent

[1] For my primary source concerning the early abbots of Glastonbury I use – apart from William of Malmesbury and the late tenth century list of abbots contained in BL, MS Cotton Tiberius B.v, vol. 1 – the fine essay published by J. Armitage Robinson in his *Somerset Historical Essays* (London, 1921). Since then, as might be expected, there has been considerably more work done on the early period in Wessex and on charters in particular. In my table I include in square brackets ([]) emended dates from E. E. Barker's unpublished M.A. thesis *Somersetshire Charters to A.D. 900* (1960) where these seem pertinent. I also note in pointed brackets (<>) some of the emendations suggested by Sarah Foot of Newnham College, Cambridge, who has been working on the chronology of the ninth and tenth-century abbots as part of her Ph.D. dissertation. At this stage, however, there are no final answers to many of the questions concerning early abbots, and any list must be considered provisional.

	'Worgret' [c.601–?]		
625			St Paulinus' supposed visit to Glastonbury
627			Edwin converted to Christianity
	'Lademund' [c.663–c.667]		
635			King Cynegils of Wessex converted to Christianity
	'Bregored' [c.667]		
664			Synod of Whitby establishes supremacy of Roman Christianity in Northumbria
670–680	Beorhtwald [c.667–676/7]		
680–705	Haemgils [676/7–701/2]		
688			Ine made king of Wessex
705–712	Beorhtwald [701/2–709/10]		St Indract murdered at Shapwick, according to the late medieval chronicles
709			Death of St Aldhelm, bishop of Sherborne, formerly abbot of Malmesbury
712–719	Ealdberht [709/10–718/9]	Church of St Peter and St Paul built by King Ine	
719–729	Ecgfrith [718/19–?]		
726			Abdication of King Ine and his pilgrimage to Rome
729	Wealhstod [not in William, rejected by Barker]		
729–744	Coengils [?–737]		
735			Death of Bede
745–754	Tunberht [737–?]		
754–760	Tyccea		
757			Accession of Offa, king of Mercia

760–762	Guba		
762–794	Wealdhun [?Wealhstod] [?Bosa]		
793			Viking raids begin in England
794–800	Beaduwulf		
802–824	Muca		
804			Death of Alcuin
824–851	Guthlac		
851–867	Ealhmund		
867–891	Hereferth <probably actually comes before Ealhmund>		
871			Alfred becomes king of Wessex
891–922	Stithheard		St Neot supposedly at Glastonbury
899			Edward the Elder succeeds to the throne
c.910			Birth of St Dunstan
922–?	Aldhun Cuthred <?> <Aelfric> Ecgwulf <?>		
940–957+	St Dunstan	St Dunstan lengthens Ine's church and adds a tower. He raises the level of the cemetery and constructs various monastic buildings	
939			Edmund succeeds to the throne of England
946			Edmund killed at Pucklechurch. Eadred succeeds to the throne
c.951			St Aethelwold leaves Glastonbury for Abingdon
955			Eadwig succeeds to the throne
956			St Dunstan's exile
?–964	Aelfric <= ?Aelfstan>		

957			Edgar succeeds to kingdoms of Mercia and Northumbria
959			Edgar succeeds to the throne of Wessex and therefore of all England
962			St David's relics supposedly brought to Glastonbury
964–c.970	Aelfstan		
c.970–975?	Sigegar		
975			Edward the Martyr succeeds to the throne
975?–1009?	Aelfweard		
978			Aethelred the Unready succeeds to the throne
984			Death of St Aethelwold
988			St Dunstan dies
c.1000			'B' writes his *Life* of St Dunstan
1009?–1019	Beorhtred		
1012			Supposed translation of St Dunstan's relics to Glastonbury
1016			West Saxons accept Cnut as king after death of Edmund Ironside
1016–1042			Cnut and his sons reign in England
1019–1024	Brihtwig 'Merechyt'		
c.1024–1053	Aethelweard		
1042			Edward the Confessor succeeds to the throne
1053–1077/8	Aethelnoth		
1066			Harold Godwinesson becomes king Battle of Stamford Bridge Battle of Hastings William of Normandy becomes king
1077/8–1096	Thurstan	Thurstan begins a new church	
1091			Translation of relics of St Benignus from Meare

1100–1118	Herluin	Herluin rebuilds Thurstan's church on a grander scale	
1120/1–1125	Seffrid Pelochin		
1126–1171	Henry of Blois	Henry builds a bell tower, chapter house, cloister, lavatory, refectory, dormitory, infirmary, the 'castellum', an outer gate, a brewery and stables	
1129			William of Malmesbury completes *De Antiquitate Glastonie Ecclesie*
1173–1180	Robert of Winchester	Builds a chamber and chapel	
	Peter de Marcy at Glastonbury		
1184			May 25. Great Fire
1186		New St Mary's Chapel consecrated. Work on Great Church begun.	
1189–1193	Henry of Sully		
c.1190			Discovery of King Arthur's tomb in cemetery
1193–1205	Savaric Fitzgeldewin, bishop of Bath and Glastonbury		
	(Master William Pica, elected 1198, but election quashed in 1200)		
1206–1218	Jocelyn of Wells, bishop of Bath and Glastonbury		
1219–1223	William of St Vigor		
1223–1234	Robert of Bath		
1235–1252	Michael of Amesbury	Carried work on the choir forward	
1252–1261	Roger of Ford		
1261–1274	Robert of Petherton	Built abbot's chamber	
1274–1291	John of Taunton	Choir completed; west end of nave and galilee built	
1275			Collapse of chapel of St Michael on the Tor

1278			Visit of King Edward I and Queen Eleanor; transfer of King Arthur's remains
c.1290			Adam of Damerham writes his history
1291–1303	John of Kent		
1303–1322	Geoffrey Fromond	Spent £1,000 on buildings: completed various parts of the Great Church	
1322–1323	Walter of Taunton	Built pulpitum at west end of choir	
1323–1334	Adam of Sodbury	Completed vaulting of nave of Great Church; worked on great hall and built a new chapel on Tor	
1331			Visit by King Edward III and Queen Philippa
1334–1342	John of Breynton	Completed abbot's great hall and worked on various other related buildings including prior's hall	
1342–1375	Walter de Monington	Extended choir by 40 feet, adding 2 bays. Completed abbot's chapel and infirmary	
c.1342			John of Glastonbury possibly finishes his chronicle
1368			Transfer of King Arthur's tomb
1375–1420	John Chinnock		
1382		Restored chapel and rededicated it to St Michael and St Joseph; rebuilt cloisters, erected or repaired the dormitory and fratry	
1420–1456	Nicholas Frome	Finished chapter house, rebuilt misericord house and great chamber; constructed bishop's quarters and a wall around abbey precincts.	

		Probably responsible for abbot's kitchen.	
1456	Walter More		
1456–1493	John Selwood	Built parish church of St John Baptist. Erected pilgrims' inn	
1493–1524	Richard Beere	Began Edgar Chapel; built crypt under Lady Chapel and dedicated it to St Joseph; built a chapel of the Holy Sepulchre at south end of nave; built the Loretto chapel; added vaulting under central tower and flying buttresses at east end of choir; built St Benignus' Church and rebuilt Tribunal	
1497			King Henry VII spends a night in the newly finished king's quarters
c.1508			Dispute with Canterbury over St Dunstan's relics
1525–1539	Richard Whiting	Completes Edgar Chapel	
1533			John Leland visits and examines library
1534			Sept. 19. Whiting and some of his monks sign the Act of Supremacy
1539			Nov 15. Whiting and two of his monks are hanged on the Tor
c.1550			Establishment of a colony of Dutch weavers on site
1723			William Stukeley's *Itinerary*
1907			June 6. Auction of ruins
1908			Site taken over by Church of England
1922			Frederick Bligh Bond dismissed.

PART ONE

ABBOTS AND HISTORY

Lancelot's vision of the Holy Grail, from a fifteenth-century manuscript. This illustrates vividly the mixture of secular chivalry and mysticism in medieval romances such as the Perlesvaus.

1

Pre-Conquest Abbots:
The Beginnings[1]

In some ways, discovering the name of Glastonbury's first abbot could be defined as a linguistic rather than a historical problem, since late-medieval local tradition suggests that there may have been holy men living on the site well before the monastic life – which revolves around the abbot (from the Greek word for father) – was invented. Presumably the very earliest foundation, if it dated back as far as the chroniclers assumed, would have been eremetic rather than cenobitic in nature and the holy men would have lived in separate huts as anchorites, not together in a monastic enclosure. This is the kind of world which the thirteenth-century author of the French romance *Perlesvaus* imagined to have existed at Glastonbury in the reign of King Arthur:

> He [Lancelot] looketh to the right, and on the top of the mountain beside the valley he seeth a chapel newly builded. ... By the side of this chapel were three houses dight right richly, each standing by itself facing the chapel. There was a right fair grave-yard round about the chapel, that was enclosed at the compass of the forest, and a spring came down ... and each of the houses had its own orchard, and the orchard an enclosure. Lancelot heareth vespers being chanted in the chapel. ... There were three hermits therewithin that had sung their vespers. ... And they told him that the place there was Avalon.[2]

---

[1] Trying to reconstruct a consecutive account of the early abbots of Glastonbury, as I have already mentioned, poses many problems, since our most reliable sources (William of Malmesbury's *The Early History* and the tenth-century list contained in British Library, MS Cotton Tiberius B.v, vol. 1) are late and contradict one another in a variety of instances. In the following chapter my main source for the 'historical' period is 'The Saxon Abbots of Glastonbury', but I do also make reference – as I did in my 'Table of Dates' – to the unpublished work by Barker and Foot. In this chapter I do not mention every abbot and I do not always list alternative dates – these do, however, appear in the 'Table of Dates'. For the earliest period I refer to the late-medieval traditions, but it should be remembered that these have little (and often no) hard evidence to support them. Both Michael Lapidge and David Dumville have gone carefully over this chapter and have provided many helpful criticisms.

[2] Although there is a more accurate modern translation by Nigel Bryant I have used Sebastian Evans' charmingly archaic version: *The High History of the Holy Graal*, 2 vols. (London, 1898), 2.133.

Writing in the mid-fourteenth century, John of Glastonbury tells us that until the coming of St Patrick in the fifth century there was an unbroken succession of twelve hermits living at Glastonbury; they had no leader and were always twelve in number in memory of the twelve companions who first settled the spot under the leadership of St Joseph of Arimathea.

The Glastonbury chroniclers – whose evidence must be used with a great deal of caution since it often represents an accretion of post-Conquest legend rather than legitimate fact – relate that when St Patrick arrived at Glastonbury in 433 (a date for which there is no historical justification) he taught the twelve hermits already on the site a communal life and he became the first abbot by their unanimous election.[3] He was succeeded in this office, so we are told, by his own disciple, St Benignus, who had followed him from Ireland to Glastonbury. Benignus, however, was not an abbot in the later, that is Benedictine, sense of the word, since he preferred solitude and lived as a hermit at Meare, coming to Glastonbury itself only on relatively infrequent occasions.

After Benignus' death a cloud descends for over two hundred years and the names of only three abbots are recorded from the British period, that is the period of Roman withdrawal leading to the subjugation of so much of Britain by the Germanic tribes. A charter associated with early Anglo-Saxon times (erroneously dated to A.D. 601), which some scholars consider to have a genuine basis, still survives; in this an unknown king of Dumnonia (a territory which included much of modern Devon, Cornwall and Somerset) grants land to the abbot Worgret, whose name, as William of Malmesbury rather maliciously (and inaccurately) puts it, smacks linguistically of legitimate British barbarism.[4] The name of Bregored was still legible on one of the ancient stone pyramids outside the Old Church in the twelfth century and a trace probably appears in an early account of the bounds of Butleigh. There may have been an earlier form of this name with Welsh components, some linguists suggest, but the form as it stands is Old English (*Bregu* as an element in personal names from the early Saxon period is attested in a variety of cases). Finally, as late as William of Malmesbury's visit in the 1120s, there appears to have been an ancient painting in the Great Church which gave

St Patrick

St Benignus

Worgret

Bregored

One of the many conjectural early antiquarian drawings of the wattled Old Church. Taken from Sir Henry Spelman's Concilia *(1639–64).*

[3] It is worth noting that even though William of Malmesbury was convinced that Glastonbury possessed the majority of St Patrick's relics, it is not altogether clear that he actually believed him to be an early abbot of Glastonbury.
[4] Barker has examined this charter closely and has concluded that it has a genuine basis. He also speculates that 'it was probably not a recent foundation over which Worgret presided as abbot.' David Dumville, on the other hand, considers the document to be a 'rank forgery'.

the names of these two as well as of a third abbot called Lademund.[5]

During the British period worship would have been conducted in the Old Church, that is the venerable wattled structure which was later covered by planking and which was still standing in William of Malmesbury's day. This church would have resembled Irish buildings of the same era and may have been – in its later rather than in its original wattled state – nearly 60 feet long, just as tradition holds. Dr Ralegh Radford points out, moreover, that the Old Church itself would probably not have existed in a vacuum and must be considered in the context of the whole island settlement. The church and cemetery at Beckery, too, may be regarded as part of the holy city, of which Ponter's Ball (the slight ridge cut by the modern road to Shepton Mallet) possibly represents the outer boundary to the east. By Radford's calculations the main living quarters would have been on the rising ground to the north of the later church and there would have been commercial suburbs surrounding the central area.

Radford has described his findings from the earliest period, those which were within the sacred precinct itself:

> The oldest remains... were those found in the ancient cemetery. Post holes were found belonging to at least four oratories of the wattled type. ... The best preserved was a small building 13 feet wide and over 17 feet long. ... There were also

John Skinner, vicar of Camerton, was firmly convinced that Glastonbury was a Roman fort. In his Diaries *(c.1797–c.1830), now preserved as BL, MS Addit. 33633–33730, he made a number of sketches of the site. This one shows Ponter's Ball as a more conspicuous landmark than it now is.*

[5] Since all three of these names have Saxon elements Barker suggests that these abbots actually represent the first recorded members of the new 'English' regime.

two mausolea within the ancient cemetery. These tomb shrines were rectangular structures, large enough to take one or two bodies. They were quite low and probably marked by a standing cross... The ordinary graves within the cemetery were rough chests formed of slabs of stone set on edge and covered with a flat stone or stones laid flush with the surface of the cemetery.[6]

A significant early feature is a ditch, or two parallel ditches, dating from the late sixth or early seventh century, and running north-south about 80 metres east of the Old Church, presumably forming a boundary of the monastic precinct. It is possible that the present Church of St Benedict replaces a much earlier chapel denoting the western boundary of the ancient enclosure. If this is the case, then the precinct must have been at least 400 metres by 125 metres.[7]

In the final analysis, there seems to be no indisputable archaeological evidence concerning a British community on what later became the monastic site and Philip Rahtz, for

Post holes in early cemetery as discovered during archaeological excavations.

[6] See 'Glastonbury Abbey', in Geoffrey Ashe, ed., *The Quest for Arthur's Britain* (London & New York, 1968), pp. 131–32.

[7] See Michael Aston and Ian Burrow, 'The Early Christian Centres 600–1000 AD', in Michael Aston and Ian Burrow, eds., *The Archaeology of Somerset* (Taunton, 1982), 119–20.

example, observes that there is no material from any of the Abbey digs which need be earlier than the eighth century. Excavations on the Tor, however, have indicated pits and buildings from the sixth century. The presence of imported pottery from the Mediterranean and south-west Gaul demonstrates far-flung trading contacts and hints at wide cultural influences. Large quantites of meat bones and two burials with heads to the south have caused scholars to disagree about the nature of the settlement: it could be a monastic type of community, but it could also be the stronghold of a British chieftain, established during this period of return to the old Celtic tribal politics based on hillforts.[8] It is at least possible that Glastonbury and its early manors formed a unit, first ruled by a secular lord occupying the Tor and then later transferred to an ecclesiastical context on the lower ground.

Under English influence, and specifically through the determination of St Wilfrid, Glastonbury Abbey finally became Roman in its organization around 673, that is, approximately ten years after the Synod of Whitby in 664. The first of the Anglo-Saxon abbots was Beorhtwald (c.670–c.680) who was *Beorhtwald* later bishop of Reculver and finally succeeded St Theodore as archbishop of Canterbury in 692. Beorhtwald was probably appointed abbot by Cenwalh, king of Wessex (642/3–672) on the advice of Cenwalh's friend Benedict Biscop and he received a generous grant of land at Meare from his royal patron in 670. In his *History of the English Church* the Venerable Bede writes glowingly about Beorhtwald, who was apparently learned in the Scriptures and highly trained in ecclesiastical matters and monastic discipline.

Beorhtwald was succeeded by Haemgils (c.680–c.705),[9] whom *Haemgils* Centwine – Cenwalh's successor after the brief reigns of Aescwine and Queen Sexburga – appointed abbot at the request of Haeddi, bishop of Winchester. Centwine, who himself was later buried in the already venerable cemetery at Glastonbury, gave Haemgils land near Quantock Wood and the island by the hill near the Tone (now Creechbarrow, Taunton). Centwine's choice of location when he made this

---

[8] For a description of the excavations on the Tor see Philip A. Rahtz, 'Excavations on Glastonbury Tor, 1964–6', *Archaeological Journal* 127 (1971), 1–81. In a recent letter Rahtz has emphasized that 'the earliest Glastonbury Christianity archaeologically could well be on the Tor, moving to the more spacious and convenient abbey site in the later seventh or eighth centuries when the Saxons gained control over the area. The Beckery Chapel sites, and a later monastic settlement on the Tor, are not attested archaeologically earlier than the later Saxon period, and were clearly daughter offshoots of the by now flourishing Saxon abbey.' He also points out the animal bones can no longer be taken as evidence against a Christian community, since the earliest Iona levels are also full of remains of meat-eating.

[9] Using early charter evidence Barker 'confidently' dates Haemgils' accession to 676/7 and his death to 701/2. He has Beorhtwald as abbot from c.667–676/7.

concession was at least partially dictated by political considerations, since the grant helped create an English presence very far west, well into British territory.[10]

Beorhtwald

The correspondence of the third Anglo-Saxon abbot, also called Beorhtwald (c.705–c.712), indicates that he knew a number of influential people. In one of his letters, for example, he recommended St Boniface, the Anglo-Saxon missionary to the Germans, as a man to be trusted with important messages. In another contemporary letter the archbishop of Canterbury asked Forthere, bishop of Sherborne, to intercede with Beorhtwald on behalf of a captive Kentish girl. Beorhtwald's response, unfortunately, has been lost. Beorhtwald also knew St Wilfrid, who presented him with land at Wedmore and Clewer. His name was engraved with those of Bregored and Bishop Haeddi on one of the two stone pyramids which dominated the abbey's cemetery.

Beorhtwald was abbot during the heyday of King Ine's long reign (688–726) and Ine made numerous grants to Glastonbury. His restoration of lost land at Brent and grants in the Polden Hills and Zoyland, in particular, gave Glastonbury an unrivalled dominance in the Somerset Levels – whose swampy environment seems to have provided the British with one of their last enclaves of independent activity. Towards the end of his reign, probably after Beorhtwald's death, Ine built a new stone church at Glastonbury; it was dedicated to St Peter and St Paul and was located to the east of the older wooden church. The new church would probably have resembled the Kentish churches being built in the seventh century, of which a good example would be Reculver, which was founded in 667 and where outlines of the seventh-century church at Reculver can still be seen. Mr W.J.Wedlake, who took part in many of the excavations at Glastonbury from the late 1920s onwards, concludes that Ine's church extended as far as the eastern end of the 'hypogeum' and that it was built in Torr burrs.

Ealdberht
Ecgfrith, Tyccea

After Beorhtwald comes Ealdberht (c.712–c.719),[11] followed by Ecgfrith (c.719–c.729). Tyccea (c.754–c.760) was abbot during the reign of King Sigeberht and received land on the Polden ridge. During Tyccea's abbacy various additions to King Ine's church were probably completed. According to the late medieval Glastonbury chroniclers Tyccea himself was originally an abbot in Northumbria and was driven west as a result of Danish invasions (although these raids did not in fact begin until around 790). When he came to Glastonbury Tyccea

---

[10] On the westward progress of the Saxons see W.G.Hoskins, *The Westward Expansion of Wessex* (Leicester, 1960), esp. pp. 17ff.
[11] Barker dates his accession to 710 at the latest, because of charter evidence linking him with St Wilfrid, who died on 24 April, 710.

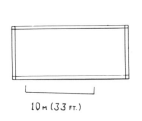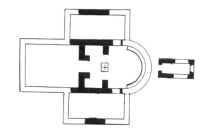

Glastonbury c.720 by Radford's scheme.

allegedly brought with him relics of St Aidan, bishop of Lindisfarne, and the bodies of Ceolfrith, Benedict Biscop and other abbots of Wearmouth, as well as remains of the Venerable Bede and Hilda of Whitby. Tyccea was buried in a beautifully wrought monument in the right hand corner of King Ine's Great Church, near the entrance to the Old Church. At least one miracle was reported to have taken place at Tyccea's tomb, when a sinner was struck blind while attempting to vandalize the monument.

By the eighth century Glastonbury Abbey had become a rich and powerful centre – it had received numerous grants of land and had consolidated great estates. Under Guba (c.760–c.762) and Wealdhun (c.762–c.794) property came from

Guba
Wealdhun

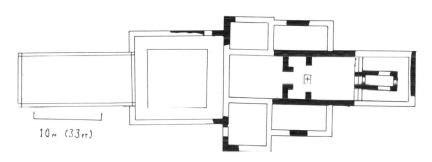

Glastonbury c.760. After Radford.

King Cynewulf. There is a grant to Beaduwulf (c.794–c.800) from Offa, the famous king of the Mercians (757–796), and Beaduwulf was also one of the abbots to attest to the confirmation of Pope Leo III's privilege of 800 hides of land to 'Kenelm'.[12] The name of Muca (c.802–c.824) appears on several documents and he received various grants of land from Ecgberht, king of the West Saxons (802–839). Some scholars

Beaduwulf

Muca

---

[12] This and similar documents suggest to Barker that at this period Glastonbury had gone through a phase as a proprietary monastery and that it had probably belonged to King Offa of Mercia. Heather Edwards, in her unpublished dissertation, has argued that 'Kenelm' can almost certainly be identified as Cynehelm, son of Coenwulf, king of the Mercians.

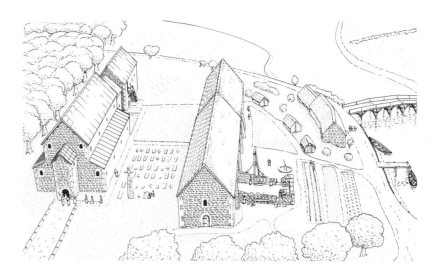

Reconstruction of the Anglo-Saxon monastery at Jarrow, as it might have looked in the late eighth century, showing the two churches, monastic buildings, the cemetery, workshops and the monks' garden. After reconstruction by R. J. Cramp.

have argued that Muca is an Irish name and that the abbots of Glastonbury were Irish during this period. As tempting as this hypothesis might seem, the name, in fact, is probably a variant on the relatively common Old English name Mucel. William of Malmesbury gives one Cuman as abbot just before Muca, a man about whom John of Glastonbury later says there is nothing worth remembering. As it turns out John is almost certainly more accurate than he realized, since it is highly unlikely that such an abbot ever existed – the name probably arose from a misreading of Muca on ancient documents and a reversal of the consonants – evidence, it seems, that dyslexia has had a long history.

Guthlac

During the abbacy of Guthlac (c.824–c.851) Danish raids began to grow in intensity and violence all over England. Raiding parties attacked Carhampton in 836 and 843, but there was strong resistance in 845 when the ealdorman Eanwulf (later to be buried at Glastonbury) led his people to a victory at the mouth of the Parrett. Somewhere around this period or slightly later the actual buildings at Glastonbury may have been damaged by the Danes and there was a corresponding decline in morale and discipline. Long after Guthlac's death Glastonbury established a local cult of the more famous East Anglian saint of the same name. Even more surprisingly, the monks of Glastonbury claimed to possess the greater part of St Guthlac's remains, which most other authorities believed to be at his attested shrine at Crowland in Lincolnshire. Over the course of centuries the community at Glastonbury, it seems, had confused the two individuals and merged them together into one local saint over whom they tried to exert a proprietary right.

Ealhmund (c.851–c.867) followed Guthlac and, even during these precarious times when Danish raids were worsening, he found a generous patron in King Aethelwulf of Wessex, who pledged to give a tenth of all his lands to the churches of his kingdom. From Aethelwulf Glastonbury received land at Doulting, Buckland Newton, Pennard, Monk Okehampton, Zoy, Puriton, Montacute ('Loggaresbeorg'), Braunton, Downhead and various other unidentified places. Many other lands came from Aethelwulf's thegns.

Ealhmund

By King Alfred's reign Glastonbury had become a strong and stable presence in a harried kingdom and he recognized his senior foundation by presenting Abbot Hereferth (867–891) with a piece of wood from the Lord's Cross, which he had received from Pope Marinus.[13] During Alfred's reign St Neot, in popular tradition held to be a brother of the king, is said to have led a life of intense study and austere discipline in the Glastonbury community. Surprisingly, there is no record that Alfred gave any land to Glastonbury. This is perhaps because he devoted his energy and resources to founding (or refounding) a monastery at Athelney, where he had lived in hiding during the brief ascendency in Wessex of the Danish attackers. Interestingly, too, Alfred sent to the continent for an abbot and monks to inhabit his new foundation rather than recruiting them locally. This may suggest a paucity of monks or poor discipline at Glastonbury.[14]

Hereferth

Hereferth's successor was Stithheard (891–922), a man of severe temperament, so William of Malmesbury relates, whose very name reflected his character, as 'stith' is the Old English word for 'stiff' or 'stern'. Apparently, too, the monastery possessed pictures of him, which inevitably showed him holding a scourge or broom. Aldhun became abbot in 922 and received many relics from King Aethelstan. It seems probable that he was succeeded by Cuthred and Ecgwulf, about whom William of Malmesbury knew nothing, even though they do turn up in the Cotton Tiberius B.v list.

Stithheard

Aldhun

Cuthred, Ecgwulf

Although Glastonbury appears to have been attracting Irish pilgrims at this time, who were keeping up some tradition of learning, it was probably more effective as a school for young

---

[13] Although the Glastonbury historians say that Alfred gave this relic to Glastonbury Abbey all that the *Anglo-Saxon Chronicle* reports (under the entry for 883) is that 'Pope Marinus sent some wood of the Cross to King Alfred.' There are also chronological problems in William's reckoning of Hereferth's dates: he is supposed to have received land from Aethelbald, son of King Aethelwulf, in 867, but this grant needs to be redated to 839×855 to fit in with Aethelbald's dates. Because of these confusions Foot tentatively suggests that Hereferth be placed before Ealhmund.

[14] Foot speculates that the monastery could even have been temporarily vacant at this time.

noblemen than as a monastery.[15] In fact, the site seems to have become more or less an appendage to the royal demesne; the monastic buildings had all but disappeared, and the church had fallen into decay. There was probably only a small *familia* of clerks living on the spot in separate cells around the abbey's precincts and religious life was at its lowest ebb for many centuries. In its spiritual and physical decay, then, Glastonbury reflected a national phenomenon; after many generations of success the monastic movement seemed to be on the verge of extinction.

At just this point, at the hour of greatest need as it were, the most important figure in Glastonbury's long history appeared on the scene. St Dunstan (940–956) was born near Glastonbury and even as a small boy he had a dream about the future buildings which would be erected on the site. Dunstan was made abbot by King Edmund I (939–946), after the latter had a miraculous escape at Cheddar Gorge through divine intervention, after repenting of his mistreatment of Dunstan. (It is worth noting, too, that during this period when the monasteries had lost much of their authority the king could arbitrarily appoint an abbot without any apparent protest on the part of the monks.) Edmund granted Dunstan numerous estates for the enrichment of the abbey. He also contributed priceless relics which he had collected, and decided to be buried at Glastonbury (a great honour for the community) after his own death. In 954 King Eadred, brother of Edmund, also conferred land on Dunstan and various of his thegns imitated him in this. Afterwards, however, there was a brief period when Dunstan was driven into exile by Eadwig, the son of Edmund, whom he had reprimanded even on the day of his coronation. Dunstan took refuge first with Arnulf, count of Flanders, and then at the monastery of St Peter at Ghent. During this period, that is 956, Eadwig gave land to the 'pseudo-abbot' Aelfsige.

On becoming king of Mercia and Northumbria in 957, Edgar presuaded Dunstan to return to England and appointed him bishop of Worcester (957), then London (959), and finally archbishop of Canterbury (960).[16] Dunstan's years of exile, although personally distressing, were crucial for the development of the English Church, since he decided to imitate the thriving monasticism which he saw on the Continent. Hence-

Dunstan

Oxford, Bodleian Library, MS Auct. F.4.32, fol.1r. Illustration of Christ with possible self-portrait of St Dunstan at His feet.

Aelfsige

---

[15] In some contemporary documents Glastonbury is called a 'royal' rather than a 'holy' island. This shift in terminology has been used by certain scholars as evidence for the secularization of the monastery, but according to Radford the two words could at the time be used more or less interchangeably in a monastic context.

[16] Eadwig had appointed Byrhthelm, bishop of Wells, as archbishop of Canterbury, but on his accession to the throne of Wessex in 959 Edgar ordered Byrhthelm back to his former see and appointed Dunstan in his place.

forth English practice would be modelled on contemporary European forms and it would be primarily liturgical and claustral, with much emphasis on psalmody and the execution of the chant. The chief office of the monks would be the solemn liturgy; the time for work would be given to teaching, writing, illuminating and craftwork – all skills at which Dunstan, as it happens, greatly excelled. It is not surprising, moreover, that, as this new learning flourished at Glastonbury, the scriptorium developed and the book collection grew. Indeed, we can surmise that many elaborate and beautifully illustrated books were produced at Glastonbury during Dunstan's abbacy and shortly afterwards, even if only a few of them have survived.

Dunstan oversaw physical as well as spiritual revival at Glastonbury. William of Malmesbury relates that

> Dunstan lengthened [Ine's church] considerably, adding a tower; and, to make its width square with its length, he added aisles or 'porticus' as they call them. The result of his labours was that, as far as the design of the ancient structure allowed, a basilica was produced of great extent in both directions; wherein, if aught be lacking of seemliness and beauty, there is at any rate no want of necesssary room.[17]

Fragment from the pre-Conquest church. Radford dates it roughly to the period of St Dunstan's revival.

This church would have been similar to the contemporary structure at Cluny. The tower was presumably constructed to house the remains of King Edmund and may well have been of considerable proportions, visible for some distance and acting as a kind of beacon for travellers. Dunstan also built a wall on the south side of the cemetery and raised the level of the ground. This, of course, explains why the monks had to dig to such a depth two centuries later when they were looking for King Arthur's grave (i.e., the original cemetery had become greatly submerged as a result of Dunstan's changes). Dunstan built a small square chapel at the west end of the Old Church which he had dedicated to St John the Baptist; this chapel later became known as St Dunstan's Chapel.[18] Excavations have revealed that at the eastern end of Dunstan's church there was a stone-lined chamber, although this feature was not mentioned in the official reports. Radford thinks it must have been a relic chamber immediately west of the High Altar.

Dunstan oversaw work on the monastic buildings as well and his cloister consisted of a courtyard measuring 180 ft. by

---

[17] See William's *Life* of Dunstan in William Stubbs, ed., *Memorials of St Dunstan* (RS 53; London, 1874), p. 271. Wedlake notes that Dunstan's building was in blue lias and that he utilized the foundations of Ine's church for the main body of his own structure.
[18] If this were an external chapel, so Radford maintains, it must have been situated over the gate of the cemetery.

120 ft., with ranges of buildings between 20 ft. and 26 ft. wide enclosing it on the east, south and west sides; the wall of the cemetery would have made the north side. Although Dunstan encouraged royal patronage, he also favoured monastic ownership in its own right rather than the widespread practice whereby the church's land was held under the crown. He consolidated land-holdings and is said to have undertaken the retrieval of many ancient rights recently lost.

Aelfstan

Dunstan's successor as abbot of Glastonbury was Aelfstan (964–c.970).[19] At this time King Edgar, who was perhaps the greatest of Glastonbury's royal patrons, gave a cross which was woven throughout in gold and silver, beautiful bells and his coronation robe to be used as an altar-ornament. Among the many precious relics which he presented was a large shrine covered in gold and silver and decorated in ivory images, containing relics of St Vincent and St Apollinaris. He himself was buried at Glastonbury in the chapter house at the door to the church.

Sigegar

There seem to have been no land grants to the next abbot, Sigegar (c.970–975), but we do know that he left Glastonbury to become bishop of Wells – a fairly common move during the period and one which could lead to further promotions, even

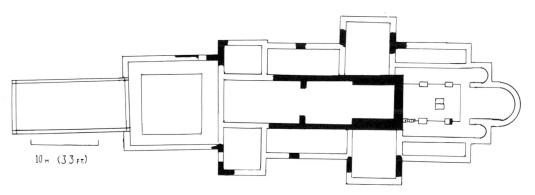

Glastonbury c.1000. After Radford.

(as in the case of Dunstan) to the see of Canterbury. In fact, four of Glastonbury's monks became bishops of Wells in the tenth century and of the six archbishops who succeeded Dunstan at Canterbury, five came from Glastonbury.

Aelfweard

For some reason William of Malmesbury does not know about Aelfweard (975[?]–1009[?]) who was actually a rather interesting character, two of whose letters still survive. These letters are good examples of the hermeneutic style practised in England during the heyday of the Benedictine reform movement and represent a strong piece of evidence concerning the central role of Glastonbury in the movement. The hermeneutic

[19] The Tiberius list puts one Aelfric before Aelfstan, but this is probably an error, and the two names should therefore be conflated.

style was ostentatious and highly cultivated, based on unusual and arcane vocabulary, much of which was coined from Greek. The production of hermeneutic writing demanded a good collection of books, a learned community and time to devote to the study of texts – all 'luxuries' emphasized both by Dunstan and his fellow reformers.[20]

The last two Saxon abbots, Aethelweard (c.1024–1053) and Aethelnoth (1053–1077/8) were responsible for a new and serious decline in Glastonbury's fortunes. Aethelweard, we are told, decided to excavate King Edgar's tomb and found the body miraculously preserved. Rather than being moved to devotion by this discovery, however, he proceeded to hack the body up in order to make it fit into the reliquary he had provided for it. In response to this violation the body began to bleed profusely and Aethelweard, in turn, became incurably insane. Not long afterwards he fell as he left the church and broke his neck. Aethelnoth was no better. He removed the gold and silver from holy books and ornaments and sold it for his own profit. He also alienated property from the monastery at Batcombe and gave it to his mother. When William the Conqueror returned to Normandy in 1067 after his conquest of England he took Aethelnoth with him, and Aethelnoth remained in exile there until he was formally deposed at the Council of London in 1078.[21]

During Aethelnoth's abbacy, that is during the difficult period on either side of the Conquest, Glastonbury remained solidly English in its loyalties and the monastery may even have provided modest refuge for local English families who had failed to redeem their land under the Conqueror. Once again its relative inaccessibility may have been of advantage to the monastery: as an island it was more secure, more independent than some of the other great English monasteries.

*Aethelweard
Aethelnoth*

[20] On this topic see Michael Lapidge, 'The hermeneutic style in tenth-century Anglo-Latin literature', *Anglo-Saxon England* 4 (1975), 67–111.

[21] Taking as his source a reference to Aethelnoth in E. A. Freeman's *History of the Norman Conquest*, Bligh Bond has portrayed these last two abbots in a much more positive light, a view which was originally suggested to him by automatic writing. See *The Glastonbury Scripts. IV. A Life of Ailnoth Last Saxon Abbot of Glastonbury* (London, n.d.). The description of the young Aethelnoth is especially lyrical: 'he sang on the fenny ways from school to cloisters the songs now lost to men with many another rare and vanished thing. Yet the dark brown deer and the tameless birds of the fenland heard and followed him. Despite long hours of unceasing toil and worship, he so reverenced the Abbey that he searched her tattered records neglected by the conquerors of Britain, and marvelled that the Man of the Desert builded Christ an Home in the wolf-haunted marshes; or in a weak moment, gained strength from the legends of the noble Warrior-Saints resting incorruptible at the foot of the high Altar. Always mindful of the poor, he frequently visited almonry and wretched hut, preaching in the uncouth tongue learned of the woodcutter, rejoicing when the miserable were healed at the spring of miracles or by a branch of the flower-filled thorn that like the wondrous Tree, the Heavenly Rood, blossomed in the winter wind of Death' (pp. 15–16).

2

After 1066:
Growth and Consolidation

The Norman Conquest was, as all the English monastic chroniclers lamented, highly disruptive to ecclesiastical life in England, and there was a universal loss of property and income. This general situation was exacerbated at Glastonbury when the priory of Montacute, established by Robert, Count of Mortain, was endowed with lands previously owned by Glastonbury. In spite of vociferous lamentations about these and similar losses, Glastonbury Abbey was nevertheless the richest monastery in England at the time of Domesday, with an income of £827 18s 8d.

Thurstan

Thurstan (c.1077/8–1096) was the first of the Norman abbots. He had been a monk at Caen in Normandy and was forced on the community by King William. As a Norman Thurstan was, not unexpectedly, a builder. Little, however, remains of his church, which seems to have been conceived on a relatively moderate scale and which was never completed. Personally, Thurstan had a strong religious fervour: he undertook the translation of the body of St Benignus from Meare to the High Altar of the Great Church[1] and gave the church two pieces of beautiful material, two censers and two candlesticks.

[1] John of Glastonbury gives a dramatic account of the event: 'The bones, when they had been unearthed, washed, wrapped reverently in linen, and enclosed in a casket prepared for the purpose, breathed forth an agreeable balsam-laden fragrance... [After eight weeks of postponement demanded by the saint through a vision to one of the monks] the bones were again brought forth from the casket, washed, and placed in the gilt shrine which had been sent for the purpose... But on the night preceding the Sunday of the translation, two men, while they were rowing on the nearby river, saw a column of light which extended up to heaven above the saint's oratory, and they pointed it out to many others. What is more, in the morning, while the holy relics were carried to Glastonbury in a boat, the two men in the same small vessel, one a monk and the other a layman, saw from afar off what was like a many-coloured arched roof in the air, shading the whole monastery; and so they had no doubt that heavenly grace had settled its pleasure upon the dwelling to which such an inhabitant had been brought... When the holy remains had reached the shore and had been carried to a suitable spot on this side of the river, about midway betwen the river and the monastery, someone standing on higher ground delivered a sermon to the people ... on the holy man's life and the reason for his translation. At the end of the sermon, when one of the holy bones had been brought forth and the sign of the cross made

He was also a man of great discretion in worldly affairs and was not afraid to challenge the bishop, asserting his rights over the neighbouring abbots of Muchelney and Athelney. In his own community, however, he met with stubborn conservatism which led to a violent confrontation and armed conflict when he rejected the traditional Gregorian chant in favour of the chant of William of Fécamp. According to the *Anglo-Saxon Chronicle*

> One day the abbot went into the chapter and spoke against them [the monks] and wanted to ill-treat them, and sent for some laymen, and they came into the chapter, and fell upon the monks fully armed. ... But they [the monks] scattered: some ran into the church and locked the doors on themselves. ... But a grievous thing happened that day – the Frenchmen broke into the choir and threw missiles towards the altar where the monks were, and some of the retainers went up to the upper story and shot arrows down towards the sanctuary, so that many arrows stuck in the cross that stood above the altar; and the wretched monks were lying round about the altar. ... What can we say, except that they shot fiercely, and the others broke down the doors there, and went in and killed some of the monks and wounded many there in the church, so that the blood came from the altar on to the steps, and from the steps on to the floor. Three were killed there and eighteen wounded.[2]

The scandal was so great and led to such shocked response throughout the kingdom that William was forced to recall Thurstan to Normandy. Later, Thurstan paid William Rufus £500 to restore him to the abbacy and he spent – the chroniclers exultingly report – an unhappy last few years there, wandering aimlessly from estate to estate. As was appropriate, too, he met a miserable end and was buried without lamentation at the altar of St Andrew in the north portico of St Dunstan's church.

Herluin

Herluin (1100–1118), also a monk of Caen, was chosen as abbot by King Henry I, but this time the choice met with the convent's approval. When he first arrived at Glastonbury Herluin had a reputation for parsimony; this he very soon belied by opening the doors to his courtyard so that all

with it above the crowd, such grace of divine generosity flowed out upon the people that those vexed with various illnesses ... were healed... In the place, furthermore, where the holy body then rested, a church was immediately built in the name of that saint... Thus St Benignus, led with festive praise into the main church and placed before the high altar, showed forth the renown of his sancity with daily miracles. In fact, such was the crowd of various people of both sexes that for forty continuous days scarcely anyone was able to reach the altar on account of the press of visitors.'

[2] See Dorothy Whitelock *et al.*, eds., *The Anglo-Saxon Chronicle* (London, 1961), p.160. Radford speculates that the 'G' version of the *Anglo-Saxon Chronicle* may represent an eyewitness account, made by one of the recalcitrant monks later banished from Glastonbury. See also David Hiley, *Thurstan of Caen and Plainchant at Glastonbury: Musicological Reflections on the Norman Conquest* (London, 1987).

petitioners might have easy access to him. He also threatened to cut off the porter's ears if the latter refused admission to the poor. Herluin tried to regain manors which had been seized at the time of the Conquest and considerably increased the monastery's land holdings. He donated several crosses of fine

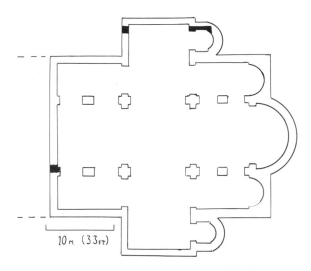

Glastonbury c.1100. After Radford.

workmanship and various ecclesiastical ornaments. One altar was so magnificent, we are told, that it would have fetched over 100 marks (1 mark = 13s 4d) of gold in Rome. Herluin enlarged the monks' quarters and, although his Romanesque cloister was slightly smaller than the one which came later, it had the north and west sides in the same position and the outer walls on the east and south running along the later walks. Herluin tore down Thurstan's church, which he considered an inadequate manifestation of the greatness of his monastery, and spent £480 on a new structure which was finally completed c.1140 under Henry of Blois. This was a cruciform building with a plan resembling that of St Albans (consecrated in 1115) but with a particularly prominent eastern chapel – planned perhaps to house the shrines of St Patrick, St Indract and King Edgar. A portion of his own tomb has been recovered during excavations and shows fine workmanship in its carving.

It is particularly fortunate that William of Malmesbury gave a detailed description of the dietary customs and clothing regulations of the Glastonbury monks during this period, since his account – which is practically unique in the annals of the twelfth century – provides a fine insight into just what the physical conditions would have been like:

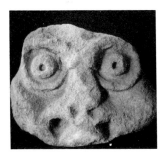

Grotesque on corbel from Romanesque church. Now in the abbey museum.

On some days of the week ... the brethren had three *generalia* [a dish of eggs or fish that was served to the whole table] and two *pitantiae* [a small dish of fish or eggs which was served to an individual monk or a pair of monks] to eat but on the other three days ... they had two *generalia* and three *pitantiae*. However, on holy days when the brethren were in copes they had cups of mead, fine wheaten cakes on the table, a measure of wine and three *generalia* and four or five *pitantiae* ... But on special festivals ... there was a greater quantity for all, depending on the dignity of the festival ... This was the custom concerning dress: each of the brethren was to have two cowls, two frocks, two shirts of linsey-woolsey, two pairs of breeches, four pairs of stockings and a new pelisse every year, and on Maundy Thursday each was to have shoes for the day time and in winter for the night and two bedcovers. They should also have ten pairs of slippers ... And this is another ration: when they are to have wine in place of beer, each of them is to have two measures a day.[3]

Life, it can be seen, was not extravagant but the monks obviously lived in more comfort than much of the lay population.

Seffrid Pelochin

About Seffrid Pelochin (1120/1–1125), who came from Seez Abbey in Normandy, little information survives. He gave the monastery a pall, a chasuble, an alb and a variety of relics: part of the Lord's sepulchre, relics of St Sebastian, St Agapitus, St Felicissimus, St Rufina, St Cyrilla, St Nympha and a piece of St Barbara's veil. Some of these relics he acquired while he was in Rome on a diplomatic mission; at this time he also obtained a papal privilege for the monastery from Pope Calixtus II. Seffrid's allegiance to Glastonbury, however, does not appear to have been absolute and in 1125 he left to become bishop of Chichester, from which position he was deposed in 1145 on the grounds of sodomy. He was buried at Chichester; many centuries later his coffin was opened and it was discovered that his episcopal ring was made of jasper and was carved with the gnostic figure of the serpent god Abraxas. In the Middle Ages, gnosticism was often associated with homosexuality – as the derivation of 'buggar' from 'Bulgar' and the suppression of the Templars suggest – and Seffrid's ring indicates that his crimes might concern his religious beliefs rather than his sexual preferences. If – as can in no way be proved – his interest in gnosticism were to date from his time at Glastonbury, then this might in turn throw light on the seemingly gnostic hints in William of Malmesbury's reference to the mysterious pattern of triangles and squares on the pavement of the church at Glastonbury:

---

[3] See *The Early History of Glastonbury*, p.163. In his review of Scott's edition (*History* 68 [1983], 493–94) D.H. Farmer objects to the translation of 'pedules' as slippers; he considers that stockings would be more appropriate.

There [in the Old Church] one can observe all over the floor stones, artfully interlaced in the forms of triangles or squares and sealed with lead; I do no harm to religion if I believe some sacred mystery is contained beneath them.[4]

Henry of Blois

If Seffrid's moral or religious character can be called into question, so too can his administrative ability. Indeed, when King Henry I invited his nephew Henry of Blois (1126–1171) to come from Cluny to succeed Seffrid as abbot, the young Henry was horrified by what he saw. The buildings, he reported, were in a state of collapse and the monks lacked even

Henry of Blois, depicted on one of a pair of plaques, copper, engraved, enamelled and gilded, made by a Mosan goldsmith. Henry is shown making a gift to a church.

the bare necessities of life. Henry, whom many modern historians rank as inferior only to St Anselm and Thomas Becket among the churchmen of his century, took immediate action and was an immense success with the monks. That he was held in such respect as a model abbot is all the more impressive when we remember that in 1129 he was made bishop of Winchester as well as abbot of Glastonbury and must have had little time to oversee his abbatial duties. Interestingly, a surviving document from the Glastonbury archives seems to indicate that he did at one point consider resigning the Glastonbury abbacy after he was made bishop of Winchester, but he obviously was unable to do so when it came to the crunch.[5] It seems possible that at some point

[4] See *The Early History of Glastonbury*, p. 67. My last suggestions are all, of course, highly conjectural and it should be remembered that even as orthodox a figure as Thomas Becket had an antique gem representing a pagan god fitted into his personal seal. Radford, moreover, speculates that Seffrid may possibly have returned to Glastonbury after his disgrace and that the Chichester tomb actually commemorates another individual of the same name. At Glastonbury itself Radford has uncovered the bones of an oldish man with buckles to hold up his hose who might well be, in Radford's view, the disgraced bishop.

[5] See *The Great Chartulary*, 3.ccxxxiv.

Henry was also prior of the nearby Cluniac priory of Montacute. When he held the deanery of Waltham he tried to buy a gem from the Holy Cross of Waltham (which had been found under miraculous circumstances at Montacute c.1035) for 100 marks.

Although elsewhere occupied much of the time, Henry kept up a close contact with Glastonbury matters and appointed very able men as priors, men such as Robert of Lewes who later became bishop of Bath. He also bought land around 1137 at Winchester from one Conon the moneylender so that a hospice could be built for future abbots of Glastonbury. Henry's accomplishments at Glastonbury are representative of the positive aspects of his character and mirror his achievements elsewhere in England as well. Keen on centralised administration and economic strength he recovered and restored to the monastery the manors of Mells, Uffculme, Camerton, Damerham, the village of Siston, Ashcott with Pedwell and Moorlinch. During his abbacy Glastonbury holdings extended into Ireland and the dependent priory of 'Ocymild' was established. In 1131 King Henry I granted him and succeeding abbots of Glastonbury the right to hold an annual three-day fair from the feast of Our Lady's Nativity (8 September): an important privilege since fairs provided agricultural landlords with a ready market for their products and also led to revenue from tolls and so forth. Henry, who acted as papal legate from 1139–1143, cunningly made sure that Glastonbury possessions, liberties and other rights were confirmed by both pope and king.

In a period which saw the full development of the obedientiary system – i.e., the allocation of the income from various estates to individual monastic offices – Henry acquired the island of Nyland and annexed it to the sacristan's office, and assigned to the sacristan a pension of 50 shillings from the church of Pucklechurch to keep a candle perpetually burning before the statue of the Virgin Mary in the Old Church. Henry gave money to the convent's kitchen and provided added salmon, honey and wine from nearby estates. Through his inspiration the principal feasts of the Virgin Mary were celebrated with more devotion and solemnity than previously. Somewhat of an epicure himself, then, he provided well for his monks, a fact which earned John of Glastonbury's pious approbation more than two centuries later: 'A suitable bestowal of bodily necessities usually encourages monks in the divine service and to a very great extent eliminates the hateful cause of grumbling.'

Henry had a passion for princely buildings and indulged in great construction campaigns at Glastonbury as well as at

Winchester and Cluny. At Glastonbury alone he built a bell tower, chapter house, cloister, lavatory, refectory, dormitory, the infirmary with its chapel, a beautiful building called the 'castellum', an attractive outer gate of dressed stone, a brewery and stables for many horses. A great connoisseur and lover of beautiful objects, he presented the church with nine precious palls, a fine tapestry, a quilt, nine copes woven with gold and jewels, two chasubles, a very valuable stole and maniple, two albs, a huge banner woven with gold, a silver cross and a great orphrey. He discovered, so the chroniclers relate, a precious sapphire (probably a round porphyry slab of a 'gradale' type used as a portable altar) which, according to tradition, had been brought to Glastonbury by St David himself but which had been hidden during the long periods of instability in the recesses of a door of the church of St Mary. He adorned this relic with gold, silver, and precious stones and had it prominently displayed in the church where it remained as an object of veneration for the rest of the history of the monastery.[6]

Henry also collected fine relics for Glastonbury: portions of the true Cross, remains of prominent saints including St Ursula, St Guthlac, the Virgin Mary, St John the Evangelist and St Benedict. Athough he did not himself produce any work of erudition, he was a supporter of scholarship and was a patron of two fine writers: William of Malmesbury (who dedicated *The Early History of Glastonbury* to him) and Gerald of Wales. He also gave more than 40 books to the Glastonbury library.

In spite of all these virtues Henry's character did have its shortcomings. His love of fine things, for example, extended well beyond any limit tolerable in a man vowed to monastic poverty and the ascetic St Bernard of Clairvaux contemptuously labelled him variously a rival pope, the old wizard of Winchester, and the whore of Winchester. Even with, or perhaps as a result of, his redoutable administrative abilities and royal connections he managed to get himself embroiled in complex and sometimes unsavory political intrigues and on occasion military skirmishes. Indeed, the contemporary chronicler, Henry of Huntingdon, referred to him with contempt as 'a new kind of monster, a monk-soldier'.[7] Nevertheless, in the twelfth century what Glastonbury needed very badly was a strong patron, an abbot capable of reorganising the financial life of the institution. For this reason, then, few abbots could

[6] In '*Mensa Sacra*: The Round Table and the Holy Grail' (*Journal of the Warburg and Courtauld Institutes* 19 [1956], 40–67) A. A. Barb has presented an ingenious argument linking this object, the Grail and the Round Table at Winchester.

[7] For an examination of Henry's career and an analysis of his character see David Knowles, *Saints and Scholars* (Cambridge, 1962), pp. 51–58.

Cambridge, Trinity College MS R.5.33 (724), fol.1r (mid thirteenth century). William of Malmesbury, The Early History of Glastonbury. *Note additions in later hand in lower margin.*

have been more suitable at the time than Henry of Blois, who in the local context at least well deserved the lavish praises heaped upon him by the Glastonbury writers.

After Henry of Blois' death the abbacy was vacant for one and a half years until Robert of Winchester (1173–80) was elected. In terms of internal policies he was an excellent abbot: he was generous to his monks and continued his predecessor's policy of handing land over to obedientiaries. In particular, he granted in perpetuity the demesne tithes of Sturminster Newton and Marnhull to the sub-prior and the sacrist to provide bread, wine and fish for conventual meals. He was especially sympathetic to the indigent and he allotted the remaining money from these estates to be distributed to poor people on his anniversary feast. Robert also gave a variety of ecclesiastical ornaments to the church.

Robert of Winchester

During Robert's abbacy, unfortunately, an acrimonious dispute with Wells came to a head. About 1170 bishop Reginald of Bath persuaded Robert to place the Seven Churches (that is, St Johns Glastonbury, Meare, Street, Butleigh, Shapwick, Moorlinch and Middlezoy), which Glastonbury had held in exempt status from episcopal and various other ecclesiastical jurisdictions since Saxon times, under a special officer to be called the abbot's archdeacon. To compensate the archdeacon of Wells for surrendering his claim to the churches, moreover, the income from the church of South Brent would henceforth be assigned to his office. The Glastonbury monks were horrified by the arrangement, which seemed in no way to be of advantage to them, and appealed to the pope to cancel it. This was, as we shall see, only the beginning of a long and desperate as well as cripplingly expensive struggle by Glastonbury against domination by the bishopric. Robert himself died in 1180 and was buried on the south side of the chapter house.

Things now started to go from bad to worse. After Robert's death King Henry II did not permit an abbatial election and drew himself on the revenues (which were legitimately his when there was no abbot) to help finance his wars in France. He also committed the abbey to the charge of Peter de Marcy, a Cluniac who was his agent in Rome and who had powerful connections in the Roman curia. Peter tried to persuade the monks to elect him as abbot, but they had heard rumours that he was irreligious, that he had a tendency to divert church funds to his own ends and that he had perhaps even engaged in mortal combat while bearing arms. To beguile the monks Peter 'feigned' a celebration of the Mass in the Old Church at Christmas. From the perspective of the community, this constituted a sacrilege since Peter was in a state of mortal sin at the time, and the church therefore stood in need of reconsecration. The evil was not, however, expiated in time and this accounted, so the later chroniclers thought, for the next calamity which befell the monastery: on St Urbans Day (May 25) 1184, there was a horrendous fire which destroyed all the buildings except a chamber and chapel recently built by Robert and a bell tower built by Henry of Blois. Gone was the beautiful Norman church, gone were the fine monastic buildings, Ine's church, the treasured vestments, ornaments, relic collections and books bequeathed by so many abbots and kings, and – most important of all – gone was the Old Church itself, universally hallowed as the first Christian church in Britain.

The only consolation for the monks was that the wicked Peter de Marcy died soon afterwards. Although no new abbot was officially appointed, Ralph Fitzstephen, the king's own chamberlain, now acted *in loco abbatis* and the king gave him carte blanche to spend the full abbatial revenues on rebuilding the church. First to be constructed, on the precise spot where the Old Church had stood, was the Church of St Mary (the

The Chapel of St Mary (the Lady Chapel), constructed on the site of the Old Church soon after the fire of 1184.

exquisite Lady Chapel of which large portions still survive). It was consecrated by Reginald Fitzjocelin, bishop of Bath, on June 11, 1186. Much later, probably during the fourteenth-century abbacy of John Chinnock, a memorial brass plate was erected on a pillar (whose substantial foundations were uncovered in 1921) with the following inscription:

> And lest the site or size of the earlier church should come to be forgotten ... this pillar is erected on a line extended southward through the two eastern angles of the same church, and cutting off from it the chancel aforesaid. And its length was 60 feet westward from that line; its width 26 feet; the distance of the centre of this pillar from the middle point between the said angles 48 feet.[8]

Ralph also repaired the outbuildings using stones from Henry of Blois' 'castellum', from the entire wall of the monastic enclosure and from the courtyard. He planned for a much larger main church to the east, laying foundations extending it 400 feet in length and 80 feet in width. (At this period, in fact, building activity was so intense that Glastonbury made exclusive use of its quarry at Doulting with the result that the Dean and Chapter of Wells – who normally had access to the Doulting quarries – had to substitute 'Chilcote Conglomerate' in their buildings. This change can still be seen in the wall of

Plate from column north of Lady Chapel.

---

[8] John A. Goodall has written an informative article on this topic, 'The Glastonbury Abbey Memorial Reconsidered', *The Antiquaries Journal* 66 (1986), 364–67.

the easternmost bay of the south aisle of the nave at Wells Cathedral.) When the Glastonbury incomes would not support the work the king himself supplied funds.

Nor did Ralph neglect the physical wants of the monks and their servants, considerably increasing their allotment of food. During Ralph's period of stewardship relics of St Patrick, St Indract and St Gildas were taken from their previous resting places in the ruined Old Church and placed in shrines. Even more remarkable was the discovery of St Dunstan's bones which – so it transpired – had long been secretly hidden in the church. This new discovery, not surprisingly, sparked a bitter controversy with the monks of Christ Church Canterbury, who also claimed to possess Dunstan's remains.

At this stage, just as Glastonbury's fortunes seemed to be improving, a new catastrophe struck: Henry II, their principal patron, died in July 1189 and his death was quickly followed by that of Ralph. The new king, Richard I, was concerned with crusading and had none of his predecessor's interest in Glastonbury; construction, as John of Glastonbury would later observe, 'therefore ceased, since there was no one to give the labourers their wages.' Richard appointed his own nephew Henry of Sully (1189–93) as abbot; he had formerly been prior of the Cluniac priory of Bermondsey. Henry was without doubt a man of intelligence, but he was also worldly and was motivated more or less exclusively by his own personal ambition. As a result his allegiance to his new monastery was conditional at best. Henry was not a builder and little construction took place during his abbacy. Still, one event of great significance and long ranging ramification did occur; that is, the discovery of King Arthur's remains in the ancient cemetery, a topic which forms the principal focus of chapter 8 of this book.

A shrewd and practical politician, Henry increased the prestige of the abbot's office by obtaining from Pope Celestine III a number of episcopal privileges: the use of the bishop's mitre, ring, gloves, dalmatic, tunical and sandals and the right to bless priestly vestments. He enlarged the holdings of various obedientiaries; in 1191, for example, he granted to the cellarer all the profits from a mill and fisheries beyond Street Bridge, except for a third part of the eels which were to be retained by the abbot himself. To regularize the arrangements begun under Robert of Winchester and to regain undisputed control over the original 'Seven Churches', he gave up all claim to archidiaconal jurisdiction in the three churches added to Glastonbury's archdeaconry by abbot Robert, relinquished Pilton and South Brent and gave the church of Huish to Wells. At this point, however, just when he seemed to be stabilizing his

Henry of Sully

Abbot's crozier found during excavations of 1951.

church's affairs, he was offered the see of Worcester and, as John of Glastonbury aptly puts it, 'he fled like a hireling who sees the wolf approaching, exposing his sheep to the wolf's teeth.'

In the next abbot Savaric Fitzgeldewin (1193–1205) Glastonbury did indeed acquire a wolfish master, one whose personal ambition knew no bounds and who saw Glastonbury Abbey as a pawn in his own political game. Savaric was well connected and the complex web of his family relationships – including his close relationship with Reginald Fitzjocelin, bishop of Bath – formed part of the background to his various strategies. He seems to have been unusually aggressive from his youth onwards and as early as 1172 he received a stiff fine for trying to snatch a bow from the king's forester in Surrey. The Holy Wars provided a natural outlet for his type of personality and he accompanied King Richard on his crusade in the early 1190s. Soon afterwards, once he had established influential contacts in Rome, he began to cast about for a suitable ecclesiastical post in England. His strategy was complicated: he planned first to have his cousin Reginald promoted to the See of Canterbury (where he would be a very powerful ally) and then to succeed himself to the See of Bath (which he planned to re-establish on a much expanded level). Reginald obtained the appointment to Canterbury in November 1191, but then died in December of the same year. Savaric, nevertheless, received priest's orders and was confirmed bishop of Bath in August 1192.

In the meantime, King Richard had been captured by Savaric's relation the German emperor Henry VI, and Savaric was appointed to act as intermediary in arranging the terms for his release. Now in a position of even greater strength than before, Savaric decided to obtain the see of Canterbury for himself. (Savaric was first and foremost a politician and never seems to have developed much of a loyalty to his assigned See. Indeed, at one point Peter of Blois, Archdeacon of Bath, had to write pleadingly to him, asking him to put in an appearance in his diocese.) Under duress Richard wrote on his behalf, but as soon as possible repudiated the letters and returned to the support of his own candidate, Hubert Walter (who ultimately got the position). Savaric had also insisted that Richard agree to an annexation of the Glastonbury Abbey to the See of Bath – and it was at this precise point that Henry of Sully accepted the bishopric of Worcester and left the monastery without an abbot and vulnerable to depredation. Savaric returned to England and summoned Glastonbury's prior, Thomas Harold, to Bath and announced that he, Savaric, was henceforth both abbot of Glastonbury and bishop of Bath; Glastonbury, in

Romanesque north door of the Lady Chapel. The doorway is part of the original design, but the elaborate sculpture groups may have been completed a generation later.

other words, had become a bishop's monastery. When the monks resisted this new state of affairs and appealed to Rome, Savaric craftily managed to obtain testimonials stating that in no other manner could the 'ancient' rift between Glastonbury and Wells be healed. He got a privilege from Pope Celestine III in 1195 confirming the union and calling him and his successors bishops of Bath and Glastonbury. This was followed by a second privilege in 1196.

At this point, King Richard – now released from the emperor's custody – began to waver and, stating that he had been coerced, decided to take the monastery back into his own hands. He therefore allowed the convent to elect their fellow monk William Pica as abbot on November 25, 1198. Savaric was predictably furious and excommunicated William and his supporters, laying an interdict on the house. Pica, a sincere and morally upright individual, was politically no match for the wily Savaric and he lost much internal support by repudiating various luxuries through which Savaric had attempted to bribe the more worldly of the monks. After imposing a strict regime on the whole community William went to Rome and presented his case to the new pope Innocent III; he received a favourable hearing from the pope and the interdict was lifted.

While Pica was in Rome Richard died and was succeeded by King John, whom Savaric won over to his point of view (through substantial bribes, according to the chroniclers). Seeing himself in a position of strength again, Savaric decided that it was now time to take Glastonbury by force and he came with a band of armed men to the monastery where he had the gates forced open. He then marched in and had himself enthroned as abbot. Those of the monks who would not submit to him were dragged out into the courtyard and severely beaten. They were then locked in the infirmary, deprived of food and water and tortured in various other ways. Indeed, the treatment was so harsh that at least one monk died of his wounds. Savaric demoted the prior Thomas Harold and appointed in his stead the former prior James – who had much earlier been dismissed because of his dissolute manner of life, and who therefore had a grudge against the community as a whole.

Figure of knight on archivolt over north doorway of the Lady Chapel. According to Bligh Bond's interpretation, this figure forms the first illustration for a sequence depicting the Massacre of the Innocents.

Even after this show of force and the calculated reorganization of the monastery, grumblings continued among the monks. Soon the resistance became so intense that one Jocelyn of Wells – later to be bishop of Bath – came back to the monastery with a troop of soldiers, laymen rather than monks. This band arrived just as the monks were about to celebrate High Mass. They pushed their way into the church and dragged off the five strongest protesters, one *per virilia*, and put them in prison in Wells where, after cruel punishments, they were deported to other monasteries. By this time Innocent III was convinced that the only hope for reconciliation lay in the union and he therefore quashed William Pica's election and confirmed his predecessor's privilege. The monks' valiant struggle at last seemed doomed to failure.

In 1202 the pope appointed several impartial judges to see that the union be properly confirmed and that Glastonbury be remodelled on the pattern of the best ordered cathedral priories. Careful instructions for the union were laid down. Glastonbury was not to decrease significantly in size nor in its duties of hospitality and almsgiving. In recent times the number of monks had been around seventy and only slightly earlier as high as eighty, but as a result of the various misfortunes of the last few years only fifty-two monks remained at the time of the union; the judges decreed that sixty would be an appropriate number in future. The judges felt that it was necessary to maintain the twenty-three hereditary servants, but there were some doubts in their minds about the need for the further eighty casual servants. Carefully managed the annual income of the monastery would run to around £800

Figure of knight with infant impaled on his sword, from the Massacre of the Innocents sequence on archivolt over north doorway.

– henceforth one quarter would go to the bishop and the other £600 to the monks. The bishop was to take possession of Meare, the abbot's house by the Lady Chapel and ten manors. Of the alien priories he would receive Kilcomman in Ireland, but the monks would retain Bassaleg in Monmouthshire and Looe Island in Cornwall.

The situation of the 23 permanent servants mentioned in the terms of union is an interesting one. These officials enjoyed hereditary tenure of their office by charter; they received a large variety of perquisites and could not be dismissed except in cases of gross dereliction of duty. By the thirteenth century these inherited positions represented an unwieldly structure and a heavy encumbrance. Not surprisingly, therefore, a gradual process of buying them out was begun. The office of the master baker, held by the Pasturel family, for example, was finally bought up in 1305 when the widow of John Pasturel surrendered claim to the laundry property (the family had intermarried with the hereditary launderers). Mistress Pasturel received a suitable house in Glastonbury for the rest of her life and each day got 2 loaves of bread and a jug of beer; on four days of the week she received a dish of fresh meat from the abbot's kitchen and on the other three days she was given a penny to buy something to eat with her bread. Each year she was provided with a suitable robe or with 2 marks to buy clothing. In other words, she received the medieval equivalent of the benefits of our modern welfare society. There were two families of master cooks by the end of the twelfth century, one of whose surname was Cox; this family had held the same position since the time of St Dunstan and did not surrender it until well into the first part of the fourteenth century. The goldsmiths, on the other hand, gave up their position in 1262. During the heyday of the system – that is during the period of Savaric's abbacy – there were also hereditary butlers, market-reeves and store-reeves, stewards of the household, ushers, keepers of the parks, stewards, and vineyard-wardens.

Soon after the judges had mapped out the terms of the union, William Pica died mysteriously in Rome and the monks suspected that he had been poisoned by Savaric's agents. They sent new monks to Rome, but in every case these individuals were waylaid by Savaric's men. The situation seemed to grow more oppressive and more hopeless practically by the day. At this dark hour, however, Savaric died suddenly and the monks – as John of Glastonbury puts it – 'catching their breath after so long an oppression beneath the yoke of servitude' began to fight the annexation with renewed vigour.

After Savaric's death, the old enemy of the monks, Jocelyn (1206–1218), was appointed bishop of Bath and Glastonbury.

Two women weeping, from the Massacre of the Innocents sequence on archivolt over north doorway.

Fortunately for the community, King John – who was probably governed by his own interests at this juncture as previously – now wrote in very strong terms to Pope Innocent III to demand that Glastonbury be restored to its former status, stating that the 'poor and wayfarers' had suffered badly as a result of the division. The Pope, however, felt it unfitting to act at once and recommended caution; he suggested that the matter be reconsidered next time there was to be an episcopal election. Soon after this King John's own disputes with the pope over the question of the appointment of Stephen Langton as Archbishop of Canterbury grew more intense and England came under papal interdict (1208–1213). No further action could take place until after the Interdict was lifted; but then, in 1215 King John gave bishop Jocelyn the official right to appoint a separate abbot of Glastonbury. As a kind of consolation to the See he also gave the patronage of Glastonbury to the bishop; the bishop was to have the naming of the abbot and custody (which included as a perquisite the substantial income arising from the monastic estates) in vacancies between abbots, and to have some of the usual feudal dues and liberties. In 1218/19 the representatives from Glastonbury and Wells met at Shaftesbury with arbitrators appointed by the new pope, Honorius III, and Glastonbury at last regained its independence, even though yet more properties and patronages had to be surrendered. Although they had wanted the dissolution at almost any price, the monks were, with good reason, disgruntled at the terms meted out to them. They felt that their losses were disastrous and they wrote pleadingly to the king asking him to remember the venerable age of their church: it was, they reminded him, a 'shining jewel of your crown, not to be so lightly thrown aside'.

During the period of overlordship by the bishop the monks had turned more and more to the prior as the real leader of the community. During Savaric's abbacy they showed great respect for Thomas Harold who manfully resisted the new regime, and they actively opposed Savaric's own appointee to the position. While Jocelyn acted as their nominal abbot Thomas was prior again. He gave the vestry a red cope with lions woven into it with silver thread and a valuable clasp. He built at least one chamber, provided for the poor and gave books to the convent: a psalter, Decretals, Biblical commentaries, missals and so forth. In other words, he fulfilled the kind of role which had traditionally been occupied by the abbot. Thomas was succeeded by Eustace Comyn, who had bravely represented the convent's point of view to King Richard in Normandy and who had endured a brief period of imprisonment during Savaric's abbacy. He was a great giver of vestments and also

Figure of seated king, from the Massacre of the Innocents sequence on archivolt over north doorway.

In 1219, Pope Honorius III issued a bull dissolving the union of the churches of Bath and Glastonbury. His seal was found during excavations in the abbey grounds.

acquired many relics for the monastery from one Peter of Spain who had brought them to England from Constantinople: wood from the Lord's Cross, bones from St Thomas of India, St Philip, St Barnabas, St John the Baptist, St Luke, St Mark, St Stephen, St Lawrence, St George, St Christopher, St Blaise, St Helen and St Scholastica. According to an unpublished fifteenth-century chronicle found in British Library, MS Cotton Cleopatra C.x., the Glastonbury convent entered the new church at Christmas 1213.

The first abbot to be freely elected by the convent after Honorius III's decree (which included a renewal of Celestine's privilege concerning the use of pontifical insignia) was William of St Vigor (1219–1223), who had in the previous year taken the agreement concerning dissolution to the Roman curia and who was an active opponent of the bishop. He was generous by nature and gave freely to both rich and poor. He believed in the importance of recreation for his monks and also, so we are told, felt that the strength of the beer should be increased. He gave the incomes from outlying churches to various obedientiaries and conceded money to the master of the works so that the building of the main church could continue. At the time of his death, however, the church could not have been completed, since his bones were deposited in the chapter house. A stone effigy, probably representing William of St Vigor, has been preserved and is now exhibited in the abbot's kitchen: he proudly wears his mitre, a defiant challenge, one feels, to the bishop of Bath.

The monks were unable to agree about who should be the next abbot and handed the decision over to an outside committee, with one proviso: that under no circumstances should Robert, prior of Bath – who had formerly been chaplain to their mortal enemy Savaric – be elected. They received their assurances on this point and the archdeacon of Wells, one of the committee members, even called the gout down upon himself as a punishment if Robert were elected. Fate, or human nature, being what it is, Robert was elected – and the gout, so we are told, was also visited upon the archdeacon. In spite of this inauspicious beginning, Robert of Bath (1223–1234) showed himself to be a remarkably fine abbot. The chroniclers relate that he was modest, pious and reasonable and that he brought back the observances of the Rule of St Benedict, which had fallen off during the recent years of tribulation. He improved finances and gave an annual gift of bread and wine to the convent for two important feast days. During his abbacy, moreover, King Henry III confirmed the traditional liberty of the Twelve Hides. In spite of all his positive achievements, nevertheless, the monks continued to

William of St Vigor

Stone effigy, possibly representing William of St Vigor.

Robert of Bath

resist Robert and he, in turn, diverted more and more of the monastic business away from the unfriendly monks and into the hands of seculars. At last, after eleven years of conflict, he decided to step down and to return to Bath. In gratitude for this decision, the monks granted him a pension of £60.

His successor, Michael of Amesbury (1235–1252) was elected by the unanimous consent of the community. The choice was a logical one, since Michael had already shown himself to be a superb administrator. In fact, when he was still chamberlain the then abbot Robert singled him out with special concessions on account of his 'faithful and profitable' service in this office. Before becoming abbot Michael had travelled widely on abbey business both in England and abroad and made shrewd contacts in the court and in the curia. He was interested in education and concerned himself with the training of the young men under his charge. His own particular bent seems to have been in legal matters and he brought to his monastery many victories in the ecclesiastical and in the civil courts. In 1243 King Henry III granted an annual six-day fair in September (at Michaelmas time) located at 'St Michael de Torr' to replace the earlier two-day event. Michael regained lost properties from the bishop and from private landlords and acquired new land. Following a national trend among monasteries Michael put much soil under plough, and increased Glastonbury's livestock holdings: at his death he left 892 oxen, 60 draught horses, 23 foals, 233 cows, 19 bulls, 153 bullocks, 6,717 sheep and 327 pigs. He gave many ornaments to the church and increased the holdings of a number of obedientiaries. He was considerate of the personal needs of the monks under his charge and in 1248 wrote to Pope Innocent IV to explain that because his monastery was situated in a cold and damp location it was often dangerous for the monks to attend services bare-headed. Might they, therefore, use skull-caps? The pope was sympathetic to the request and informed the archbishop of Canterbury of his affirmative decision. Michael was an enthusiastic builder both on abbey estates and at home. He oversaw the construction of a sea wall at Brent Marsh, added ten mills to abbey properties, and erected almost 100 new houses inside and outside the abbey precincts.[9] He kept a close eye on tenants and in 1243, for example, Geoffrey de Langelegh had to explain why he was maintaining 'one hundred and fifty goats and twenty oxen and cattle beyond the

[9] On the identification of the mills and on Michael's general policies in this area see Richard Holt, 'Whose were the profits of corn milling? An aspect of the changing relationship between the abbots of Glastonbury and their tenants 1086–1350', *Past and Present* 116 (1987), 3–23. Taking mills as a representative (and profitable) example, Holt notes that Michael made it his policy to get properties previously held in customary tenure back into the abbot's direct holding.

number which he and his ancestors were wont to have, to wit, sixteen oxen only.' Michael founded St Mary's Hospital with a hall and chapel at the eastern end. The roof was removed from this structure in the fourteenth century and the two rows of cubicles were converted into two rows of small cottages. As late as 1958 the south side was demolished, but fortunately the rest remain as the almshouses on Magdalene Street. Within the monastic enclosure itself Michael carried work on the choir forward and the transepts at last took on a recognizable form.

Glastonbury, 1856. A photograph by Colonel Verschoyle.

By 1252 Michael's eyesight was failing; he felt old and worn out and decided that it was now time 'to pass on to the contemplative life of Mary's rest which he had now earned by the active services of Martha'. The monks reluctantly accepted his resignation and rewarded him generously for his contributions: he received £160 a year, the manor of Meare, a food allowance and a large chamber and chapel at Glastonbury for his own use – the total of his pensions and perquisites forms an instructive contrast with the terms of abbot Robert's settlement seventeen years before. Michael died the next year and was, suitably, the first abbot to be buried in the new church, before the altar of St Thomas in the north transept. His epitaph laid particular stress on his accomplishment in breaking the chains of Glastonbury's bondage to the episcopal see.

The monks decided to elect their next abbot by ballot among themselves, as was one of the options, rather than trusting to the judgement of an outsider. There were two main candidates – Roger of Ford and Robert of Petherton – and the election was hotly contested. Although Roger of Ford (1252–1261)

Roger of Ford

emerged as victor, a feeling of bitterness remained and contributed to the mixed success of his abbacy. Roger had been born in Glastonbury, had presumably been educated there, and had shown himself an intelligent scholar and an able administrator. He was the author of a *Mirror of the Church* – which survives unpublished as MS Cotton Tiberius B.13 in the British Library – and at the time of his election, when he must have been a relatively elderly man, he was the monastery's chamberlain. Obviously a shrewd politician (he had earlier convinced the community at Wells that he would be an ally if elected abbot) and a highly litigious individual, he immediately consolidated his contacts with the royal court. Once he felt he had the favour of the king he decided, previous sentiments to the contrary, that he would confront William Bytton I, bishop of Bath and Wells, over a variety of questions of jurisdiction. He threw himself enthusiastically into his legal battles which turned out to be extremely expensive. To help finance litigation he put the monks on short rations and also tended to neglect the petty details of daily life in the cloister. The monks were affronted by his lack of interest; and hungry men, of course, quickly become restless. The community, therefore, appealed to the bishop as their patron to make a visitation, knowing full well that the bishop himself had a number of grudges to settle with Roger. The bishop came, although he had just recently been to Glastonbury, and after two days of examination he decided that Roger should be deposed. Roger, however, was shrewd enough to anticipate the bishop's verdict and on the day of his deposition directed his own men to drive the bishop's guard out of the convent. The bishop then retreated to the refectory, surrounded by friendly monks, and tried to take stock of the situation over a leisurely lunch. During this pause Roger gathered up assorted treasures and marched out of the main gate with his supporters and headed for the royal court. Stunned and chagrined, the bishop acted upon his prerogative as patron and chose Robert of Petherton as abbot at the more or less unanimous request of the remaining monks. Robert was quickly consecrated at Wells, then returned to Glastonbury where he very publicly celebrated mass before the High Altar. Next day he presided in chapter – rearranging certain obediences and attempting to make a distinct administrative mark, new and separate from Roger's policies.

Meanwhile, Roger was being assiduous in his petitions at court and obtained a judgment in his favour. The king, moreover, considered that he, not the bishop, held the right of patronage and therefore was irked with William Bytton's action. Roger returned with the king's officers and demanded to be reinstated, to which move the bishop responded by

Thirteenth-century seal of Glastonbury Abbey, showing the Blessed Virgin flanked by St Catherine and St Margaret. In the centre arch of the base is a church. On the reverse are representations of St Patrick, St Dunstan and St Benignus.

Seal of Robert of Petherton.

Robert of Petherton

excommunicating him. Ignoring the excommunication, Roger summoned the porter and took possession of the keys of the monastery. The servants were loyal to him and respected the king's decision, but most of the monks, rallying under the prior, appealed to the apostolic see. Roger and Robert both journeyed to Rome to present their cases and eventually – in 1259 – a cardinal was appointed to settle the case. He ruled in Roger's favour, but also insisted that both parties acknowledge guilt, that the settlement be amicable, and that Robert be compensated by the income from two manors.

Although very old by this time, Roger felt altogether rejuvenated by the decision and forthwith threw himself into a violent dispute with the bishop over four manors which both Glastonbury and Wells claimed. He obtained the services of the best lawyers he could find and planned complex strategies, but just as everything was in place for the legal battle Roger suddenly died while visiting the bishop of Rochester's manor at Bromley in October 1261. His body was taken to Westminster and buried there. In his will he showed himself propitiatory to the monks and left money to the chamberlain to provide fish, wine and spices for the community on the anniversary of his death. On every All Soul's Day he asked that clothing be distributed to the poor in his memory.

Immediately upon Roger's death, the prior and convent re-elected Robert of Petherton (1261–1274) as abbot. As it happens, the choice was politically sound, since Robert already felt entitled to the office and would have heartily opposed any other candidate and since – as the chroniclers sensibly point out – Robert already received the income from a variety of abbey estates. By the time of his election Robert was approaching middle age. Tall in stature and by nature literary in interests, he turned out to be a good and effective administrator. During the previous period of legal battles discipline had badly fallen off and his first concern therefore lay with re-establishing the Rule as a model of behaviour. He next set about paying the various debts contracted by his predecessor, acquiring new lands and reorganising other holdings. He was especially skilled at turning agriculture to profit through demesne (i.e., direct) farming, although in this he was, in fact, following a national trend. Robert did a moderate amount of building at various outlying estates and at Glastonbury itself he built the abbot's chamber and a gate near the grange, together with fine new cattle barns. In 1266 King Henry III granted several new annual fairs on abbey estates.

During Robert's abbacy, at a time when Glastonbury's internal affairs appeared to have returned to an even keel, a new danger threatened: Walter Giffard, who was a close friend to Henry III, was made bishop of Bath and Wells and then appointed chancellor of the realm. He immediately revived old disputes and obtained letters from the king stating that Glastonbury fell under episcopal patronage. Backed by the king he forced the abbot to surrender the four manors, which Roger had tried to retrieve, as well as the patronage of six churches. The only hopeful sign for the monastery during this crisis was that Prince Edward consistently opposed the pact between his father and Giffard.

In 1272 Henry died and Prince Edward succeeded him as Edward I. Although dying of tuberculosis himself, Robert sent John of Taunton as a messenger to the new king, who produced a writ stating that he alone was patron of the abbey, that the election of the abbot was entirely in the king's hands and that it did not concern the bishop. John rushed back with the good news which he conveyed to the bedridden abbot: at peace, Robert died the next evening which, as it happened, was Easter Eve. Ostensibly out of respect for the festival, but actually out of fear that everything was not yet in place to make the king's writ effective, the monks decided not to announce Robert's death until after Easter. The Dean of Wells and the bishop's steward somehow heard rumours about Robert; they therefore turned up on the scene and insisted on speaking with the abbot. The bluff was called and the community was forced to announce Robert's death on Tuesday, when the Dean and steward in turn demanded fealty and put their bailiffs into the manors. Meanwhile, the custodian of Bristol Castle, who had also heard the rumours, arrived to take possession for the king and on Wednesday managed to chase off the bishop's men in what turned out to be a definitive victory. Robert, who seems to have been forgotten in all the excitement, now received full funeral honours and was buried at the feet of Michael of Amesbury before the altar of St Thomas Becket in the north transept.

Not surprisingly, the monks made a great show of soliciting the permission of the king before they chose their next abbot, John of Taunton (1274–1291), who soon set to work at exploiting the king's benevolence on the patronage question. As usual, however, there were setbacks and complications. The worst came when King Edward's close friend Robert Burnell was made bishop of Bath and Wells in 1275 and persuaded the king to make various concessions of money and land from Glastonbury's holdings to the bishopric. Edward also held back a number of promised liberties until the monastery made certain payments to his treasury. The financial problems were exacerbated when on September 11, 1275 a large earthquake occurred, totally destroying the ancient Norman chapel of St

Seal of John of Taunton.

John of Taunton

Michael on the Tor and badly damaging the chapter house. (Earthquakes seem to have been an architectural hazard in this region at the period; on December 21, 1248, for example, a roof-boss was dislodged at Wells Cathedral as the result of an earth-tremor.)

In spite of his personal loyalty to Burnell King Edward had an even more powerful allegiance to Glastonbury because of its Arthurian associations. He saw his various military campaigns as Arthurian adventures and he cultivated an image of himself as *Arthurus redivivus*.[10] After his first victorious expedition into North Wales in 1277, Edward forced Llywelyn to do him homage and not long afterwards he claimed the crown of Arthur from the Welsh – a trophy which, unlike the Stone of Scone (another of his imperial trophies), was soon afterwards permanently lost. At Easter 1278 he and Queen Eleanor, accompanied by Robert Kilwardby, archbishop of Canterbury, came to Glastonbury to celebrate a major Arthurian event timed to coincide with the consecration of the High Altar.

Before the king's arrival, Walter de Everslegh, vice marshal to the Earl Marshal, arrived to organize accommodation for the royal party, but he was prevented from doing his work because the ancient liberties of Glastonbury forbade anyone – no matter how important – from exercising his office within the Twelve Hides. Richard Pyk, who was the guardian of the liberties of Glastonbury, was delegated in his place, therefore, to perform this and various other functions.

The king and his entourage arrived soon after this episode and were elegantly accommodated and treated with suitable respect. Nevertheless, when the king wished to hold assizes on Easter Monday it was pointed out that ancient precedent forbade him from doing so within the Twelve Hides. Voluntarily, therefore, he moved the assizes to the village of Street. On Tuesday the whole court was entertained at the monastery's expense and at twilight King Arthur's coffin – which up to this time had probably been stored in the Treasury – was opened to reveal two separate chests decorated with Arthur and Guenevere's portraits and their arms. In her portrait the queen was shown fully crowned, but Arthur was represented with a battle-damaged crown, his left ear cut off and marks from the blow which slew him. When the caskets were opened the king's bones turned out to be of a great size, the queen's of a delicate beauty. (For moderns, unused to the cult of relics, it is hard to imagine in what this beauty might have consisted.) The next day, that is the Wednesday, King Edward wrapped his illustrious predecessor's remains in a precious pall and

10 On this topic see Roger Sherman Loomis, 'Edward I, Arthurian Enthusiast', *Speculum* 28 (1953), 114–27.

Queen Eleanor did the same with Guenevere's, and the relics were replaced in the chests, although the head and knee joints of each were temporarily kept out to be shown to the people to encourage their devotion. The caskets were finally reverently placed in a stately mausoleum before the High Altar, that is, in the most appropriate position for a saintly founder's tomb.[11] In this highly public ceremony Edward was clearly emphasizing that he was the legitimate successor to Arthur as king of all Britain. John Leland saw the mausoleum as late as the 1530s and described it as black marble, having two lions at each end and an effigy of the king at the foot.[12] For some reason it was completely destroyed during the Dissolution – although even the arch-Protestants of the period were devotees of the Arthurian cult – and only the base of the cavity where it had been placed remained intact. The site was excavated in 1931 and is now marked with a plaque on the surface of the grass.

During his abbacy John of Taunton tried to increase Glastonbury's land holdings and took possession of the earlier appropriated churches of Doulting and East Brent. In 1283 he was granted a yearly fair for four days at the feast of St Dunstan. He was one of the two abbots presiding over the Provincial Chapter of the Black monks when a new and radical set of constitutions, aimed at imposing dietary reform, increased theological study, and regularity throughout the order, was approved. In his own church the west end of the nave and the Galilee were completed. John constructed outer chambers, dovecots and a new gate. He gave numerous ornaments to the church: 'a crystal cross, two beautiful brocades woven in gold designs of leopards and birds, an indigo cape with castles and lions woven in gold and varius other costly ornaments for the altar.' According to the local chroniclers, John was a doctor of theology, but no record of this degree is found in the Oxford archives. It is certain, however, that he was a good scholar and particularly interested in theology: as abbot he acquired over forty volumes, which were later stored in the Galilee itself – these concerned Biblical subjects for the most part and some were written by contemporary authors. In 1291 John left Glastonbury to attend the funeral of Queen Eleanor and caught a cold which led to serious complications. Soon afterwards he died and was buried near his immediate prede-

Modern plaque indicating location of Arthur's tomb before the High Altar.

---

[11] In 1368, after he had extended the length of the choir, Walter de Monington moved the tomb again, so it would continue to occupy its prominent position before the High Altar. At this time the tomb was opened and the enclosed account of Edward I's visit noted down; this survives in Oxford, MS Bodleian Ashmole 826, fol. 107.

[12] See Leland's *Assertio inclytissimi Arturii regis Britanniae* in W. E. Mead, ed., *The Famous Historie of Chinon of England* (EETS, OS 165; London, 1925), p. 76; also my 'Polydore Vergil and John Leland on King Arthur: the battle of the books', *Interpretations* 15 (1984), 86–100.

cessor on the south side of the north transept.

About the next abbot, John of Kent (1291–1303), we know relatively little. He seems to have worked at furnishing the completed choir and its altars – giving a large and precious cross, an ivory statue of the Virgin Mary and various altar ornaments. He also provided episcopal equipment of the sort the abbot of Glastonbury was entitled to enjoy: a finely wrought pastoral staff, a mitre and gloves adorned with gold and precious stones, and a magnificent ring called 'Caman'. He freed the monastery from a large debt owed to a merchant of Lucca. In the late thirteenth century, Italian merchants dominated the English wool trade, and this debt probably arose because an earlier abbot had sold wool in advance to the merchant and the subsequent yields did not measure up to the contract. John provided an income for the pittancer to use to supply the convent with good wine, fine fish and spice every year on his anniversary; if good wine could not be found, he stipulated, there should be an increased allotment of spices. On the anniversary, moreover, the sacrist was instructed to find four candles, each weighing one pound, to burn round the abbot's tomb while Evensong of the Dead and Dirge were being sung, and also while High Mass was being sung in the choir. A candle of a half pound was to burn continually from the beginning of the service for the Dead until the end of High Mass. In general, then, John seems to have been an adequate but unexciting abbot, many of whose interests appear to have concerned creature comforts.

The next abbot, Geoffrey Fromond (1303–1322), did much to raise the monastic community to one of its highest levels of productivity. The name Fromond, a surname and not a toponymic, suggests relatively gentle birth, as do references to other Fromonds in high positions in contemporary Glastonbury records. Although pledged to religion, Fromond maintained a concern for his own immediate family and towards the end of his life made sound financial provisions for three of his sisters. Surviving registers from his abbacy give us no sense of what he was like as an individual – they describe neither his spiritual life nor his feelings about his colleagues – but they do show us that he was sharply attuned to contemporary economic trends. For example, he preferred to rent estates for cash rather than produce crops for sale, as these were less in demand than previously. He was keen to define property rights and to establish specific boundaries of the estates. He continued the policy established by his predecessors of resuming control over lands which had gradually fallen into the hands of the families of hereditary servants, completing the absorption of lands held by the bakers and the launderers and taking over more of the cooks' properties.

Although careful and perhaps aloof, Fromond was not unnecessarily strict with the monks and he made certain that their allowances of food and clothing were generous. As a result he was popular and when John Drokensford, bishop of Bath and Wells, made his visitations, no serious complaints were lodged concerning the abbot's regime. In fact, the bishop was somewhat piqued by the solidarity of the monks and railed against their illicit oaths of secrecy. That Fromond used the increased income which he had managed to generate for the physical glory of the monastery must also have pleased the community at large. He spent £1,000 on buildings; during his abbacy, for example, the central tower of the Great Church was completed and the eastern part of the nave vaulted. Indeed, work on the church had, by now, progressed so far that Fromond had the church dedicated and gave many beautiful ornaments (over £200 worth) to it. Fromond seems to have

View of the ruins about 1800, from Warner's Antiquities of Glaston-bury *(1826).*

taken only a nervously conservative interest in the outside political world and kept well out of the problems surrounding Edward II's reign. For a number of years he managed to avoid attending parliament on the grounds of ill health, for which there is no supporting evidence in his vigorous activities on his own turf.

Walter of Taunton's abbacy (1322–23) only lasted for approximately a month. At the time of his election on December 7, 1322, he seemed the natural choice, having proved himself an intelligent and able prior. Unfortunately, his death occurred before the end of January, presumably through some kind of sudden illness. For some time before he became abbot

Walter of Taunton

he seems to have been taking over abbatial duties and had a pulpitum (choir screen) built at the west end of the choir, whose decoration included 10 large statues. He also had a cross designed for the church which featured images of Christ, Mary, and St John. He gave 10 copes decorated with scenes from saints' lives and a number of vestments. He seems to have been particularly devoted to St Dunstan and presented his shrine with two silver basins, two silver platters, and six silver saucers with five silver vessels to go with them. As prior he had shown himself interested in theology and law and at his death left two summas and several standard works on canon and civil law.

After Walter of Taunton's unexpected death a quick search had to be made for a successor and the choice fell on Adam of Sodbury (1323–1334), a capable individual who had previously been both cellarer and sacrist. Probably a native of South Gloucestershire where the monastery had a number of holdings, Adam turned out to be a first-rate choice from an economic point of view. Although he does not appear to have had a university degree, he showed an interest in scholarly books and acquired a number of historical texts, a copy of Bartholomaeus Anglicus' massive encyclopedia *On the Properties of Things*, and a new legendary. In books as in other areas he had excellent taste and he gave the monastery a beautiful Bible, finely illustrated psalters and benedictionals and a stone tablet on which were skilfully carved four stories from the life of the Virgin Mary. The list of gold and silver ecclesiastical ornaments he assembled is long and almost cloying. He loved fine materials and acquired three sets of silk of which the first was red and delicately embroidered with designs of purple beasts and eagles, the second green with red griffins and peacocks and the third green with purple beasts and birds. He obtained relics of St Catherine and a gold ring worn by Thomas Becket at the time of his martyrdom.

The statement by John of Glastonbury that Sodbury built a large and excellent clock has caused much speculation among scholars. Some of the more sceptical of modern authorities have argued that the allusion is to a clepsydra (i.e., water clock) rather than to a mechanical clock in the modern sense, but the Latin description does seem to make quite clear that the reference is to a mechanical device. Unfortunately, however, it cannot be proved that John Leland alludes to the same clock when he notes that in the church there was a: 'Horologium. Petrus Lightfote monachus fecit hoc opus.' Nor, in spite of recurring rumours to the contrary, does there seem to be any connection between this instrument and the clock now found at Wells Cathedral, which was made c.1390. It is tempting, on

Adam of Sodbury

the other hand, to imagine that Chaucer is thinking of this very machine when he tell us that: 'Wel sikerer was [Chaunticleer's] crowing in his loge / Than is a clok or any abbey orloge.'

Clocks were beginning to become more common in this period and at Durham Priory, for example, the first mechanical clock appeared late in the fourteenth century. Richard Segbroke, a Durham monk, used this new instrument as a reference point when he wrote a summary of his priory's horarium. The timetable at Glastonbury Abbey would have been roughly similar. According to Segbroke, the monks got up for matins at midnight and the service took about an hour. In summer and on various winter feasts prime followed at 6 or 6:30 a.m. and lasted for thirty minutes. The morrow mass was sung at nine o'clock and was followed by the daily chapter meeting at ten. This was succeeded by high mass at eleven. The monks then had dinner at noon and were allowed a period of rest until two o'clock when the service of nones took place. Vespers began at four and was followed by a break which lasted until supper at some time between 6 and 7 o'clock. The last office of the day was compline, after which the community was supposed to retire, although many monks took strolls in the garden or found various other diversions.[13]

Music appealed to Adam and he gave five large bells for the campanile; he also had six new bells cast for the tower of the abbey church. He had an organ constructed and assigned twenty marks a year for the maintenance of four chantry priests, specifying that they should 'daily serve with their melodies chants in the chapel of the blessed Virgin.' As elsewhere, during the sung offices the choirmaster would have led his young choristers through the intricacies of 'playnsange, prikenot, faburdon, dischaunte and countre'. Adam spent £1,500, we are told, on actual building: he completed the vaulting of the nave of the great church of St Peter and St Paul, the walls of which were painted with portraits of kings, saints and benefactors, and to which he gave many statues. He had chapels dedicated to St Silvester and St George constructed and united the Galilee to St Mary's Chapel. He worked on the great hall and built a new chapel on the Tor; the standing tower is fifteenth century and incorporates the west end of Adam's chapel. Adam provided the sacristan with money for distribution to the monks on the anniversaries of himself, his parents and John of Breynton, who would ultimately succeed him as abbot. In general he was concerned about the monks' physical well being and made special allowances for monks on holiday as well as providing fine accommodation and food.

St Michael's Tower, Glastonbury Tor, in the late eighteenth century before restoration.

[13] See R. B. Dobson, *Durham Priory, 1400–1450* (Cambridge, 1973), pp. 69–70.

When Adam became abbot he inherited a number of debts, but he showed himself to be a shrewd manager and successfully continued his predecessors' policies of consolidation, and got back the properties of the last of the hereditary servants. In 1327 he made an agreement with the Dean of Wells over boundaries in the moors north of Meare after a particularly acrimonious dispute in which the bishop had demolished various dikes and sluices and had deliberately fired the moor all the way from Burtle Priory. Even after the agreement both sides continued to accuse the other of rustling cattle. By various kinds of strategies and through tidying up vaguely defined rights to other holdings Adam managed to increase the abbey's annual income by £200. He also challenged (without success, as it happens) the bishop of Bath and Wells over the question of the jurisdiction of the archdeaconry of Glastonbury. He built a sea wall near Brent and windmills at Shapwick and Meare, chapels at Meare, Pilton and Doulting and a new church at Shapwick. He seemed especially interested in Meare and had the church reconsecrated in honour of St Benignus. Ever mindful of physical comfort, he also added rooms to his manor there and put up stone farm buildings which are still in use. It is possible that the surviving stone barn at Glastonbury, justly famous for its cruciform shape and the fine carved evangelist emblems over the doors, was built during Adam's abbacy, although it may, in fact, date from slightly later in the century.[14]

The Abbey Barn, Glastonbury, now the Somerset Rural Life Museum.

Unlike his immediate predecessors Adam was actively involved in the national political scene. Having disputed with Hugh le Despenser and therefore being unsympathetic to Edward II's rule, he attended the meeting of temporal and spiritual lords at the time of the king's deposition and was

[14] Several other fine barns associated with the abbey survive: at Pilton, at Doulting, at Mells and at West Bradley.

Abbey barn at Doulting.

vocal in his opposition to the king. He was then appointed one of the delegates to take the motion that the king should abdicate in favour of his son to Kenilworth. Afterwards, when Edward III came to the throne, Adam assiduously cultivated him and in December 1331 he persuaded Edward and Philippa to visit the monastery as royal patrons. A description of their arrival survives.[15] First, Queen Philippa, attended by the king's sister, dismounted at the door of the church where she was received with much honour by the richly vested Convent; they then all solemnly processed to the choir. After she made her prayers her people offered a web of silk sprinkled with gold drops, which was later made into a chasuble. Next, they proceeded to the treasury where the prior described the antiquities and wonders. Having seen these she retired to her guest-chamber and, passing on her way through the cloister which the Convent had decorated throughout, saw the many gifts they were going to give to the king. After she entered the little cloister leading to the guesthouse she received her own gifts about which she expressed herself enthusiastic. Soon afterwards the king arrived on horseback and was received by the abbot in pontificals and another procession was formed before they returned to the choir. When the king had risen from his prayers, a cloth of gold as long as the altar was offered. He too saw the treasury, received magnificent gifts and then retired to the chamber which had been prepared for him at the end of the infirmary cloister. The ensuing entertainment

Figure of king on corbel on Abbey Barn.

15 See *The Great Chartulary of Glastonbury* 1.lxxiv–v; 194–95.

was lavish, and Adam spent £800 on food, accommodation and ceremony. It was, however, money well spent since he managed to obtain a number of rights and privileges from the king at this time. Most importantly, Edward agreed that in future the monks could administer their own properties during vacancies between abbots, although the king would still receive certain cash payments. Usually this right was extremely expensive to obtain and given out grudgingly, since the incomes during the vacancies could amount to a healthy sum. Edward also re-affirmed ancient liberties and let the monks appropriate the churches of Sowy, Ditcheat, Wrington and Sturminster Newton, on the manors of which they would henceforth have the right to hold markets and fairs.

It seems appropriate that the most interesting document surviving from Adam's abbacy concerns temporal rather than spiritual matters: it is an account of the garden in 1333–34.[16] At this time the chief gardener was one Thomas of Keynsham, who had four men working under him. His garden included an orchard, a vineyard, a herb garden, vegetable plots, flower beds and some pasture. Normally much of the income came from pasture, but in this particular season the herbage and nettles of the great garden were sold for only 4s 3d because three horses belonging to the cellarer and another monk had grazed there. The revenue from the garden produce totalled 58s 2d: 3 tuns of cider brought in the largest income, followed by 54 bolts of linen, 16 stones of hemp, and then smaller quantities of onions, madder plants, leeks and apples. The expenses included garden tools (a sickle, an axe, 5 new spades and 4 iron hoes), gloves and seeds (4 bushels of beans, 2 bushels of hemp and perhaps some linseed). Ten moles, we are told, were captured in the garden at a cost of 3d. This was a dry season, the gardener states, and the hay crop suffered. The weather did not, however, hurt the grape harvest which produced 1 pipe or four barrels of wine and 70 gallons of verjuice – both of which commodities were rendered to the cellarer. Local wine was popular with the monks who – according to various accounts – had fairly discerning palates. The monks also consumed large quantities of their own cider, and made a point of storing apples and pears for winter eating. The names of the spices which the gardener planted are not specified, but the total issue of seed for the year was two pounds. The monks grew and used what by our standards appear to be immense amounts of garlic: 3,000 cloves for seed, 2,000 for the abbot's kitchen, 6,000 for the larder at the inn. Leeks and onions were in great demand as was madder, which was employed for medical

[16] See Ian Keil, 'The Garden at Glastonbury Abbey: 1334–4', *Proceedings of the Somersetshire Archaeological and Natural History Society* 104 (1959–60), 96–101.

purposes, dye and perhaps for the preparation of cheese rennet.

The policies and goals of John of Breynton (1334–1342) were very similar to Adam's, under whom he had served ably as prior. Probably born in Breinton in Herefordshire, he may well have spent time as a young monk at Oxford and in his will he left £40 for a lodging to be built for Glastonbury monks at Oxford. He also provided 20s for them to buy a processional cross. When he was prior John built a hall, kitchen and domestic structures for the prior's office and had beautiful stairs made at the entrance to the orchard. He successfully challenged both the bishop of Bath and Wells and the archdeacon of Wells regarding territorial claims. Once elected abbot, he made sure that the question of the control of the vacancy of the monastery, so carefully obtained by Adam, be securely recognized by the crown. He next turned his attention to building and finished the abbot's great hall, which had already been constructed as far as the top of the windows; this was a major task and cost £1,000. He then completed the abbot's chapel and built a long chamber next to the abbot's chamber, added a wall and set up a *piscina* nearby. He added to the endowment for the monks' kitchen, redeemed two fiefs in the abbot's kitchen, authorized the building of a new windmill at Walton and acquired various other bits of land. He spent 500 marks on St Dunstan's shrine and made the final payment on a magnficent gold chalice earlier acquired by Adam. He gave a number of ornaments to the treasury including an interesting collection of five pontifical rings (which, of course, the abbot of Glastonbury was entitled to wear): one with a large sapphire, the second with a red stone in the fashion of a man's head with a crown, the third with a white stone in the fashion of a man's head, with wings coming together at the back, the fourth with a red amethyst, and the fifth with a white stone in the fashion of a man's head with a black bird on the joint of its face.

As it turns out, John's concern with muniments has been a principal factor in allowing modern writers to reconstruct Glastonbury's history. John appointed a keeper of records who was to have the assistance of a junior monk and an annual budget of a mark, of which half was to be spent on the preservation of records and half was to go to himself. To the abbot the time seemed right for a consolidation of all the abbey archives in the form of a huge book of records which has since come to be known as the *Great Chartulary of Glastonbury*. The compiler listed 1,335 documents which were apparently housed in one or more vaulted chambers and stored in pigeon-holes. He worked his way right through the muniments and made copies of all relevant texts. The documents can be divided, roughly speaking, into seven sections: (1) spiritualities (archidiaconal jurisdiction in the Seven Churches, churches appropriated to Glastonbury, churches from which Glastonbury drew a pension); (2) documents concerned with the relationship of the monastery to the diocesan; (3) deeds concerning Burtle Priory, of which Glastonbury had the patronage; (4) papal and royal privileges; (5) deeds concerned with the feudal position of Glastonbury; (6) deeds concerned with Glastonbury estates; (7) a detailed examination of Glastonbury estates, place by place and manor by manor.

In studying the *Great Chartulary*, masterfully edited by Dom Aelred Watkin, scholars have learned a great deal about the monastic officals, the history of the various obedientiaries, what positions existed in the abbey hierarchy, who held them, how much income was assigned to the position and from which estates it was derived. The *Great Chartulary* makes many allusions to the prior, who was aided in his duties by a subprior and a third prior. The prior was the second in command and oversaw much of the day-to-day running of the monastery, especially when the abbot was away (as he needed to be much of the time), when there was a vacancy between abbots, or during periods of dispute over the abbacy. The prior was, moreover, a natural, but not inevitable, candidate as succeeding abbot. The archdeacon of Glastonbury also held a key position and had full ecclesiastical jurisdiction over the Seven Churches (St John's Glastonbury, Meare, Street, Butleigh, Shapwick, Moorlinch and Middlezoy). Although the archdeaconry brought in little income, it was a symbol to the monks of their long tradition of independence and they struggled hard to prevent any infringement by the episcopal see on their archidiaconal privileges. The almoner's job was to dispense alms to the poor and sick, in which important social office he was assisted by a sub-almoner. John of Breynton also created the position of intern almoner; this official was in charge of distributing the scraps collected from the monastic table. The titles of the other positions listed in the *Great Chartulary* more or less describe the functions attached: cellarer, cook, gardener, granger, guardian of order, guest master, infirmarian, medar (in charge of the mead), novice master, pittancer, precentor, refectorian, sacrist (in charge of the altars, sacred vessels and fabric of the church) and warden of the Lady Chapel. Each officer held control of the income of certain properties attached to his office. In 1303, for example, we learn that the prior held Beckery; the chamberlain had Deverill and East and West Monkton and he was to provide clothing, shoes, spices and knives for the community from this income; the sacrist held West Bradley, Nyland and a rent in

Glastonbury, with which income he was to find the lights and preserve the ornaments of the church; the almoner held lands within the Twelve Hides, a rent in Glastonbury and land in Walton with which to maintain 13 clerks at the University and distribute alms for the house; the medar, hostilar, infirmarian and precentor held rents in Glastonbury for carrying out their duties; the cook had the manor of Uplyme in Devon and £188 15s from other manors. His, it can be seen, was a demanding and expensive profession.

Walter de Monington (1342–1375) took his surname from a small village in Pembrokeshire. Even though there are no surviving records linking him with Oxford either before or after his ordination as a priest in 1336, a number of factors indicate that he was an intelligent and bookish individual who strongly advocated university education for his monks. We know, for example, that of the 63 monks admitted to the monastery during his abbacy at least nine attended university and two received doctorates in theology (the most rigorous of academic degrees, demanding 16–17 years of gruelling study).[17] He built four chambers for the monks studying at Oxford and provided ecclesiastical ornaments for their chapel. The letters in his unpublished register for the years 1352 to 1366 show that he had a strong personal concern for the spiritual as well as the physical well being of the young scholars.[18] In 1360 Monington sent two Glastonbury monks, John Lange and John Loccombe, to Gloucester College and entrusted them to the care of a slightly older Glastonbury man, William Nye. Monington laid down sensible rules for the young monks: they were not to leave the house without permission nor to entertain in their rooms, and they were to keep all regular feasts unless granted dispensation. Loccombe, however, soon fell into bad company and Monington had to reproach him and another Glastonbury monk, Robert Samburne, for foolish overspending. In 1361 he wrote to the young reprobates, reprimanding them for hunting, fishing and trespassing. Although Samburne continued to have some financial problems, his general behaviour seemed to improve after this point and in 1365 Monington sent him another letter expressing pleasure in his assiduous scholarship; the abbot also conferred a young monk to his care. Loccombe, on the other hand, did not mend his ways and by 1366 he was recalled to Glastonbury and Thomas de la Mare, abbot president of the Black Monks, required Monington to inquire

Walter de Monington

---

[17] See my 'An Annotated Edition of the List of Sixty-Three Monks Who Entered Glastonbury Abbey during the Abbacy of Walter de Monington', *The Downside Review* 95 (1977), 306–15.

[18] This is found in British Library, MS Arundel 2, fol. 1–86. I plan eventually to produce an edition of the register.

into the charges of incontinence laid against the renegade monk.

Although a highly busy and effective abbot, Monington himself found time for scholarship and was an avid book collector as the list of books acquired during his abbacy shows. Monington was abbot during the period of great controversy over the teachings of John Wycliffe and even though Monington himself did not appear to interest himself actively in the Lollard question, one of his monks, Nicholas Fox, transcribed a manuscript – now Oxford, MS Oriel 15 – which contains a number of tractates debating the topic: works by Richard Fitzralph, Roger Swineshead, Wycliffe himself and others.

Monington's epitaph informs us that he was a young man when he was first made abbot and it is not clear what, if any, major official position he held previously. It is significant, moreover, that none of the older monks resented his election. What this suggests is that he must have had a fine administrative skill which manifested itself even when he was a junior monk. And, as it happens, a man of genius was needed during the mid-fourteenth century; Monington had been abbot for only six years when the first of several crippling waves of plague overwhelmed England and completely upset the economy and cultural life of the country. In Somerset, as elsewhere, one of the most pronounced long-term consequences of the Black Death was a serious decline in the whole agricultural system. As the size of the population shrunk so too did the price of crops and the value of land. For the most part landlords suffered severe difficulties, but Monington showed himself unusually shrewd and managed to keep up Glastonbury's income against all odds: he gained properties, consolidated other holdings, added a retaining wall at Meare, a seawall at Brent, a dovecot and barton wall at Pilton, ox and cow houses and barns at Butleigh, Lympsham, Walton, Street, Batcombe, East Pennard, Badbury, Ashbury and Sturminster Newton. He built a watermill in Glastonbury and windmills at Zoy and Uplyme. He improved manor houses and built a fishhouse at Zoy. Although Monington followed a national trend and rented an increased number of farms for cash rather than having the monastery's reeves oversee the operations, he did nevertheless continue to farm many of the estates. Monington kept with him a slightly later copy of the *Great Chartulary*, known as the *Secretum Domini*, and this permitted him to be clearly informed about the status of each of the estates.

Surprisingly, the monastic community itself at Glastonbury does not seem to have been decimated by the plague: there were around 50 monks for the full length of Monington's abbacy and, since it can be shown that Monington admitted an average of only two monks a year and still kept a stable population over 33 years, there could have been no period of sudden increase in mortality. Most of the monks Monington admitted came from nearby estates and there is a complete gamut of social backgrounds: from boys of aristocratic families to the sons of poor labouring folk. Many came because of a genuine vocation or at least through a love of learning. Some, however, probably simply liked the prospect of a comfortable, perhaps even comparatively opulent, life. One monk, whose name was Henry Brekebeke, entered the monastery because he wanted to escape the clutches of Christine Courteney, whom he had foolishly promised to marry. Although Christine complained to the authorities about his breach of promise Henry managed to stay safely ensconced in the monastery.

Fortunately, the account of the abbey granger (that is, the official responsible for grain supplied to the abbey) for 1361–62 survives and gives specific data about one aspect of the monastic farming operations.[19] What is most impressive is the vast quantity of wheat and other grains produced to supply the 50 or so monks, the pensioners, the huge retinue of servants and the large numbers of horses and other livestock. Much of the wheat went to the abbey baker, who prepared fine wastel bread for the monks and, as the little dogs belonging to Chaucer's Prioress well knew, wastel – a term which is related linguistically to the modern French word for cake, *gateau* – was the best grade of bread in daily use. The servants received 'cural', an inferior wheat or various mixtures of wheat and other grains. Considerable quantities of malt were needed for brewing. The poulterer required grain for fattening fowls for the abbot's table and for special feasts. Judging by the granger's account, indeed, the quality of food and drink on special occasions such as the visit of the Black Prince (the entertainment of whom cost the abbot £40) must have been superb. At the other extreme of entertainment Adam de Stodleigh, the almoner, took pulses and beans to provide pauper soup in Lent and soup for the servants. Finally, John Penpons, the abbey doctor – who must have been a highly respected individual during these precarious times – was singled out to receive a special allowance of oats for his horses: a few years earlier he had already been granted food, shelter, a horse and £2 a year.

Early in the abbacy the bishop received complaints that Monington was overly severe and that he needed to improve the quantity and quality of the monks' food. Certainly, by the 1360s, that is during the time for which his register survives, he showed himself to be a sympathetic and considerate abbot.

[19] See Ian Keil, 'The Granger of Glastonbury Abbey, 1361–62', *Somerset and Dorset Notes and Queries* 28 (1963), 86–90.

Throughout his abbacy, however, he did continue to attempt small reductions in expense and on one occasion, at least, this almost got him into serious trouble. By tradition the king had the right to grant two corrodies (which basically functioned as pensions) at Glastonbury at any given time. Usually these were given to wounded soldiers and retiring members of the royal household, but they did periodically go to people as exalted as Thomas More. In 1357 King Edward provided letters of recommendation for one John of Odiham. To save money, Monington seems to have procrastinated on the matter, as he did in the case of various other corrodies. Apparently the king was not amused and soon afterwards we see Monington writing obsequious letters to Queen Philippa – with whom he was on good terms and who later gave expensive ornaments to the Lady Chapel – beseeching her to intercede with the king on his behalf in order to avoid the consequences of royal displeasure.

Monington's administrative skill and his ability to retrieve himself from potentially difficult situations brought him to the attention of other establishments. He rose to a senior position in the English Chapter of the Black Monks and in 1363 the canons of Wells chose him as their next bishop: the choice, however, was contested and another candidate finally got the position.

Monington was an enthusiastic builder and spent over £1,100 on the abbey. He extended the choir by 40 feet, adding two bays, and had the interior refaced in freestone panelling. He made provisions for the ambulatory and gave 22 statues for the great screen. He also completed the abbot's chapel and the infirmary. The list of ornaments he gave, whose total value came to 1445 marks, is extensive and shows a strongly developed aesthetic sensibility. When we think of Walter de Monington, then, it seems at first tempting to conjure up the analogy of Chaucer's Franklin. Like the Franklin, Monington enjoyed beautiful things; he seems to have been socially adept and he knew how to manipulate his estates for considerable material gain. This may not, however, be the key to his personality. Indeed, we might ultimately do better to compare him with his friend and fellow abbot Thomas de la Mare. Thomas, abbot of St Albans, also lived an outwardly flamboyant life. He was a scholar, a munificent superior, president of the English Chapter of the Black Monks, and a magnificent builder, who made St Albans stunningly beautiful and provided for himself unusually elegant and splendidly furnished apartments. Such, he felt, should be the external life of a prince of the church. His personal life, however, tells quite a different story. He rose before midnight from a spartan bed and recited

Abbey church. Arch leading from north transept to choir, 1858.
A photograph by Colonel Verschoyle.

lengthy prayers. In any spare moment of the day or during the
enforced physical inactivity of periods of travel he recited the
Penitential Psalms or the Office of the Dead. He wore a hair
shirt under his splendid outer garments and ate only once a
day. He loved his monks as a father and forgave their foibles –
for example, ringing the bells to announce the first office of the
day when the younger brother in charge of this chore
overslept. He administered personally to the sick and afflicted
and though he had loved hunting and hawking as a boy he later
refused to take part in such sports even as a spectator. His
personal devotional life, then, was rigid and austere in spite of
a public life of pomp and urbanity. Monington's surviving

writings suggest that his mode of living might have been similar.

John Chinnock (1375–1420) probably professed around 1365, which made him relatively junior at the time of his election as abbot. Early in 1375, he had succeeded John Crosse as receiver when Crosse became prior. Surprisingly, after Monington died in July, Chinnock rather than Crosse was chosen to replace him. Chinnock's election was all the more unexpected since there was a much more likely candidate, Thomas Coffyn, who was several years senior to Chinnock and who had been grooming himself for the position. Coffyn, who seems to have been formidably intelligent and who also had the support of a sizable number of the monks, refused to accommodate himself fully to his defeat and he remained actively antagonistic to Chinnock on a local, national, and international level for many years. Indeed, the relative failure, or at least lack of brilliance, of much of Chinnock's abbacy is probably a function of this unresolved quarrel.

Coffyn was a dedicated scholar (he had received a B.Th. by 1380 and a D.Th. by 1408) and he obtained the support of the chancellor of Oxford in his attempt to overturn Chinnock. Indeed, in the early 1380s feeling ran so high at Oxford in his favour that royal protection had to be provided for visiting Glastonbury scholars, such as Richard Hunesworth, who supported Chinnock. Chinnock, for his part, had Coffyn declared an apostate in 1381 and orders for his arrest were issued to the king's sergeant-at-arms. Coffyn took his case to Rome and by 1387 had returned to England with bulls annulling the election of 1375. This time the abbot retaliated by having the king issue a warrant for Coffyn's arrest. At this point, just as things were coming to a crisis, some sort of reconciliation was effected and Coffyn returned peacefully to his monastery. By 1393 he was an elector of visitors for the Provincial Chapter of the Black Monks and ultimately he was made prior at Glastonbury.

When Thomas Arundel, archbishop of Canterbury, made a visitation to the abbey in 1407/8 during a vacancy of the bishopric of Bath and Wells, there were numerous rumours of 'bitterness and dissention' among the monks and Coffyn seems to have been particularly vocal in his complaints. After hearing Coffyn mention old age, bodily weakness, and general dissatisfaction with Chinnock's regime Arundel allowed him to retire, and realizing his vulnerability he stipulated that Coffyn should always have an honorable chamber, a servant, a yearly pension, and all things proper to his estate and doctoral dignity. As it happens, Coffyn outlived Chinnock and did not die until 1423 when he must have been in his nineties. During the last year of his life he obtained a papal grant of plenary remission and licence to have a confessor of his own choice.

In 1385 John Harewell, bishop of Bath and Wells, made a visitation to Glastonbury and gave a variety of injunctions concerning the management of the archdeaconry of Glastonbury. Fortunately, the archdeacon's account from a few years later has survived and it gives us a good idea of the scope of the office.[20] Most of the archdeacon's income (73s 1d) came from the fines he levied as a corrector of moral faults, although he did also earn 23s from mortuaries and 66s from the acquittance of wills. On the debit side, he paid his summoner 6s 8d – a miniscule sum which helps explain why summoners had a need to supplement their incomes in a variety of ways, as Chaucer makes ironically obvious in the portrayal of his Summoner who was willing to grant

> ... for a quart of wyn
> A good felawe to have his concubyn
> A twelf-monthe and excuse hym atte fulle.

In the 1340s Edward III seems to have visualized founding an order based on the Round Table and became keenly interested in Glastonbury's version of the Arthurian/Joseph of Arimathea legend as promulgated by John of Glastonbury. Later, when Edward lost enthusiasm for the project Walter de Monington decided to let the Joseph story fall back into obscurity.[21] In Chinnock's abbacy two factors made the Joseph legend suddenly much more relevant. One of the results of the Great Schism was the development of the Conciliar movement; theorists now argued that councils were superior to the pope in some areas and that precedence in councils should be determined by the dates of foundation of the various national churches. If Joseph of Arimathea did establish a church at Glastonbury, then Glastonbury (and England itself) ranked among the most senior of churches. Combined with this national issue was the local question of supplement of income. If more money could not be generated from the estates, then there was still the possibility of encouraging a larger volume of pilgrims, which Joseph's fame as a Glastonbury saint would certainly do. It is not surprising, then, that shortly after he became abbot Chinnock commissioned a new copy of John's chronicle – containing a fully developed account of Joseph's mission to Glastonbury and his building of the wattled Old Church – to be written. In 1382, moreover, Chinnock restored

---

[20] See Ian Keil, 'The Archdeaconry of Glastonbury in the Later Middle Ages', *Somerset and Dorset Notes and Queries* 28 (1963), 129–33.
[21] On the appropriation of Joseph's name as guardian of the Grail and evangelizer of Britain, see below pp. 87–93.

a small ruined chapel in the cemetery and had it rededicated to St Michael and St Joseph of Arimathea. Conspicuous in its decorations was a lifesize triptych featuring Joseph's role in the Deposition. Not much later, Chinnock caused a large manuscript (3 ft 8 in × 3 ft 6 in) containing John's account of King Arthur, St Patrick, the translation of St Dunstan, the story of St Joseph's mission and various other excerpts to be written in an elegant book hand. It was mounted on a folding frame and was set up in a conspicuous place in the church where it could be read by visitors.

There are no written statistics to indicate how many new pilgrims were attracted, but there are a variety of other indications that the legend 'caught on'. As a result of the Joseph association Chinnock quickly managed to win primacy among abbots at a national synod; later the English Church demanded and obtained parity with other apostolic churches at the councils of Pisa (1409), Constance (1417), Siena (1424) and Basel (1434).[22]

The evidence of Arundel's 1408 visitation suggests that towards the end of his abbacy Chinnock was not altogether effective as abbot. The most vocal of his antagonists was a relatively junior monk, John Polglas, who said that the abbot 'had drawn to himself and kept round him men who were immature, weak-minded, improvident and dishonest, not punishing offenders as he ought to do, and that, owing to his example, inferior guardians and rulers of the order had not dared or cared to punish or correct offenders.'[23] On the other hand, the spirit of disobedience among the monks themselves had, as Arundel pointed out, 'been strengthened by conspiracies and meetings in corners, and nightly potations and private feastings too long continued.' The situation was so serious that Arundel felt it necessary to discharge nine of the abbot's most important officials. Chief among these was Chinnock's old supporter from Oxford days, Richard Hunesworth, who was now outer cellarer and who had in 1399

[22] See Valerie M. Lagorio, 'The Evolving Legend of St Joseph of Glastonbury', *Speculum* 46 (1971), 209–31. Even in England it was not universally accepted that Joseph qualified fully as an apostolic founder. The anonymous fifteenth-century annotator to Robert of Gloucester's chronicler is representative when he notes beside Robert's standard account of Britain's evangelization by Phagan and Deruvian: 'Thus com lo Cristendom in to Brutayne londe. But there were erst some preueliche Cristendom hadde fonge. As at the place of Glastyngbury Joseph of Arimathie lyuede there in Criste's lay. with hys companye.' There is a similar treatment of the topic in Lambeth Palace Library, MS 84, on which see Lister M Matheson, 'The Arthurian Stories of Lambeth Palace Library, MS 84', *Arthurian Literature* 5 (1985), pp. 70–91, at 73–75.

[23] See Ian Keil, 'Profiles of Some Abbots of Glastonbury', *The Downside Review* 81 (1963), 359. Keil also supplies information about Frome, More, and Selwood. In 'The Abbots of Glastonbury in the Early Fourteenth Century', *The Downside Review* 82 (1964), 327–48 he examines the careers of Fromond, Walter of Taunton, Sodbury, Breynton and Monnington.

obtained a papal indult to hold the office of chamberlain for life. Arundel labelled him a troublemaker and deprived him of his offices, sending him at what must have been a relatively advanced age to end his life in disgrace at Hyde Abbey. Other monks were shown to be guilty of a variety of faults, including incontinence, and Arundel ordered that no brother was to go outside the bounds of the monastery, especially to places where women would be likely to be met, without special licence from the abbot. Those who broke this rule would be suspended from entering the church until they had completed a three-day fast; they would also be forbidden to go outside the bounds of the cloister for a whole year.

In the context of these stringent recommendations by Arundel we should remember that during the late fourteenth and early fifteenth century many superiors had trouble with monks guilty of sins of the flesh. At Durham Priory, for example, where there was a strong prior at this period, several monks were accused of committing adultery with Durham women and various others were reproached with 'the horrible synne of sodomye' – a sin perhaps hinted at in Arundel's recommendation that no brother at Glastonbury was to take to himself a clerk without a special indulgence from the abbot, and that all such clerks, as well as other youths in the monastery under the age of twenty, be forbidden from all places of the order; they were to go straight across from table to church or school. Hunting with hounds was to be prohibited and no one was to keep hounds inside or outside the monastery, except that the abbot might keep a reasonable number for the use of the parks and the warren of the brethren. (One is reminded both of Chaucer's Monk who kept fine greyhounds and whose lust was 'Of prikyng and of huntyng for the hare' and of the Prioress and her 'smale houndes'.) Arundel was also concerned about laxity in church attendance and suggested that absence from matins, mass or from the other canonical hours should be punished by withdrawal of the whole pittance for the day; absence from vespers or compline would lead to withdrawal of the pittance for the next day. A second offence was to be punished by withdrawal of wine and ale as well as of the pittance; and a third by fasting on bread and water. Breaking of the rule of silence would lead to similar punishments. Finally, Arundel observed that some of the buildings at Glastonbury needed attention and recommended that £120 be set aside yearly and spent on the construction and repair of the church, the refectory, the dormitory and the chapter house; the sum was to be deducted proportionally from the goods assigned to the abbot's table and the goods pertaining to the table of the convent or any other offices or administrations in the monastery.

From a financial point of view and from an examination of Arundel's recommendations, then, one might be tempted to deduce that Chinnock had long been ineffectual and a bumbler – or, as Arundel puts it more mildly, he had become somewhat lukewarm and remiss and needed to be more diligent in future. Problems arising from his inefficiency, moreover, did not end with his death. As late as 1443, Nicholas Frome had to prosecute one Bartholomew Downton of Lyllington in Dorset because he would not give up his accounts from the period when he was receiver in that county for Chinnock. Before condemning Chinnock too severely, however, we should take into account several other factors. On the most general level, the psychological wounds of the Great Schism of 1378 were still being felt on many levels and there seems to have been a gradual slackening of authority even in the hierarchical world of the monasteries – at the time of his visitation Arundel stated that the clear cause of 'the fury of dissention and root of bitterness which made the monastery a byword and a scandal in all the country round had its beginning in an impatient spirit of disobedience.' Traditional religious devotion seems also to have suffered from the Lollard movement and at least some of Chinnock's monks probably lacked a vocation. These problems were made more acute by the relative separation, on a financial and personal level, between the abbot and the rest of the community. By 1408, too, Chinnock was an old man, worn down by years of conflict with Coffyn who, as prior, should have been his strongest ally.

On the positive side, Chinnock made a number of contributions to the life of his monastery. In particular, he had managed to rebuild the cloisters with thin long buttresses, probably improving fenestration and the carrells. He also erected or repaired the dormitory and the fratry. In a modest way, too, he began the trend of buying London properties, a policy of diversification away from agricultural holdings only. He also appropriated the benefices of Longbridge Deverill and Butleigh church along with Baltonsborough chapelry. Chinnock's main administrative interests had been on a national level and from 1387 until 1399 he was president of the English Chapter of the Black Monks. Probably, therefore, he was often absent from Glastonbury and his attentions may well have been concentrated elsewhere. It is worth noting, too, that as late as the 1390s Glastonbury had a good reputation for discipline and in 1398 Thomas Lemyngton, a monk of Winchester, moved to Glastonbury because he desired a stricter life.

In 1390–91, Geoffrey Chaucer seems to have been appointed a subforester in North Petherton. Although we do not know for certain that he actually ever went to Somerset in connection with this position it is tempting to speculate that he did go and that he visited Glastonbury Abbey at the same time. From a modern perspective at least this putative visit would constitute one of the high points of Chinnock's abbacy.

As a young man Nicholas Frome (1420–1456) devoted himself to a life of scholarship and must have spent a number of years at Oxford where he ultimately obtained a D.Th. After he became abbot, he kept up his academic involvement, and although he produced no work of scholarship himself he did encourage John Matthews to write a *Mirror for Monks*. He seems to have remembered his university days with pleasure and was interested in the physical and mental well being of young monks studying at the university. During his abbacy Thomas Knyght, one of the younger Glastonbury monks, acted as *prior studentium* at Gloucester College, Oxford.

Nicholas Frome

By 1408 Frome held the position of almoner, from which he was ignominiously ejected at the time of the Arundel visitation and banished to St Augustine's Canterbury. It is not altogether clear how much time, if any, he spent in exile, since by 1414 he was listed as receiver at Glastonbury. He must have been popular with his fellow monks and when Chinnock died he was chosen as an obvious candidate for abbot; on 22 September, 1420 he made his profession of obedience to bishop Bubwith at the chapel of Dogmersfield manor in Hampshire.

As a spiritual lord, Frome threw himself wholeheartedly into politics and during the minority of Henry VI ranged himself on the side of those who tried to minimize the role of Humfrey, Duke of Gloucester. In 1434, acting as the chief representative of England's apostolic church, he attended the council of Basel and wrote a letter – now preserved in a Trinity College, Cambridge, manuscript – describing his experiences. At this council the Castilian ambassador expressed extreme scepticism about Joseph of Arimathea's mission to Britain and challenged the English to prove that he ever really came. He also referred to a counter legend, recorded in the *Golden Legend*, which narrates that Joseph was not freed from prison until 70 A.D., in which case he could not have come to England several years earlier. Although Frome and his fellow English delegates stoutly maintained their position and continued to uphold the Glastonbury tradition throughout the council, Joseph's name would never come up again in the conciliar context. In 1435 Frome was one of the English ambassadors appointed to treat for the reformation of religion and peace with France. His loyal services did not go unnoticed and ultimately generated a variety of rewards, including a royal grant of exemption 'from all collection, levying, receiving of tenths, taxes, tallages, and other quotas, and subsidies granted by the clergy of the province of Canterbury or otherwise without the said diocese.'

In 1435 John Stafford, bishop of Bath and Wells (1425–1443), commissioned Frome to make a visitation on his behalf to the nearby small monastery at Muchelney, about which a variety of unsavoury reports were circulating. Discipline had, indeed, disintegrated and ultimately it was recommended that the monks be categorically forbidden to leave the abbey for pleasure trips, hunting expeditions, or to attend public spectacles. (The latter probably included performances by travelling minstrels, mummers and players who came to the monastery.) Frome, who was a practical man, recommended that a small, relatively secluded, external gate at Muchelney be permanently blocked up, since – as it was euphemistically phrased in the report – laundry women and others were using it at all hours of the day and night.

Although discipline at Glastonbury itself seems to have been maintained during Frome's abbacy, he did come into conflict with at least one monk, Richard Fowey, who was – as it appears – of noble birth and perhaps therefore less tractable than some of his more humble brethren. In 1435/36 Fowey was accused of incontinence – a perennial problem during the period – and appealed to bishop Stafford, who granted him at the pope's command a dispensation 'in respect of the charge of disobedience and rebellion' against his abbot. The matter did not end there, however, and in 1445 Bishop Thomas Bekynton (1443–65) appointed commissioners to hear a case in which Fowey and another monk sued their abbot on account of unjust imprisonment and other grievances. Although the results of this particular case are not known, problems like this were an inevitable corollary to the possession of personal wealth by individual monks, who felt a strong degree of independence and who also had the private resources to use in appeals to episcopal courts and to the pope. Indeed, a variety of monks during Frome's rule obtained papal privileges or confirmation of rights, and these by nature lessened the superior's authority.

Given his ambitious nature, it was predictable that Frome would disagree with his local bishop and he entered into a bitterly acrimonious dispute with Bekynton. During the course of a regular visitation in 1445 the ever vigilant bishop discovered some unspecified irregularities, but was called away before he could legislate on them. When Frome acted on the problems under his own jurisdiction, the bishop objected and annulled the abbot's actions. Bekynton twice put off a new visitation, presumably to chasten Frome, who then said he could wait no longer to enforce discipline. The bishop replied with a very bitter letter, in which he expressed the hope that the physical blindness from which the abbot was suffering had not spread to his mind. The quarrel now extended to the question of the archdeaconry, which the abbot claimed was free from episcopal interference in the matter of proof of wills. In a symbolic act of defiance he ordered the churches in the archdeaconry to discontinue the traditional custom of ringing bells when the bishop passed through the area. The bishop, in turn, informed the pope that at Basel Frome had supported the conciliar movement and had publicly spoken against the pope. At this point, the pope turned the case over to Cardinal John Kemp, archbishop of York, using terms hostile to the abbot. When he later became convinced of Frome's loyalty, though, he revised his opinion and set forth a more favorable commission. How Kemp finally resolved the dispute is unknown, but there does seem to have been some sort of reconciliation, since in July 1455 Bekynton stayed in the spacious new bishop's quarters at the abbey as a guest of the now extremely aged abbot.

In 1447 – during the dispute with Bekynton – Henry VI granted Glastonbury a charter 'in respect of the king's pious regard for the abbey'; the charter, which extended the judicial privileges within the liberty of the Twelve Hides, could not have pleased the bishop and his supporters. As well as increasing prestige and extending legal rights, Frome worked hard at improving finances: he cut down on demesne farming, improved bookkeeping and invested in London property. With a sound financial situation, Frome could embark on a vigorous building programme, of which the bishop's quarters were one aspect. At long last the chapter house was finished. Frome then built or rebuilt the misericord house and the great chamber of the abbot's lodging – during the fifteenth century, as farming land was increasingly rented out, abbots had less need to travel from manor to manor and therefore set about renovating their own monastic lodgings on a grander scale.

Most impressive of all Frome's projects, perhaps, was the great embattled wall which was constructed around the abbey precincts and of which parts survive; it was remarkably similar, perhaps competitively so, to Bekynton's wall about the close at Wells Cathedral. It is likely, too, that Frome rather than his predecessor was responsible for the fine abbot's kitchen with its four fireplaces and octagonal roof crowned by a lantern; this was the model for at least two nineteenth-century university laboratories, at Oxford and Toronto, and one cannot help

Gateway on Magdalene St. This was the main approach to the abbey buildings. Immediately inside was an open courtyard from which the church and the abbot's hall could be reached.

but wonder if this suggests something important about the comparative values of the two cultures. Certainly fifteenth-century abbots were expected to keep a kind of permanent open house and had occasion for large and complex cooking facilities. At Durham Priory, for which we still have records, we know that in the fifteenth century Prior Wessington obtained malmsey and other sweet Mediterranean wines from London, got his oysters and salmon from Northumberland, and ordered a bewildering array of imported 'spices' – pepper, figs, raisins, rice, dates, saffron, sandalwood, currants, cloves, anise, ginger, cinnamon and mace.[24] He was expected to have banquets when a distinguished guest came to Durham, when episcopal agents arrived on business, and for the celebration of a great variety of feast-days. In fact, cellarers' accounts show that virtually every week of the year there were banquets of some sort. The Glastonbury calendar would have been similar.

Like his immediate predecessor, Frome remained abbot for a considerable number of years; unlike Chinnock, however, he does not appear to have been particularly young when elected. Indeed, judging from the evidence of a variety of lists, it would seem likely that he professed around 1380, at which time he would probably have been at least 20. This suggests that he may have been close to a hundred by the time of his death. It appears, too, that he was vigorous until the end and he shows

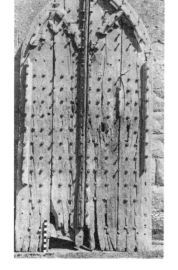

Late medieval door from abbot's kitchen.

[24] See Dobson, *Durham Priory*, p. 104.

60

no slowing down of energies or desire to retire.

Like Walter of Taunton in the fourteenth century Walter *Walter More*
More (1456), who had acted as sacrist during the latter part of
Frome's abbacy, was abbot no more than a matter of months.
He was chosen on 7 May, 1456, the crown gave its assent to
the election on 13 May, and he then died some time before
7 November when the king granted permission to find a
successor. The process leading to More's election had run very
smoothly and he was the unanimous choice of the nine
delegates appointed to find an abbot. In the next case,
however, the preliminaries were more complex than the
election itself; this was probably not a result of dissension but
a function of confusion over the sudden death of More. Two
delegates from the earlier group were nominated to choose
seven others, but they were unable to agree and so they
resigned. It was then decided that two scrutators should be
appointed to interrogate each member of the community
privately. Half way through this process the prior and convent
changed their minds and appointed seven delegates to join the
earlier two to recommend an abbot. This group began work,
but soon resigned because it could not come to a decision.
Finally, a panel of three was appointed to take the votes of the
community; after all this, they quickly brought in a vote which
would have been unanimous except for the abstention of the
elect himself and after a number of false starts John Selwood *John Selwood*
(1456–1493) was thus made abbot.

Selwood had been receiver under the two previous abbots

The abbot's kitchen, from a Victorian engraving.

The rebus of John Selwood on the south aisle of Meare church.

and predictably showed his own greatest strengths in economic matters: for example, he ended all demesne farming and the estates at last were held exclusively by rentiers. In this policy of giving up farms run by bailiffs in order to rent the land out to individual tenants Selwood followed a national trend among major landlords. He continued accounting reforms and ultimately increased the annual income by £62. His relations with the crown during a difficult period of history seem stable, if minimal, and he undertook a minor land transfer at the request of Richard III. He improved the church buildings in a number of the parishes in the archdeaconry and his rebus appears on the church of Ashcott and on the south aisle of Meare Church. It can also be found on buildings at Ditcheat, High Ham, Ivy Thorn Manor and Norwood. His dealings with the monks seem peaceful, if perhaps somewhat slack. Nevertheless, Bishop Robert Stillington (1466–91) ordered a commission to

Parish church of St John Baptist, with its fine perpendicular tower. In 1856–57 the church was restored by Sir George Gilbert Scott.

The George and Pilgrims Hotel.

visit Glastonbury in 1472 because 'of the common report that the abbot has been careless and negligent in matters spiritual and temporal and that other persons there have been guilty of various crimes'.[25] The abbot of Abingdon also planned a visit on behalf of the Chapter of the Black Monks, but Selwood appealed to the pope, saying that Glastonbury 'needed no visitation, correction or reform by the said abbot of Abingdon who they allege is an enemy of the said abbot of Glaston-bury'.[26] The pope made a compromise ruling and said that the abbot of Abingdon could come only if he were accompanied by the diocesan. There is no surviving record to indicate whether he actually did come or not after the papal injunction.

Selwood appears to have made no additions to the main claustral church; rather, he devoted his energies to the con-

[25] See Keil, 'Profiles', p. 369, who is translating from bishop Stillington's registers.
[26] See Keil, 'Profiles', p. 369, who is quoting from Selwood's petition to Pope Sixtus IV.

*Stone figure of un-
identified king at
Wedmore.*

struction of the still intact parish church of St John Baptist, on the tower of which he had his arms carved. In East Brent he built a manor house, a rather grand establishment, consisting of a chapel, hall, parlour, large and lofty chambers, store house, cellar, pantry, kitchen, chambers above, other sumptuous apartments and a magnificent portico. Two stone figures of unidentified kings now found in the garden of Porch House, Wedmore, appear to have been rescued from the ruins of this house by Dr John Westover in the early eighteenth century. John Leland refers to the still standing manor house in Norwood Park 'a mile by est from Glaston.' Selwood was also aware of the need for accommodation of the increasing numbers of 'middle class' pilgrims; those who were not important enough to be invited to stay with the abbot but who needed some sort of adequate housing. He therefore undertook construction of a pilgrims' inn which, of course, continues its function today as 'The George and Pilgrims'. Early in the twentieth century Bligh Bond thought he found traces of a tunnel from the Inn leading to the Abbot's Gateway. The income from the inn was assigned to the chamberlain's office.

In the final analysis, it is difficult to come to any conclusion about Selwood's degree of commitment to his religious vocation. He does not seem as corrupt as his friend Hugh Sugar, the notorious treasurer of Wells who misappropriated funds for his own lavish entertainments, and we do not have complaints about the excessively fashionable dress of his monks, such as those set forth by archbishop Bourchier who censured coped caps, short jackets and beaked shoes. On the other hand, his interests do seem worldly rather than pious or even academic and perhaps it is fitting that a hostelry is one of the most enduring memorials to him.

3

Beere and Whiting:
Indian Summer and Fall

Selwood was abbot for 37 years and towards the end of his abbacy he appears to have become senile. The monks, therefore, were anxious to have a strong new leader and immediately on Selwood's death petitioned Henry VII for permission to appoint a successor. They made an obvious choice in Thomas Wason, a learned scholar with a B.Th. from Oxford and a man who had already shown himself to be a highly capable prior. During the process of their decision making, however, they forgot to consult their bishop, Richard Fox (1492–94); he was predictably irate and set about rendering the election null and void. The king acknowledged his point, and Fox then decided to put forward his own candidate, Richard Beere, whom he had ceremoniously installed on 20 January, 1494. This inauspicious beginning could have resulted in a tense or even badly weakened abbacy – as was the case a century earlier when John Chinnock was abbot – but Wason seems to have been an eminently reasonable and generous individual who supported the new abbot wholeheartedly. Indeed, he may even have been pleased to escape from the time-consuming administrative tasks and ceremonial duties of the position, since there are indications that he was strongly attached to his own studies. He was particularly interested in the history of his monastery and around 1500 made for himself a copy of John of Glastonbury's chronicle, which survives as MS Ashmole 790 in the Bodleian collection at Oxford. In this manuscript Wason notes passages where John used other sources, particularly the *Annals* by the great early fourteenth-century writer Nicholas Trevet. Wason also owned another very learned work – a set of commentaries by Trevet and the theologian Thomas Waleys on St Augustine's *City of God*.

What led Fox to choose Beere instead of Wason is not obvious, unless it was simply a desire to exert his own authority over the recalcitrant monks. In any case, Beere proved to be an excellent choice – as one layman later put it, 'good, honest, virtuous, wise and discrete, as well as a grave man, and for those virtues esteemed in as great reputation as few in England at that time of his coat and calling were better accounted of' – and some historians consider him the greatest abbot of Glastonbury since St Dunstan.[1] The 1490s were a period of political unrest in the south and Beere was soon called upon to show his mettle. Early in 1497 between 6,000 and 15,000 Cornish rebels, resisting the heavy taxation levied by Henry VII, passed through Glastonbury on their way to storm London. Later in the same year Perkin Warbeck assembled his rebel forces at Taunton; on 21 September, the king's advance guard arrived at Glastonbury and was sheltered by the monks. After Warbeck's troops were disbanded Henry himself came to Somerset. He spent the first Sunday of October with the new bishop, Oliver King (1495–1503), at Wells and on Monday he came to Glastonbury as a greatly honoured guest of the abbot, lodged magnificently in the newly completed king's quarters (which John Leland some fifty years later said was situated by the abbot's great chamber earlier built by Frome).

In 1503 Beere was chosen to head an embassy to congratulate Pius III on his elevation to the papacy and also to negotiate a dispensation for Katharine of Aragon to marry her brother-in-law, Henry, Prince of Wales. Pius died on 18 October, and so the aims of the mission were not satisfactorily completed; Beere returned to Italy in February 1504 and en route to Rome delivered the Order of the Garter to the Duke of Urbino, at which time he seems to have been deeply impressed by the shrine erected for the newly fashionable cult of Loretto. According to legend the Holy House, that is the reputed home of Jesus in Nazareth, had been miraculously transported through the heavens in 1295 and fetched up intact at Loretto – as a result, in modern times Our Lady of Loretto has been designated as the patron saint of aviators. Beere entered Rome itself on 12 May and rendered obedience to the new pope, Julius II, on 20 May; he then remained in Rome for a longish period of time, involved in various other negotiations. He returned to Glastonbury full of enthusiasm for Italy and contemporary humanistic thought. The whole course of his future intellectual life seems to have been moulded by the trip which he commemorated in the very architecture of his monastery when he built the chapel of Our Lady of Loretto near to the chapel of St Thomas in the north transept of the church. Some modern archaeologists think that the chapel must have been a substantial piece of masonry exterior to the church, although Radford considers it to have been an internal

---

[1] See F. A. Gasquet, 'Blessed Richard Bere', *The Downside Review* 9 (1890), 160.

structure near the door in the north side of the north transept. In this case it may well be the small standing structure which appears in a seventeenth-century plan of the site.

We get an unusual insight into Beere's management of local affairs through the records of a legal case peripherally connected with his nephew and namesake.[2] As abbot of Glastonbury Beere was lord of a very large number of manors, including that at Mells, where one of the tenants, Thomas Samuel, died leaving an infant daughter Jane. The lord of the manor was automatically the child's guardian and had the right of tendering a suitor whom his charge could not reject without a forfeit – on the principle that all land was held for military service and by remaining unmarried (and thus husbandless and childless) an heiress was unable to fulfill this duty. In casting about for a suitable husband for Jane, who was relatively wealthy, Beere thought of his own nephew, a promising student at the thriving monastic school. At this stage Jane still seems to have been a very small girl, far too young for marriage, and the junior Richard – who had not been fully consulted on the matter – had quite different ideas for his own future. He was in fact so agitated that he left Glastonbury precipitously and travelled up to the Inns of Court in London. After a brief period pursuing a career in law, however, he decided he had a religious vocation and entered the London Charterhouse, where he stayed until his martyrdom in 1537.

That Beere would suggest a relation for Jane's spouse seems practical rather than rapacious; that he bore no grudge after Richard defected – and he even sent one of his servants up to London to enquire after his nephew's health – shows an admirable flexibility and generosity of spirit. In any case, the abbot did not forget about his responsibilities to Jane – and to his own family – and he soon arranged for Jane to be married to one of his great-nephews; he received a present of £40 from his niece as a recompense for this service. Later his niece tried to get some of the money back because she considered the bride to have been too young; perhaps she was offended when Jane played at 'squynce and divers other and childish parts' at her mother-in-law's house on the day of the wedding. On the money issue the abbot remained obdurate; his loyalties were more absolute to his monastery than to his family and he 'would by no means remit one penny, answering that it belonged to the whole house and not to him.' Ultimately the marriage was consummated and a son and then a grandson was born, who, like his grandmother, was orphaned early, and made ward of the new – at this point lay – lord of Mells; this

---

[2] On this episode see 'Blessed Richard Bere', 158–63.

was none other than John Horner whose role in the dismemberment of the Glastonbury estates has been immortalized in the nursery rhyme.

The Manor House at Mells, home of the Horner family.

During the late fifteenth and early sixteenth centuries an academic degree was of great advantage to a monastic career. Indeed, the Provincial Order of Black Monks was almost entirely dominated by a small number of monks trained at the university. Policy as well as desire, therefore, dictated that Beere should finish his studies and he incepted for his D.Th. at Oxford in 1504.[3] His love of learning was profound and his intellectual habit of mind interesting: it can be argued that in terms of the history of ideas he stands – like a colossus as it were – with one leg in the medieval past (as his interest in John of Glastonbury's history of the monastery indicates) and one leg in the new humanist world of classical revival and exciting new Biblical scholarship. Even the great Erasmus admired his erudition and wrote him a letter on 4 September, 1524.[4] In this letter Erasmus expresses his regret that they have never met and although he reminds Beere that Beere's chaplain had earlier offended him by misguided criticism of his talents as an editor of Jerome, he does nevertheless respectfully defer to Beere's

[3] See A. B. Emden, *A biographical register of the University of Oxford to A.D. 1500*, 3 vols. (Oxford, 1957–59), 1.150.
[4] See Peter G. Bietenholz and Thomas B. Deutscher, *Contemporaries of Erasmus. A biographical register of the Renaissance and Reformation*, 3 vols. (Toronto, 1985–87), 1.128–29.

opinion concerning aspects of his new translation from Greek of a portion of the New Testament. Even more significantly, Erasmus expresses his pleasure at Beere's generosity towards Richard Pace during the course of the latter's studies – and Pace was closely involved in the new humanist school at St Paul's. Clearly, Beere was involved in the most radical intellectual currents of the period and it is possible that he initiated educational reforms at his own monastic school.

Beere was fascinated by St Joseph of Arimathea to a greater degree than any other abbot in Glastonbury's history. During the first years of his abbacy he had several copies of John of Glastonbury's chronicle transcribed for the monastic library and this text, of course, prominently featured Joseph's role in early Glastonbury history. One of the copies was made by the monk William Wyche and also included a continuation of the history of the abbey up to Beere's own time. A variety of factors may have influenced Beere in his veneration of Joseph. Certainly, the Arthurian legend was undergoing one of its periodic revivals and Sir Thomas Malory had not long since completed his Arthuriad; in his preface to the printed edition, moreover, William Caxton underscored Glastonbury's Arthurian connection. The West Country rebellion and ensuing royal displeasure may have also made Beere want to compensate by positing strong positive associations for the area. Mostly, however, he seems to have been a natural entrepreneur and Joseph constituted first-rate material for exploitation. Beere established a prominent shrine to St Joseph and a hymn and collect dedicated to the saint were featured in the local calendar. Around 1502 an anonymous *Life* of Joseph of

Lady Chapel with St Joseph's Chapel below. From a sepia print.

Arimathea was composed – which was then published in 1520 – and it refers specifically to St Joseph's Chapel (as the newly dug out crypt under the Lady Chapel was now called), to the Holy Thorn, and to miracles achieved in St Joseph's name. One William Good, who grew up at Glastonbury during this period describes the chapel: 'There was likewise at Glastonbury, in a long subterranean chapel, a most famous place of pilgrimage, which was made to a stone image of the saint [St Joseph] there, and many miracles were wrought at it ...'[5] In other words, under Beere's management, we at last see the appearance of a fully developed, carefully orchestrated cult designed to attract pilgrims. Beere also created an Arimathean coat of arms – a white shield with drops of blood scattered over the white field and a central green, knotted cross, flanked on either side by a golden ampoule – contemptuously mocked by the pragmatic nineteenth-century antiquary Richard Warner as 'an escutcheon charged with R. Bere's fanciful arms: a cross between two beer flagons.' The shield can still be found in a number of places, such as the battlement of the north side of the church of St Benignus, on the outside of the east wall of the chapel of abbot Beere's almshouses (now St Patrick's Chapel), and at the back of the manor house at Sharpham Park.

Beere's great energy manifested itself in a huge spurt of building activity. In the main church he made a number of improvements. Apart from the Loretto Chapel and St Joseph's Chapel, he showed a timely concern for the condition of the central tower which was in some danger of collapse, probably because he had made some additions to it: he therefore added vaulting and supported the piers with inverted arches, perhaps similar to the scissor arches at Wells Cathedral, which had been added c.1338–48 when the tower at Wells had also seemed about to fall down. He then added flying buttresses at the east end of the choir. Leland describes this stage of restoration work: 'Bere arched on both sides the Est parte of the churche that began to cast owt. Bere made the volte of the steple in the transept and under 2 arches like S. Andres crosse, els it had fallen.' At the south side of the nave Beere added a chapel of the Holy Sepulchre. His greatest modification to the church, however, was the construction of the Edgar Chapel at the east end, although the chapel was not fully completed until the time of the next abbot. The Edgar Chapel was roughly similar, so it seems, to Henry VII's chapel at Westminster and measured 52 × 25 feet before the addition of an apse. It also had a strong resemblance to the surviving Lady Chapel at Gloucester Cathedral. It was probably constructed to rehouse the relics of

[5] On Good and his story see J. Armitage Robinson, *Two Glastonbury Legends* (Cambridge, 1926), pp. 46–7, 66–7.

St Dunstan and this may in part account for archbishop Warham's angry letter to abbot Beere concerning Dunstan's remains, which Canterbury also claimed to possess. Glastonbury was unusual among English churches in having its Lady Chapel to the west and the new chapel therefore came in a capitular position. When completed the Edgar Chapel made Glastonbury the longest ecclesiastical building in England, longer even than Old St Paul's. In front of the High Altar Beere added a magnificent antependium made, Leland says, 'of sylver and gilt'. To provide lodging for secular priests who served in the great church and for the chaplains known as clerks of Our Lady, he had new accommodation constructed within the abbey precincts. On the north side of the church near the gate Beere erected in 1512 a group of almshouses for seven to ten poor widows. We learn from a slightly later document that there were fairly strict rules concerning admissions to the almshouses. None of the widows could be a practising physician or midwife nor have any other means of livelihood. Nor were they permitted to possess any holdings or goods apart from the alms of the hospital. All the widows were to keep a common table and each was to have a habit of black 'burnett' made of three yards of broad-cloth and bearing the arms of St Joseph of Arimathea. Each widow was to have two waggon-loads of fuel annually; each year 2,000 pieces of peat were earmarked for that purpose. The houses have only recently been destroyed, but the chapel still stands (now rededicated to St Patrick) and contains some of the abbey's original stained glass.

John Buckler's drawing (1825) showing chapel of Beere's almshouses. The chapel is now dedicated to St Patrick. BL, MS Addit. 36381, p.278.

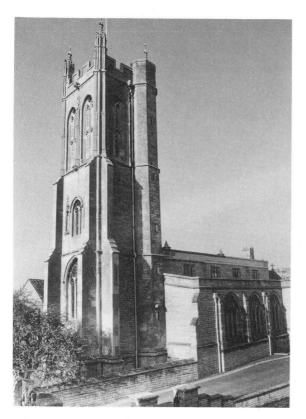

The parish church of St Benignus, now called St Benedict's.

Tribunal building on High St. The elaborate stone front replaced a half-timbered facade.

Outside the monastic enclosure Beere had a new church built to the honour of St Benignus. It was designed in a typical perpendicular style with a double arcade of four bays. Above the front entrance there is a corbel which can transform itself from bishop to devil depending on the position of the spectator – one wonders how closely Wells was associated with this *jeu d'esprit*. Genuinely charitable, Beere rebuilt the leper hospital at West Monkton. He was also concerned with justice and rebuilt the older Tribunal in stone. As the early twentieth-century Anglican divine and local antiquary, C. L. Marson, points out, the very form of this building was rich in symbolism: 'Its plain parapet and bold cornice give it a severe touch: the bay window with the six lights (of creation) make it alert, and the long window of eight lights on the ground floor is to let the light of blessedness shine upon the unhappy, for whom human justice was too coarse to do right, eight being the sign of blessedness. Over the door are two panels, to give the word of entry in the king's name.'[6] Like other contemporary abbots Beere felt the need for a place of retreat not too far

6 *Glastonbury* (London, 1925), pp. 92–3.

from the monastery, where he could escape from the constant pressures of day-to-day monastic life and where the monks, too, could come for annual periods of relaxation, appropriately known as *ludi* (games). He therefore rebuilt the manor house at Sharpham for his own use; this remained intact after the Dissolution, but it was unfortunately completely refashioned in 1799. Nowadays it is perhaps more famous as the birthplace of the novelist Henry Fielding. Further afield, Beere constructed lodgings for members of the community whose business took them to London.

By the early 1520s Beere would have passed well into middle age, but he still seems to have been active in local concerns and interested in wider reaching affairs as well. In 1522 he was a member of Cardinal Wolsey's retinue when the emperor Charles V was met at Dover and escorted to Richmond. In September 1524 Erasmus expressed a hope that he would meet Beere at some time in the future. By January 1524/25, however, the abbot had died; he was buried under a plain marble slab in his Chapel of the Holy Sepulchre. Beere was sadly missed by his monks and he was long remembered by the lay community with fondness and respect; it speaks much that almost fifty years later a local husbandman could testify with conviction that his former master had been 'just and upright in all his ways and for so accounted of amongst all sorts of people.'[7]

After Beere's death the prior Henry Coliner called the forty-seven resident monks together and gave them five days to deliberate on the question of how to choose their next abbot. When they met again they were unable to agree among themselves on the name of an obvious candidate and decided to elect by compromise – that is, to entrust the choice to a responsible outsider – deciding that Cardinal Thomas Wolsey should take charge of the matter. John Islip, the abbot of Westminster, had come to Glastonbury to help oversee the proceedings and it was probably he who scrutinized the local scene and suggested to Wolsey who the choice should be. In any case, on 3 March, Wolsey gave a commission (signed by Thomas More and two other witnesses) to a deputation of three monks who had come to York Palace: the document speaks highly of the abbot elect, Richard Whiting (1525–1539), whom it describes as 'watchful and circumspect' as well as 'upright and religious ... commendable for his life, virtues and learning.'[8]

At the time of his election Whiting held the position of

Richard Whiting

---

[7] See 'Blessed Richard Bere', 162.

[8] See Francis Aidan Gasquet, *The Last Abbot of Glastonbury and his Companions* (London, 1895), p. 33.

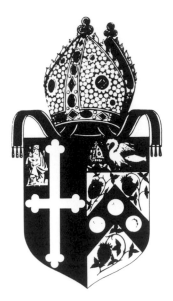

The arms of Richard Whiting.

chamberlain to the abbey. Born in the Wrington area, he came from the younger branch of a distinguished family which had strong ecclesiastical connections. In the late fifteenth century a Richard Whiting, probably his uncle, was chamberlain at Bath Abbey, another near relative later professed as a nun at Wilton, and after the Dissolution two nieces became nuns at the English Franciscan house at Bruges. Little is known of Whiting's early life, although it can probably be assumed that he attended Glastonbury's own monastic school. There is no evidence that he attended university before he took the first step towards the monastic life and became an acolyte in 1498. After passing through the orders of sub-deacon and deacon he was ordained to the priesthood on 6 March, 1501. We know almost nothing about his next quarter of a century, although there is a tradition that he taught in the monastic school. After he became abbot, certainly, many young men of noble family were boarded in his household and began their education – in the widest sense of the word – under his supervision.

Unlike his immediate predecessor, Whiting had little sympathy for the new learning or scholarship in general, but music seems to have been an important aspect of his life. In 1534, an agreement was drawn up between the abbot and one James Renynger, singing man, under the terms of which Renynger would receive a salary of £10 a year, a livery gown (or else 13s 4d), two loads of wood and a dwelling in return for undertaking the duties of organist and instructor of the song school.[9] Renynger's duties were not negligible. He was expected daily to sing and play the organ at services in the Lady Chapel and in the Choir and also to provide music for the abbot's entertainment at Christmas and at other feasts. His pupils were to number six and were to be taught 'pricke songe and descaunte'. The abbot would provide 'clavyngcordes' so that two of the children at any given time could be learning to play the organ; they, in turn, it was assumed, would number among Glastonbury's future organists. The terms of the indenture makes clear that the position was for Renynger's lifetime and Renynger continued to receive his salary even after the Dissolution; he was still drawing his £10 as late as 1569.

Names of the contemporary monks at Glastonbury are found in six lists dating from 1524–5 to 1538–9.[10] At the time of Whiting's election there were 46 monks present; at a visitation in 1526 there were 51; in 1532–3 there were at least 52 monks and in 1537–8 55 names are recorded. Allowing for regular

[9] For a transcription of this document see Dom Aelred Watkin, 'Last Glimpses of Glastonbury', *The Downside Review* 67 (1948–9), 76–79.
[10] See Robert W. Dunning, 'Revival at Glastonbury 1530–9', *Studies in Church History* 14 (1977), 213–22.

mortality figures this means that at least 8 men were recruited after 1533. In the context of the first half of the sixteenth century, when most monasteries were finding it more and more difficult to keep up their numbers, these figures seem impressive and suggest that Whiting created a stable and comfortable atmosphere in his monastery. The younger monks, in particular, turned to Glastonbury's illustrious past for their names in religion. Royal patrons are memorialized – Arthur, Centwine, Ine, Aethelstan, Edgar; names from the great relic collections appear – Aidan, Bede, Basil, Urban, Apollinaris, Ambrose, Oswald, Ultan; and figures from Glastonbury's own history are recollected – Arimathea, Phagan, Deruvian, Gildas, Yder, Indract, Neot. The names stand like a living catalogue, a testimony to the wealth of ties which Glastonbury maintained with the English past and the whole Christian heritage.

Whiting was meticulous about business affairs, which he often supervised personally. One John Lyte, for example, borrowed £40 from the abbot.[11] On the Friday after New Year's Day 1538 he came to Whiting immediately after the latter had dined and they adjourned to the 'little parlour upon

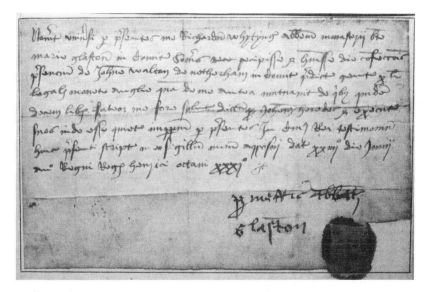

Document with Abbot Whiting's signature in museum in Tribunal building.

the right hand within the great hall' where Lyte gave the abbot £10. In midsummer Lyte returned on a Sunday while high mass was being sung; the two men walked in the abbot's garden and when they got to 'an arbour of bay trees' Lyte

[11] See *The Last Abbot of Glastonbury*, pp. 75–76.

handed over the last £30. Whiting, we are told, was very glad that the money was all in gold and could be counted quickly since he did not want to be observed doing business. He also gave Lyte 'eight angels nobles' on condition that the latter would set up the abbot's arms in the new buildings he was just erecting. On another occasion, very shortly before the Dissolution, Whiting went to visit his niece and her husband Robert Burgess who were tenants at Mells.[12] Their tenements were in bad repair and the abbot agreed to finance extensive improvements to the house as well as to the fulling and grist mills. 'Robert Burges', he is reported to have said, 'I know your tenemente and howse was greatly decaied therfor what ye bestow on it hit shal be alowed.' Later, of course, Burgess could not collect the money and petitioned the king for reparation. Whether he got a sympathetic hearing or not remains unclear.

At the time of the Dissolution King Henry VIII's financial clerk went carefully through the Glastonbury accounts and brought a complete set of obedientiary rolls back to London with him; these were eventually transferred to the Public Record Office and have therefore survived intact into modern times.[13] They give an intimate insight into the details of day-to-day life at the very last moment of English monasticism. Each of the obedientiary rolls is divided into entries for income – primarily from land rentals, pensions and church collections – and expenses, which vary radically from office to office. The sacristan's outlays, for example, include the price of several thousand altar-breads, hogsheads of wine and oil, 1,100 pounds of wax for altar candles, the repair and washing of vestments, the price paid to priests for daily masses, gifts to the students at Oxford, a boar presented to the abbot on Christmas Day, large eels for him on another occasion, a feast for the community on St Brigit's Day and so forth. The pittancer lists some of the extra food provided during Advent and Lent: on the Monday after Advent he gave the monks pea soup and fresh fish to supplement their regular rations, on Tuesday vegetable soup and fritters fried in oil, on Wednesday fish soup flavoured with pepper, cinnamon, raisins and 'la potell de mustadell'. Chief among the infirmarian's expenses come supplies and labour to run and maintain the four infirmary stills where cordials and liqueurs were produced for the sick. The water system at the infirmary also caused difficulties and the sick themselves (who seemed to enjoy prolonged stays at the infirmary, especially after bloodletting) needed great quantities of oats for porridge,

12 See 'Last Glimpses of Glastonbury', 79–83.
13 See Dom Aelred Watkin, 'Glastonbury, 1538–39, As Shown by Its Account Rolls', *The Downside Review* 67 (1948–9), 437–50.

butter, milk, fresh fish, cheese, ginger, cinnamon, geese, pasties and joints of meat. The almoner spent large sums on food, clothing and shrouds for the poor. On Mid Lent Sunday the precentor relieved the austerity of the season somewhat by giving a fine feast which cost 45s. This official was in charge of the Chapel of St Michael on the Tor and spent a fair sum on its maintenance, including the wage of a labourer who was to scythe the nettles growing on the Tor itself. On the feast of the Dedication of the Church the cook supplemented the regular meal with extra supplies: a corn gruel, three flagons of milk, a half pound of sugar, pepper and saffron, twelve suckling pigs and three pounds of large raisins; on Lady Day he provided six salted salmon with sugar, pepper and saffron; on Easter Day six lambs and a quantity of Easter eggs; on Corpus Christi Day a number of meat pasties as well as the usual spices and malted barley. During the last quarter of 1538 alone the cellarer of the hall (i.e., the abbot's great hall) listed a consumption of over 56 quarters of bread, 90 oxen, 3 cows, 1 bull, 144 sheep, 6 calves, 7 pigs, 62 pigs' trotters, 174 pounds of butter, 11 stone of cheese, a quantity of salt fish including 381 cod, 290 hake, 18 salmon and 497 white herrings. The amount of fuel consumed, too, was immense: 27,000 bundles in one year. Other minor, but indicative, expenses with which the cellarer had to cope included 6s 8d for decorating the abbot's hall with evergreen on great festivals and 2s 3d for painting and ornamenting the boar's head at Christmas. Finally, the chamberlain – who drew much of his income from the 'new Inn at the sign of St George' – had a miscellaneous variety of expenses: thatching the roof of the house of a certain widow, paying the wages of the

Model of abbey church as it may have been shortly before 1539. Constructed by N. J. W. Gaffney to the scale 1 ft–1/16 inch, and displayed in museum in abbey grounds.

conventual washerwoman, the tailor, the barber and so forth. Doles to the poor in 1537 totalled £140 16s 8d. Perhaps the most ironically ominous, and unconsciously prophetic, of the entries is the 4s spent to have Thomas Drewe strip ivy – which is so intimately associated with ruins – from the church.

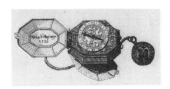

Abbot Whiting's watch and seal, engraved for Warner's Antiquities of Glastonbury. *They have since disappeared.*

Abbot Whiting's chair.

John Thorne's chair.

Surviving documents suggest that Whiting was an agreeable, conventional, perhaps even slightly bland individual. He had honesty of character and charm of personality, but appears to have lacked deep piety or profound political foresight. That his style of living suited the grandeur of his office – and at the time of the *Valor Ecclesiasticus* in 1535 Glastonbury's annual return of £3,311 7s 4d constituted the second greatest monastic income in the country – is made abundantly clear from the various accounts. Several of Whiting's elegant personal possessions survived the Dissolution: in particular, his beautiful watch and private seal, only recently lost, his richly embroidered chasuble, now at St John's Church, and the splendidly carved chair, now at the Bishop's Palace at Wells.[14] (This, by the way, should not be confused with the less grand and commonly reproduced Glastonbury chair which was given to the Bishop's Palace by descendants of Whiting's sister and which belonged to John Thorne – one of the two monks to be later martyred with Whiting.)

Whiting's whole style of life was that of a country gentleman and, from our perspective, he seems almost an anachronism, Chaucer's innocently naive Franklin suddenly dropped down into the dangerous polemic world of vying court and religious factions. As it turns out, nevertheless, Whiting's gentle epicureanism may have helped his monastery limp along as long as it did. During the second half of the 1530s, especially, Whiting tried to satisfy the ever accelerating demands of those in power. Request after request was satisfied: More's corrody went to Cromwell himself after the former's disgrace, the livings of churches were given to friends of the ecclesiastical commissioners, and on one occasion when a demand for a living could not be met because it had been assigned to a friend of a different royal protégé Cromwell had a simple solution; he suggested that a new sinecure be forthwith discovered. The old abbot submitted patiently, writing to Cromwell that 'If you request it, I must grant it.' It is characteristic that one of his last letters was to Arthur, Lord Lisle, apologizing for prosecuting servants of one of Lisle's retainers for stealing five cygnets: what particularly upset Whiting was that as a result of this theft he was unable to present the cygnets as gifts to the executors at the time of the funeral of his friend Sir John

[14] Another chair associated with Whiting, bearing a crozier and his initials, is found at Kingweston Church.

78

Fitzjames 'which grieved me more than twenty times the value of them.'[15] The cry is that of the beleaguered country squire rather than the religious militant. During these last years, nevertheless, even hostile visitors could not help but respond well to him. John Leland, who was generally unsympathetic to monks and abbots, refers to him as 'a man truly upright and spotless of character and my sincere friend' – although the politically astute antiquary later prudently expunged the compliment from his manuscripts.[16] When he came to Glastonbury in August 1535 Richard Layton, perhaps the most fanatic of the king's monastic visitors, also admired his host, but by 1539 he repented this weakness and wrote to Thomas Cromwell, the vicar general, that Whiting 'apperithe nether then, nor now, to have knowyne God, nether his Prynce, nother anny parte of a good Christin man his religion. ... I am a man, and may arr, and cannot be sure of my judgementt to knowe the inwarde thoughte of a monke, beinge fayre in worldly and outward apparaunce, and inwardly cankerede as now by your discrete inquisition apperithe.'[17]

One of the king's policies in dealing with the monasteries consisted of a shrewd application of the sound military tactic of dividing to conquer. Royal regulations cut abbots further and further off from their monks and from the community at large. At Glastonbury, Whiting's judicial powers over the archdeaconry, the Twelve Hides and the town of Glastonbury were dissolved and this led to costly delays and inefficiencies in all sorts of local cases. In 1535 a regulation was passed ordering all religious superiors to remain strictly enclosed. Sir John Fitzjames, who was at this time the abbey steward, wrote to Cromwell on Whiting's behalf and asked that this rule be at least somewhat relaxed. He also pleaded that something be done about the new system which permitted any monk who felt he had grounds for complaint to leave the cloister at the abbot's expense to report on his superior: 'Peradventure there be sume of his brodiers would be gladde to be abrode and to make untrew surmyse, so the abbot may paye for ther costes... Wherfore, it may please you ... to make it if the complaynannt prove his complaynt to be trow, then to have his costes, or elles not.'[18] Glastonbury, Fitzjames concluded in his petition,

[15] A copy of Whiting's letter is found in Muriel St. Clare Byrne, ed., *The Lisle Letters*, 6 vols. (Chicago, 1981), 5.547–48.
[16] This statement, crossed through, is found in the manuscript of Leland's *Commentarii de scriptoribus Britannicis*, on which see my 'The Manuscript Remains of John Leland, the "King's Antiquary"', *Text* 2 (1985), 111–20.
[17] See Henry Ellis, *Original Letters, Illustrative of English History*, 3rd series, vol. 3 (London, 1846), p. 247.
[18] Quoted in David Knowles, *Bare Ruined Choirs. The Dissolution of the English Monasteries* (Cambridge, 1976), p. 222.

did not need to be so strictly overseen, since it had kept 'as good religion as any house of that order within this realm.' This was the same opinion to which Layton had reluctantly come the year previously: 'At Bruton and Glastonbury there is nothing notable; the brethren be so straight kept that they cannot offend; but fain they would if they might, as they confess, and so the fault is not with them.'[19] Layton, it can be seen, wore his prejudices – as others might their hearts – upon his sleeve.

After several years of constantly increasing external pressure, morale within the monastery had disintegrated considerably.[20] In 1538 a bishop's visitation was made; these visitations of course were designed as forums for complaint, but nevertheless the mood does seem unusually querulous even if the actual faults – except for one recurrent case *de peccato sodomitico* – seem relatively venial. What is most disturbing is the police state atmosphere, where the king's dictatorial injunctions are constantly cited as one monk reports on the others. Predictably, there is a strong tension between abbot and monks, seniors and juniors: the old have the best food, the juniors, *au contraire*, are disrespectful, the prior has favourites, the abbot is incompetent and invites some monks more regularly than others to his table and so forth. William Brittock complains that he cannot have meat and drink for his kinsfolk when they come to visit. Various other monks observe that the convent ale has become inferior in quality. One individual suggests that the abbot has taken to himself sums of money which ought to be at the disposal of the whole community. The relics, another observes, are carried in procession with small devotion. What is saddest of all perhaps is the discernible decline in the quality of education. The novices complain that they have to pay up to 20 shillings a quarter for their own education and the schoolmaster has to exist on a pittance. William Joseph regrets that a grammar master is hired only just before and after times of visitation and 'for lack of lectures and other teaching the brethren doth diverse tymes play at dice and cards.' The prior and his cronies, apparently, have resisted learning and have tried to dissuade the abbot from pursuing his duties in this area. Books, moreover, seem to be missing and the services are so long and tedious that little time is left for the young men to devote to study. John Neot, who has been away at Oxford for somewhere between seven and twelve years, is the object of considerable envy. John Pantaleon, in particular, feels that he would profit more fully than Neot from a stay at the

[19] See *The Last Abbot of Glastonbury*, p. 66.
[20] On the situation at Glastonbury during this period see 'Revival at Glastonbury 1530–9'.

university. Various other monks point out that, in spite of all his education, Dan Neot can 'nother preache nor reade.'[21] All in all, Glastonbury did not produce any great scholars in the 1530s and only two monks took degrees, although at least six or seven attended the university during this period, which slightly reversed the downward trend of the the two previous decades. The criticism of the royal commissioners that Glastonbury had only three bachelors 'meanly learned' is partially – but only partially – justified.

From the very first inklings of trouble Whiting tried to co-operate with the king and his agents. He had signed the petition to the pope concerning the royal divorce and had subscribed to the oath accepting royal supremacy. By 1539 he seems to have reached a point of despair and asked to be excused from the spring session of parliament on the grounds of an unspecified illness which made travel impossible. This ostrich-like move, however, did nothing to slow down the fate which was about to overwhelm his monastery. The act of suppression of 1536 had condemned only houses with an annual income of under £200 or those which might wish voluntarily to surrender. The 1539 act added a retrospective clause concerning monasteries which 'shall happen to come to the king's highness by attainder or attainders of treason.' By the summer of 1539 few of the great monasteries remained undissolved. Glastonbury, in particular, seemed tantalizingly desirable:

> We [the commissioners] assure your lordship [Cromwell] it is the goodliest house of that sort that ever we have seen ... a house mete for the kings majesty and for no man else; which is to our great comfort ... The house is great, goodly and so princely as we have not seen the like; with 4 parks adjoining ... a great mere ... well replenished with great pikes, bream, perch and roach; 4 fair manor places belonging to the late abbot, the furthermost but 3 miles distant, being goodly mansions.[22]

The sequence of events from September through November is not altogether clear. In mid-September Cromwell reprimanded Layton for having praised Whiting and about a week later the three chief visitors – Layton, Richard Pollard and Thomas Moyle – descended unexpectedly like the three avenging furies on Glastonbury. The abbot was away at Sharpham Manor and they went to examine him there; he was broken in spirit and in poor health 'being but a weak man and sickly', old and

---

[21] Just before the Dissolution Neot returned to Glastonbury as guestmaster and was replaced at Oxford by Pantaleon.
[22] These two letters are quoted by G. H. Cook, *Letters to Cromwell and others on the Suppression of the Monasteries* (London, 1956), pp. 242–44.

presumably worn out. They interrogated him unmercifully and demanded that he 'call to mind what he had forgotten and tell the truth.' Sharpham was searched but no compromising correspondence with the abbot of Reading or others was found; indeed, the most incriminating items they could discover were a letter 'against the divorce of the king's majesty and the lady dowager, which we take to be a great matter, as also divers pardons, copies of bulls, and the counterfeit life of Thomas Bequet in print' and various bits of hidden treasure. The pickings, in other words, seemed slim – but, confident that the abbot had a 'cankered and traiterous heart' the commissioners dragged Whiting off to the Tower of London for more prolonged interrogation.

On 2 October the inquisitors sent a letter to Cromwell enclosing a now lost book with proof of 'divers and sundry treasons' committed by Whiting; he was then subjected to continual examinations by Cromwell himself. Nevertheless, as late as 25 October, the French ambassador, Charles de Marillac – usually a highly reliable source – knew of no more seriously damaging evidence than the book on the divorce. Cromwell was determined, however, to be rid of the abbot and noted to himself in his book of remembrances 'The abbot of Glaston to be sent down to be tried and executed at Glaston'. Whiting was not tried in London, then, or brought before parliament but was shipped back to Wells for the trial which took place at the Bishop's Palace on 14 November. Ultimately the charge of treason was abandoned for the simpler charge of 'robbery' – which seems particularly ironic since Henry's own men at that very moment were busily dismantling the whole monastery. As a final coup de grace Whiting was tried in the company of common criminals and deprived of all dignity. He handled himself with great decorum and refused to be baited. The jurors, hand selected, came to a hasty verdict of guilty and the final journey took place on 15 November.

In the company of two of his monks, John Thorne, the treasurer, and Roger Wilfrid, one of the youngest members of the community, Whiting was taken across the moors to Glastonbury. At the abbey gates he was attached to a hurdle and dragged through the town and up the Tor, where three gallows had been set up. Pollard tried to obtain incriminating evidence from him until the very last moment, evidence that subsequently could be used against others, but the abbot remained silent. Whiting and his faithful supporters seemed fully reconciled to their fate; as the accounts say, Whiting, one monk on either side of him 'took his death patiently, asking pardon of God and the king for his offences.' It is hard to evoke the drama of the final scene. At the best of times the Tor presents a daunting spectacle; in the late autumn with a constant wind blowing it has a formidable, almost supernatural, aspect and it is small wonder that in medieval legend it has been associated with the earthly entrance to the underworld. On this occasion, Whiting's age and gentleness must have made a stark contrast to the barrenness of the hill and the brutality of his tormenters. Indeed, in some ways the hanging can almost symbolise the ending of the English monastic movement and the Tor witnessed on this wild November day the apotheosis of the Crucifixion scene in the medieval mystery plays. Whiting himself may not have been a particularly Christ-like figure, but the *mise en scène* of his martyrdom certainly had many of the props used in the traditional representations of the event.

One more indignity still awaited Whiting after his death; there was no place for Joseph of Arimathea and his tomb in this Crucifixion drama. As soon as Whiting was dead, his head was struck off and his body cut into quarters; one quarter to be displayed at Wells, one at Bath, one at Ilchester and one at Bridgwater – the head was placed over the great gateway of the abbey itself. Glastonbury, Britain's *Roma secunda*, which had survived the assaults of the Saxons, the Danes, the Normans, all forms of civil and ecclesiastical dispute, was now at last destroyed in a final needlessly brutal act – an act which, so local legend would later relate, had long been prophesized:

> The meere: a great water, forth of the whiche is taken micch fyshe romenge to ye foote of ye Torr, which torr is a great hill: whereon Abbot Whiting was executed. A prophesi when a whiteng on ye torr is caught: Then shall ye Abbey comme to nawght.[23]

---

[23] This note, possibly recorded by Stephen Batman, is found in Oxford, MS Bodleian Douce 363, fol. 106r.

PART TWO

CULTURAL LIFE

St Joseph of Arimathea. Fifteenth-century stained glass window from All Saints Church, Longport.

4
Saints[1]

I. ARTHURIAN SAINTS

Such, felt the monks and historians of Glastonbury, was the sanctity of their monastery that the author of the verse *Lyfe* of St Joseph of Arimathea (published in 1520) could confidently affirm that 'Sothely glastenbury is the holyest erth of england.'[2] By the fourteenth century the monks had laid claim to a startling number of relics and remains of saints, many of whom, they felt, had also had close associations with the church during their lifetimes. These saints fall into several categories. First, and in many ways most exotic, is the small group of Arthurian saints – that is, saints venerated at Glastonbury whose biographies contain some reference to the legends of King Arthur.

St Joseph of Arimathea is perhaps the most illustrious of the *Joseph of* Arthurian saints, although his official life, as promulgated at *Arimathea* Glastonbury in the late middle ages, contains no direct references to King Arthur's world:

> 'When our lorde Ihesu Criste was crucefyed, Ioseph Ab Arimathia asked of Pylate the bodye of our Lorde and leyde it in a clene Sendell and put it in a Sepulcre that no man had ben buryed in, as the Euangelyst[es] testifie ... [Later] he became disciple to seynt Phylyp, & of hym he and his sone Iosefes were baptised; and he was a messenger fro Ephese bytwyxt seynt Iohn Euangelyst and our Ladye, and was at her departynge with other disciples; he was a Constaunte precher of the worde of god as he had herde of our lorde and of our Lady, and conuertyd moche people; after, he, with his sone Iosefes, went into Fraunce to seynt Phylyp and he sent Ioseph and his sone with .x. others into Brytayne & at last they came to a place then

---

[1] Before embarking on a discussion of Glastonbury saints I need to reiterate that I am for the most part describing the traditions as they existed in the fourteenth century, that is, at the period when the surviving relic lists were produced and when John of Glastonbury composed his chronicle. The relationship between medieval hagiography and historical fact is often a tenuous one and many of the *Lives* seem to be pure inventions. What they do show, however, is just how holy a place Glastonbury was held to be in the high middle ages.

[2] Ed. Walter W. Skeat (EETS, OS 44; London, 1871), pp. 35–52.

called Inswytryn, nowe called glastonburye ... And after, by monycion of the Archaungell gabryell, they made a Churche or oratory of our Lady & there they lyued a blessed lyf in vigylles, fastingz, & prayers. And two kynges, seynge theyr blessid lyfe, though th[e]y were paynymes, gaue to eueryche of theym a hyde of lande, whiche to this day be called the .xii. hydes and there they dyed; and Ioseph was buryed nygh to the sayd oratory.'   (Prose *Life* of Joseph [1516]; ed. Skeat, pp. 33–4.)

The material in the first section of this extraordinary narrative derives from the brief references to Joseph found in the Biblical Gospels, supplemented by the fuller account contained in the apocryphal *Gospel of Nicodemus* and the *Transitus Mariae*.[3] In these early scriptural texts, however, there is no hint that Joseph had collected any of the Holy Blood at the time of the Deposition or that he ever travelled into continental Europe. At Glastonbury itself, moreover, there is no indication that Joseph was the object of particular veneration before the late twelfth or early thirteenth century. What, then, led to the identification and why does Joseph qualify as an Arthurian saint? Here, we have two quite distinct traditions – one romantic and one 'historical' (at least by medieval standards) – which ultimately converged in a process which provides a model of the ingenuity displayed in the hagiographical writings of the high middle ages.[4]

In the late twelfth century Joseph's name turns up in the relatively surprising context of the French Grail romances when, in an early continuation of Chrétien de Troyes' unfinished poem *Perceval ou Le Conte du Graal*, it is narrated that the nebulous object described by Chrétien is none other than the very dish in which Joseph collected Christ's blood after the Crucifixion. Like the mysterious lance, which, as various scholars postulate, seems to have accompanied the cup even in the original preliterate (and therefore by definition hypothetical) story and which had become identified as the lance used by the blind Longinus to pierce Christ's side, the elusive Grail is seen in the continuation as a relic from the Crucifixion, one closely linked to an important Biblical personage. The connection may have arisen originally through a kind of association of ideas: if the lance came from Longinus, then the cup, too, needed a historical point of reference from the same period and Joseph would easily spring to mind since

[3] Valerie M. Lagorio has written a series of important articles on this topic; in particular, see her 'The Evolving Legend of St Joseph of Glastonbury', *Speculum* 46 (1971), 209–31.
[4] See Valerie M. Lagorio, 'The *Joseph of Arimathie*: English Hagiography in Transition', *Medievalia et Humanistica*, New Series 6 (1975), 91–101.

he is often portrayed in medieval art standing at the foot of the Cross.

Stories about the history of the Grail – and the operative term here becomes history as the Grail becomes more and more associated with a Biblical and therefore historical past – continued to be produced over the next half century. Sometime shortly before 1200 one Robert de Boron undertook to write a five-part sequence of poems concerning the complete history of the Grail (now visualized as the vessel from which Christ and the apostles drank at the Last Supper) and its travels from the Holy Land to Britain. The first segment was to concern *Joseph d'Arimathie*. Robert saw the Grail as a literal relic from the Holy Land; his job was to explain how it was transported through space and time to the fifth-century court of King Arthur. Specifically, Robert tells us, the final destination of the Grail – although not Joseph himself – is 'En la terre vers Occident / Ki est sauvage durement / En vaus d'Avaron' [in the land to the West, which is very wild, in the Vales of Avalon]. The context suggests that by Avaron, presumably an error for Avalon, Robert meant Glastonbury.

Slightly later, the long prose romance, *Perlesvaus*, takes up the same story and weaves the various strands into a long and coherent narrative. The anonymous author of *Perlesvaus* relates that Joseph collected the Holy Blood at the time of the Crucifixion and was later imprisoned by the Jews for burying Jesus. Miraculously escaping from prison Joseph travelled to Britain where he became the ancestor of an unbroken line of valiant knights. His niece, Iglais, was the mother of Perlesvaus, the hero who would achieve the Grail with the aid of Joseph's red-cross shield. Joseph himself placed the shroud of Christ in the Perilous Chapel and after his death his own body was buried outside the Grail castle. When Perlesvaus departed from this castle he took Joseph's body with him on the red-cross ship which carried him to the Other World.

In a colophon at the end of the romance the author of *Perlesvaus* refers to his source and tells us that: 'The Latin from whence this history was drawn into Romance was taken in the Isle of Avalon, in a holy house of religion that standeth at the head of the Moors Adventurous, there where King Arthur and Queen Guenievre lie, according to the witness of the good men religious that are therein, that have the whole story thereof, true from the beginning even to the end.' In fact, some of the geographical references in this text are so direct and when carefully examined so seemingly accurate that certain commentators have argued that *Perlesvaus* or its prototype must have been composed at Glastonbury. Be this as it may, the Glastonbury community had certainly acquired a copy of

Fragment from fourteenth-century copy of Perlesvaus *at Wells Cathedral.*

this romance by the fourteenth century at the latest and incorporated aspects of it into their own foundation story.[5]

The last major French Grail sequence was composed early in the thirteenth century in prose and is now usually referred to as the Vulgate cycle. In these romances (and especially in the *Estoire del Saint Graal*, which would become one of John of Glastonbury's main sources in his description of the evangelization of Britain) the geography is vague, but the details concerning Joseph's role as apostle to England are very

[5] It seems quite possible that the fourteenth-century fragment of *Perlesvaus* I have recently unearthed at Wells Cathedral was copied from a French exemplar in the Glastonbury library, possibly the very version used by John of Glastonbury when he compiled his chronicle.

specifically and convincingly visualized. The accounts of Joseph's missionary activities, moreover, are presented in terms very similar to those used in the *vitae* of recognized saints. For the French audience for whom the cycle was originally written the geographical aspect of the story would have remained peripheral, but when the romances were transported to Britain, and especially to Glastonbury, it was inevitable that the place of action would suddenly seem considerably more important. A change of context was bound to produce a quite different reading of the text.

In these French romances Joseph is presented as a real person, a verifiable historical fact, as it were, by which the Grail can be solidly located in the real world. Since even the earliest traditions as they have been recorded make the Grail manifest itself in King Arthur's kingdom, it seemed logical to the French writers that Joseph, like Arthur himself, should

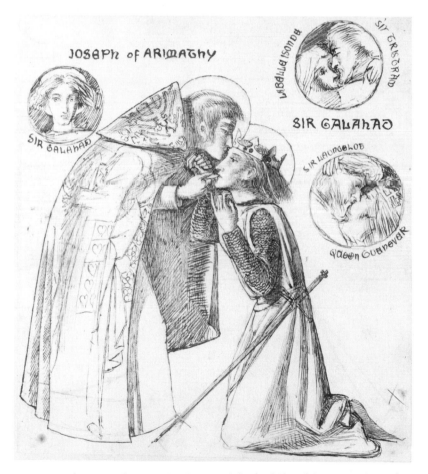

Simeon Solomon. The Death of Sir Galahad while taking a portion of the Holy Grail administered by Joseph of Arimathea. *Solomon was one of a number of late nineteenth-century artists who illustrated Arthurian themes.*

ultimately arrive at the otherworldly Avalon so lyrically described by Geoffrey of Monmouth: 'The Island of Apples, which men call the Fortunate Isle ...' By the time when the later Grail romances were being written in France, however, the concept of Avalon had evolved in a dramatic fashion in England itself. After c.1190, when King Arthur's body was 'found' in the cemetery at Glastonbury, Avalon was no longer seen as a vague place in the mists of Celtic tradition. If Arthur were buried at Glastonbury, so the argument ran, then Glastonbury must be identical to Avalon, where Arthur was transported after receiving his fatal wounds. This identification did not, of course, make much difference to the French romances, which were concerned with an imaginary *matière de Bretagne* rather than with local church history, but it did have immense implications for Glastonbury Abbey's own development. For many centuries Glastonbury writers had assumed that theirs was the oldest ecclesiastical site in England. There was the tradition, first recorded c.1000 in the anonymous biography of St Dunstan, that the first preachers of Christ in Britain had found at Glastonbury a church built by no skill of man and consecrated by Our Lord himself to the honour of his Virgin Mother.[6] Even William of Malmesbury, that most careful of twelfth-century historians, felt that there might be some truth in the theory of an apostolic mission to Glastonbury, since there seemed to be ample evidence that France had been visited by St Philip. William pointed out, however, that no specific information had survived on the topic and that it was, therefore, useless to speculate any further. What the Grail romances did (partly by coincidence, since they appeared about the same time as the Glastonbury excavation took place) was to suddenly bring to light new evidence on the topic. They were a practically miraculous solution to a hitherto insoluble problem.

In the mid- to late thirteenth century the inevitable occurred and the following marginal note appears in one of the manuscripts of William of Malmesbury's *The Early History of Glastonbury* beside the section describing the earliest history of the monastery: 'The book of the deeds of the famous King Arthur bears witness that the noble decurion Joseph of Arimathea, together with his son named Josephes and very many others, came into great Britain, now called England, and ended his life there ... Again in a later part of the book, about the search for a vessel called there the holy grail, almost the same thing is recorded where a white knight explains to Galahad, son of Lancelot, the mystery of a certain miraculous shield which he entrusts to him to bear because noone else

[6] For possible evidence suggesting that the dedication to the Virgin dates back at least to the sixth century and the time of Gildas see Ashe, *Avalonian Quest*, pp. 141–44.

St Joseph's chapel, constructed by Richard Beere. From a sepia print, 1860.

could carry it, even for a day, except at great cost.' Soon after this insertion appeared in William's text, John of Glastonbury composed his chronicle; in it the process is carried one stage further. Now the Grail itself has been expunged and replaced by an ecclesiastically respectable relic, two cruets containing the blood and sweat of Jesus.[7] The romance elements of the evangelization story have been eliminated and Joseph has become an altogether credible apostolic saint. His pedigree, as John propounds it, also provides a justification for Glaston-

[7] As his authority on these relics John quotes from an ancient prophecy by Melkin the Bard, a so-called British magus who lived before Merlin. The language of the prophecy, which was probably put together in its present form in the thirteenth century, is singularly obscure and defies precise translation: 'The Isle of Avalon, greedy in the burial of pagans, above others in the world, decorated at the burial place of all of them with vaticinatory little spheres of prophecy, and in future it will be adorned with those who praise the Most High. Abbadare, powerful in Saphat, most noble of pagans, took his sleep there with 104,000. Amongst them Joseph de Marmore, named "of Arimathea", took everlasting sleep. And he lies on a forked line close to the southern corner of the chapel with prepared wattle above the powerful venerable Maiden, the thirteen aforesaid sphered things occupying the place. For Joseph has with him in the tomb two white and silver vessels filled with the blood and sweat of the prophet Jesus. When his tomb is found, it will be seen whole and undefiled in the future, and will be open to all the earth. From then on, neither water nor heavenly dew will be lacking to those who inhabit the most noble island. For a long time before the Day of Judgement in Josaphat will these things be open and declared to the living.' For a discussion of some of the strange oriental allusions in this text see my 'Melkin the Bard and Esoteric Tradition at Glastonbury Abbey', *The Downside Review* 99 (1981), 1–17. There is an early reference to Melkin's prophecy outside a Glastonbury context in the *Flores Historiarum*, ed. H. R. Luard, 3 vols. (RS 95; London, 1890), 1.127.

bury's status as the most senior church in England, one which should take precedence over most continental foundations as well. No wonder that the recorded late medieval Glastonbury prayers to St Joseph were effusive: 'Heyle, tresour of Glastenbury moost imperyall, / In sauour smellynge swete as eglantyne; / Now shall thy name flourysshe ouerall, / Ihesu for thy sake the bell of mercy doth rynge.' Naturally, too, miracles and healings came to be associated with St Joseph of Glastonbury and he attracted a large following among late medieval pilgrims.

Gildas

Modern historians still make use of Gildas' *Concerning the Ruin and Conquest of Britain*, perhaps written around 540. Gildas describes his work, the title of which indicates its general tone, as an admonitory letter to his fellow Britons; in it he reproaches them for the deplorable moral and physical state into which they have let themselves and their country fall, a state which accounts, by Gildas' reckoning, for God's repudiation of them. Fortunately, Gildas moves beyond polemic in certain sections of the work and includes a homiletic history of Britain from Roman times down to his own day. What is particularly interesting about this work from the point of view of Arthurian studies is that although Gildas refers to the Battle of Mount Badon, which he says took place in the year of his birth, he never alludes specifically to King Arthur.

In the middle ages Gildas was considered an eminent historian, but he was also venerated as a major British saint. By the tenth century at the latest he was commemorated at Glastonbury, where his feast was celebrated on 29 January. At the invitation of the Glastonbury community, so it seems, Caradog of Llancarfan, known far and wide for his ability to reconstruct saints' lives, wrote a *Life* of Gildas (c.1140).[8] According to Caradog Gildas was born in the Clyde Valley, one of the twenty-four sons of Caw, the ruler of a small Scottish kingdom, who was later driven into exile in Anglesey. The brothers of Gildas were all brave warriors, but Gildas himself – later to become universally known as 'the Wise' – was attracted to scholarship and religion. He mastered the seven liberal arts under the tutelage of St Illtud at Llantwit Major (Llanilltud Fawr) and then spent seven more years studying in Gaul. He brought many books back to Britain with him and became famous for his learning and for the austere piety of his life: 'He use to fast like the hermit Antony ... he used to pray clad in goat's skin .... It was his habit to go

---

[8] For references to Gildas and commentators on his *Life* see Elissa R. Henken, *Traditions of the Welsh Saints* (Woodbridge, 1987), pp. 135–40.

into a river at midnight, where he would remain unmoved until he had said the Lord's Prayer three times …. He used to sleep moderately, and lie upon a stone, clothed with only a single garment.' Before long, Gildas became the most renowned preacher in Britain. Only once did this gift desert him: when St Nonnita, pregnant with St David, appeared in a church where he was preaching, he was unable to speak. After the angel of the Lord explained to him that the silence was a miraculous indication of the superior evangelizing skills of the boy in St Nonnita's womb Gildas decided to bequeath Wales to St David's ministrations, and he himself travelled over to Ireland where he converted much of the population to Christianity.

Meanwhile, so Caradog relates, Arthur had become king of all Britain. Hueil, Gildas' elder brother, who was a proud as well as a brave man, refused to accept anyone as overlord.[9] Setting up his headquarters in Scotland he waged war on Arthur and pillaged up and down the coast. Arthur pursued him and they met in battle on the Isle of Man, where Arthur killed the young renegade, his worthiest foe.[10] Gildas was, of course, desolate, but refused to denounce his brother's murderer. The two men met soon afterwards at Llancarfan, just as Gildas was setting out on pilgrimage to Rome; there was a tearful reconciliation and Arthur joyfully accepted the penance laid upon him by the attendant bishops and set about a general reformation of character. At Llancarfan itself, tradition maintained, Gildas made a beautiful copy of the Gospels during the year when he substituted for St Cadog as abbot. This book was adorned with gold and silver and kept as a precious relic.

After other adventures, including a sojourn of seven years as a hermit on the desolate island of Steep Holme in the Bristol Channel, from which he was driven by pirates, Gildas came by ship to the island of Glastonia (the name means 'glassy isle' in both British – or Welsh – and English by Caradog's etymology) where the abbot welcomed him and where he immediately began teaching the brethren and the local laymen and composing his *Concerning the Ruin and Conquest of Britain*. At this time the king of the Summer Region (i.e., Somerset) was Melwas, who had wickedly abducted Guenevere, the wife of King Arthur, and had brought her to his fortress at

[9] The medieval Welsh romance *Culhwch ac Olwen* proudly boasts that Hueil 'never petitioned the hand of a lord'.

[10] In a sixteenth-century chronicle written by Elis Gruffudd we are told that problems first arose when Hueil took one of Arthur's mistresses. Arthur was wounded in the knee in an ensuing combat between the two men, but made peace on condition that Hueil never mention the wound. Later, when Arthur disguised himself as a woman to visit a girl in Rhuthun, Hueil saw him dancing and mocked the bad knee. After returning to his court the offended Arthur summoned Hueil and cut off his head in revenge for the broken promise.

Glastonbury Tor, an invulnerable position because of 'the fortifications of thickets of reed, river and marsh.' After a year's search Arthur discovered where his wife was hidden and gathered together his forces in Cornwall and Devon to lay siege to Glastonbury. Thereupon Gildas and the abbot of Glastonbury approached Melwas and persuaded him to return Guenevere to Arthur; peace was thus restored. The kings met at the Church of St Mary and both endowed the monastery with many lands and privileges in commemoration of the peaceful settlement of their differences.

Feeling that he was nearing the end of his earthly sojourn Gildas obtained permission from the abbot to take up the life of a hermit again. Near Glastonbury and not far from a river, he built a little chapel dedicated to the Holy and Undivided Trinity and lived a life of prayer and penance there. (Later there was, in fact, a chapel dedicated to St Gildas himself, which was known in the romances as the 'Chapel Adventurous'.) When Gildas felt death approaching he asked the abbot to bury him at Glastonbury Abbey, the place he loved above all others. The abbot granted his request; Gildas thereupon expired and 'amid very loud wailing and with most befitting funeral rites, he was buried in the middle of the pavement of St Mary's church; and his soul rested, rests, and will rest, in heavenly repose.'[11]

St Kea

'Lantocai' is the ancient name for Leigh in Street, which was owned by Glastonbury Abbey as early as 681 when Haeddi, bishop of Winchester, gave three 'cassati' at Leigh to the abbot Haemgils. The original name 'Lantocai', that is the church of Kea, indicates a possible Glastonbury provenance for yet another Celtic holy man, St Kea, who is more generally associated with Devon, Cornwall and Brittany.[12]

From Kea's *Life* we learn that he was a contemporary of Gildas. He was trained at Glastonbury and then became a hermit nearby at the location to which his name would later be attached. Before he set out on his wanderings (these almost statutory migrations in the lives of the early Celtic saints) he acquired a bell from St Gildas – famous in hagiographical tradition as a bell-maker – at the nearby 'Chapel Adventurous'. This bell would ring, so it was revealed, when Kea arrived at the place where he was meant to settle. In due course, when he got to a wood by a river just south of modern Truro, now

[11] Alternate traditions link Gildas with Brittany; these are described by Henken, pp. 135–140. In the Breton *Life* Gildas is credited with the miraculous resuscitation of the beheaded daughter of the Count of Vannes who had been married to a Cronus-like figure, notorious for killing his wives the moment they conceived. Gildas also shows a miraculous ability to create glass from a rock when building his oratory by the river Blavet in Rhuys.
[12] On Kea see H. M. Porter, *The Celtic Church in Somerset* (Bath, 1971), pp. 60–61.

known as Old Kea, the bell rang of its own accord, a sign that the wanderings were over. Kea and his companions thereupon cleared the land, built a little chapel and dwelling cells nearby and began their eremitic life. After a variety of adventures Kea emigrated to Brittany and set up a second monastery at Cleder (c.472) in the reign of Hoel the Great. For this new monastery he brought relics from Cornwall and a book of the gospels which he had earlier written himself.

After Kea's departure from Greater Britain to Lesser Britain (i.e., Brittany) a series of catastrophes occurred in the former location. Taking advantage of the absence of his uncle King Arthur in Gaul, the rebel Mordred usurped the throne and incestuously married Queen Guenevere. Hearing of this, King Arthur handed over his affairs in Gaul to the care of another nephew named Hoel and returned home to challenge the usurper who, for his part, had already contracted an alliance with the pagan Saxons. In panic over the Saxon deluge, the English bishops sent word to Kea, who was universally renowned for his skill in diplomacy as well as for his sanctity. He returned to Britain and appeared before Arthur with plans for a peaceful solution to the dispute. Unfortunately, however, 80,000 Saxons had already landed on the coast and so it was impossible to avoid a war. In despair over the sad fate awaiting his country, Kea decided to return to Brittany. He passed through Winchester en route and there visited the despondent Guenevere whom he persuaded to forsake the world and become a nun. Back at Cleder Kea himself fell mortally ill and died, his *Life* states, in October 495. He was buried quietly in the oratory of his hermitage, where his tomb was subsequently discovered and where many miracles occurred.

In the *Life* of Kea, which survives only in a very late and corrupt version, there are a number of striking overlaps with the legends of St Gildas and with the whole Arthurian saga. Both saints are associated with Street and the 'Chapel Adventurous'. The bell cast by Gildas – who in his capacity as bell-maker also provided bells for St Brigit and St Cadog – forms an important component in the account of Kea's early quests. The names in both *Lives*, moreover, have similarities. Kea, of course, immediately brings to mind King Arthur's own foster brother Sir Kay. Gildas' brother, with whom King Arthur waged mortal battle, was Hueil, a close variant on the name of Kea's second patron King Hoel. The long Arthurian episode in the *Life* of Kea – where Kea returns to Britain (perhaps even to Glastonbury) to meet Arthur and propose a peace-treaty with Mordred – is structurally very similar to the ambassadorial episode in the *Life* of Gildas, where Gildas mediates between Arthur and Melwas at Glastonbury. What these parallels between the two *Lives* may suggest is that Glastonbury was somehow associated with the development of some of the most important Arthurian hagiographical traditions.

St Collen

The otherworldly aspect of Glastonbury – hinted at in the Melwas episode of the *Life* of St Gildas – is made even more explicit in another, peripherally Arthurian, saint's life, namely the *Life* of St Collen, which survives only in a Welsh redaction of the sixteenth century.[13] According to Welsh tradition, Collen – whose name is commemorated in Llangollen in North Wales and in Brittany – was the grandson of Coleddog, a man described in the Welsh Triads as one of the 'Three Ineloquent Men of the Court of Arthur'. After his education in Orleans Collen undertook a heroic encounter on behalf of the pope with a pagan called Byras. He then came to Glastonbury where he eventually set up his hermitage in a quiet spot beneath a rock on the side of Glastonbury Tor. One day he heard two men discussing Gwynn ab Nudd; when they said he was King of Annwfn and of the fairies, Collen was exasperated and interrupted them, explaining that Gwynn and his company were only pagan demons. His interlocutors begged to differ and informed him that he would soon have to confront Gwynn face to face. Not long afterwards, indeed, Gwynn's messenger arrived and ordered Collen to come to speak with Gwynn on the top of the Tor by midday at the latest. After two refusals, which led to threats by the messenger, Collen equipped himself with holy water and climbed the Tor, where he saw Gwynn's habitation: 'the fairest castle he had ever seen and around it the best appointed hosts, and many musicians with every instrumental and string music, and horses with boys on their backs, the fairest in the world, and girls of noble aspect, lively activity, lightfooted, lightly dressed, in the flower of young age, and every dignity which was known to the court of a powerful king ...' When the saint entered the castle he was taken to Gwynn, sitting in a chair of gold, and was offered food and drink, both of which he wisely refused, since he knew that fairy-food is notoriously dangerous. The king then asked him if he had ever seen men better dressed than the courtiers in their red and blue. Collen retorted that these were evil colours: the red on the one side meant burning and the blue on the other intense cold. He then sprinkled holy water over them and they all vanished, leaving nothing but green mounds and the desolate hillside.[14]

---

13 See Henken, pp. 221–26.
14 Elis Gruffudd seems to be referring to a variant of this tradition when he observes that 'they [the English] talk much more about him [Arthur] than we do for they say and strongly believe that he will rise again to be king. In their opinion he is sleeping in

One of the fascinating aspects of this legend is the identification which it makes between Glastonbury Tor and Annwfn, the Celtic Otherworld, the region so lyrically described in the story of 'Pwyll, Prince of Dyfed' in *The Mabinogion*. In Welsh myth, moreover, Gwynn had a role very similar to that of Melwas in the *Life* of Gildas. Indeed, the Gildas and the Collen stories independently seem to indicate that Glastonbury/Avalon had a pervasive place in medieval Celtic myth and that the very names bring together a whole range of otherworldly meanings: 'Annwfn', 'Isle of Glass', 'Isle of Apples', 'Summer Region' and so forth. The historical validity of the etymologies is considerably less important than the fact that they could all easily be made, and that through them Glastonbury could accrue to itself a wealth of Celtic legend, the same kind of legend which would be so successfully transformed elsewhere into the Arthurian *matière de Bretagne*.

II. CELTIC SAINTS

Why so many Irish saints figure in the Glastonbury calendars is a vexed question, one which has not been completely resolved even by the the most sophisticated techniques of modern scholarship. Certainly there was an Irish influence in the South West as early as the seventh century when St Aldhelm berated one Heahfrith for succumbing to the allurements of Irish learning.[15] Under the year 891 the *Anglo-Saxon Chronicle* refers to an Irish presence in England as the result of the travels of Irish pilgrims: 'Three Gaels came to King Alfred in a boat without any oars from Ireland, which they had left secretly, because they wished for the love of God to be in foreign lands, they cared not where.' Around 1000 'B', the author of the *Life* of St Dunstan, refers specifically to an Irish community at Glastonbury:

> Irish peregrini, as well as other flocks of the faithful, sought this aforementioned place called Glastonbury with great veneration, especially because of the renown of the younger [or older, depending on the manuscript] St Patrick, who is said to lie buried in that church.

a cave under a hill near Glastonbury and indeed if one could give credence to many diverse people from that district he appeared and conversed with many people in many strange ways three hundred years ago.' I owe this reference and the translation from the Welsh to Dr Ceridwen Lloyd-Morgan, National Library of Wales, Aberystwyth.

[15] A. S. Cook, 'Who was the Ehfrid of Aldhelm's Letter?', (*Speculum* 2 [1927], 363–73) identified this individual as the Ecgfrith who later became abbot of Glastonbury. In his discussion of this letter to Heahfrith (*Aldhelm. The Prose Works*, trans. Michael Lapidge and Michael Herren [Cambridge, 1979], p.145) Michael Herren queries this identification on linguistic grounds and concludes that Cook's case is dubious.

Medieval monumental slab with a carved figure representing St Patrick, from Faughort churchyard, Co. Louth, and now in the National Museum of Ireland.

In his late eleventh-century *Life* of St Dunstan, Osbern of Canterbury, who had visited Glastonbury and who was not himself particularly sympathetic to the aspirations of the monastery, takes up the same point:

> Many distinguished scholars, eminent both in sacred and profane learning, who quitted Ireland to embrace a life of voluntary exile in England, chose Glastonbury for their habitation, as being a retired but convenient spot, and one famous for its cult – a point of special attraction, this, for the exiles – of Patrick, who is said to have come after a lifetime of miracle-working and preaching the gospel, and to have ended his days there in the Lord.[16]

That there was an Irish community at Glastonbury before the Conquest, then, seems virtually certain. What is not clear, however, is whether the first Irish pilgrims came to Glastonbury because they had heard stories linking St Patrick with Glastonbury or whether their presence itself accounted for the formation of the legends.

Relatively recently, in the 1920s, a fragment from a Glastonbury manuscript of the late thirteenth century turned up at West Pennard, where it was functioning as the cover for a late sixteenth-century book of accounts. This fragment contains an Anglo-Norman verse rendering of the famous Glastonbury charter of St Patrick and gives a succinct account of the fully developed St Patrick legend at Glastonbury:

St Patrick

I [Patrick] was sent on a mission into a region
That is called Ireland, a very wild land,
By the Pope Celestine who caused me so to do
To preach to that folk our belief. ...
[Afterwards] I departed thence doing harm to none
And returned straightway into Britain ...
I came into an isle that had to name Ynswitrin,
So was it called of old time in the British tongue,
In the which I found a place delectable ...
There found I several brethren well indoctrinate
And well instructed in the Catholic faith ...
They came there after those saints
Whom saints Phagan and Deruvian had left there ...
And, because I found them humble and peaceable,
I made choice rather to be with them, though I should be feeble,
Than to dwell in a royal court in vigorous life ...
But, because we all had one heart ...
We chose to dwell together
And to eat and drink in one house
And in one place sleep under a rule.

---

[16] For Osbern's *Life* see William Stubbs, ed., *Memorials of St Dunstan* (RS 53; London, 1874), pp. 69–161.

The Bewcastle cross, mid seventh century to mid eighth century. Probably similar in shape to the Glastonbury pyramids.

So, though I liked it not, they chose me chief
And by fraternal force made me their guardian ...[17]

Another section of the charter tells us that St Patrick later climbed the Tor and found a ruined oratory with an ancient volume containing the 'Acts of St Phagan and St Deruvian', the so-called second-century missionaries. Patrick then appointed two Irish monks, Arnulf and Ogmar, to remain and administer at the chapel on the Tor. The charter also gives the names of the twelve hermits whom St Patrick found living on the spot when he arrived at Glastonbury: Brumban, Hyregaan, Brenwal, Wencreth, Bantommeweng, Adelwalred, Lothor, Wellias, Breden, Swelwes, Hinloernus and another Hin. The names are puzzling: at first glance they seem neither Irish, Welsh, English nor Norman. In his researches into the history of Glastonbury Abbey, however, Dom Aelred Watkin made a comparison of these names with William of Malmesbury's account of the names engraved on the larger of the two ancient pyramids which stood so prominently in the old cemetery:

Pyramid	*St Patrick's Companions*
1st storey:	
(Image of a bishop)	BRUMBAN
2nd storey:	
(Image displaying royal pomp)	
HER ...	HYREGAAN
SEXI ...	
BLISWERH ...	BRENWAL
3rd storey:	
WEMCREST	WENCRETH
BANTOMP	BAMTOM-
WINETHEGN	MEWENG
4th storey:	
HATE	·ADE-
WULFRED	WALRED
EANFLED	
5th storey:	
(Image)	
LOGWOR	LOTHOR
WESLICAS	WELLIAS
BREGDEN	BREDEN
SWELWES	SWELWES
HWINGENDES	HINLOERNIUS
BERN	
ALTERA	ALIUS HIN[18]

---

[17] See Robin Flower, 'A Glastonbury Fragment from West Pennard', *Somerset and Dorset Notes and Queries* 17 (1923), 205–17.

[18] 'The Glastonbury "Pyramids" and St Patrick's "Companions"', *The Downside Review* 63 (1945), 30–41.

The similarities are, of course, remarkable. What probably happened was that the person who first assembled the material for St Patrick's charter looked at the pyramid with its images and weathered names and decided that he had found a memorial commemorating the names of the hermits. It is not, then, a question of blatant forgery but of over-ingenious detective work. Modern historians might not agree with the solution of the mystery, but the method cannot be dismissed out of hand.

In his chronicle John of Glastonbury supplies us with a variety of other details he 'discovered' about St Patrick's mission to Glastonbury. St Patrick, John tells us, was born in Britain in 361 and was a nephew of St Martin of Tours.[19] At the age of 16 he was abducted by Irish pirates and spent six years as a slave to a cruel Irish chieftain called Milchu. Miraculously he was directed to a piece of gold hidden under some turf and was thus able to redeem himself from slavery. After serving as a disciple to St Germanus of Auxerre, he travelled to the Roman *curia*. He was then sent back to Ireland in 425 by Pope Celestine I. Having converted the Irish he returned to Britain on a floating wooden altar and landed at Padstow in Cornwall. He arrived at Glastonbury in 433 and remained there as abbot until his death in 472. He was then buried in a beautiful shrine and remained there until the fire of 1184. After this catastrophe his bones were dug up and placed in a new shrine covered in gold and silver where they continued to be venerated for the rest of the life of the monastery.

Throughout the middle ages and even after William of Malmesbury, at the time considered a thoroughly dependable authority, gave his *imprimatur* to some of Glastonbury's claims in his now lost *Life* of St Patrick, there continued to be unresolved doubts about the Glastonbury cult of St Patrick elsewhere in England and Ireland. To begin with, the Irish themselves had an early hagiographical tradition that there had been more than one Patrick. In the eighth century, for example, a hymn was composed which stated that 'When Patrick departed this life, he went first to the other Patrick: together they ascended to Jesus the Son of Mary.'[20] The Patricius Senior, so some scholars now suggest, might have been Palladius, the Roman deacon who was sent to Ireland in

[19] There continues to be much dispute about St Patrick's dates, although it is generally agreed that he lived in the fifth century. In his unpublished Ph.D. dissertation, *Medieval Irish Saints' Lives: a study of the three Latin Collections* (Cambridge, 1987), Richard Sharpe surveys the field and concludes that 'Objections can be found to all dating-models proposed, but dates lying outside the fifth century are still less convincing.'

[20] See H. P. R. Finberg, 'St Patrick at Glastonbury', in *West Country Historical Studies* (New York, 1969), p. 78.

431 by Pope Celestine. If there were two Patricks, the question inevitably arises concerning the identity of the one commemorated at Glastonbury. Interestingly, when the Kalendar now found in the *Leofric Missal* was composed at Glastonbury c.970, both saints appear: the feast of Patrick the bishop is found under 17 March and Patrick Senior is found with a very high rating under 24 August.[21] This may suggest that the earlier tradition at Glastonbury concerned Palladius/Patrick, but it was later transformed when the monks realized that they might actually possess the relics of the greater and more prestigious saint.

Nor does the matter stop here. In the fourteenth century John of Glastonbury's fellow historian and arch-rival Ranulf Higden, a monk of Chester, noted in his *Polychronicon* that there was a third Patrick, an Irish bishop who died in 863. Here, Higden postulated, lay the solution to the conflicting traditions. The saint of the Irish was, as the Irish generally claimed, buried at Down and it was the much later bishop who ended his days at Glastonbury. Needless to say, John was not impressed by Higden's reasoning.

In the later middle ages, then, as conflicting accounts circulated more and more widely about the number of Patricks, their dates, and their final resting places, so too did doubts arise in the minds of the Glastonbury monks concerning the identity of their Patrick. The solution to these doubts came in a miraculous manner. A certain monk, who had long been pondering the matter, was vouchsafed a dream-vision in which it was confirmed that the Patrick buried at Glastonbury was, indeed, the apostle of the Irish and no lesser individual. This form of proof satisfied the community and provided the last word on the topic at the time, but it is, of course, somewhat less convincing to modern scholars. What, then, are the facts? How did Glastonbury come to appropriate Patrick so firmly into its roster of saints? H. P. R. Finberg, who made detailed studies of early charters from south-west England, has suggested that *patricius* is a title as well as a name and that in the early English kingdoms it was applied to members of the royal family who served as underkings. When the Irish *peregrini* came to Glastonbury, Finberg speculates, they might well have found an ancient monument with this title engraved on it. What, in this case, would be more natural than to assume that the term applied to their own national apostle, about whose burial place there was some confusion even in Ireland?[22] Other scholars, however, feel the association is even more

---

[21] Edited by Francis Wormald, *English Kalendars before A.D. 1100* (London, 1934), pp. 44–55.
[22] See 'St Patrick at Glastonbury', p. 84.

intimate. R. P. C. Hanson, for example, observes that even if St Patrick was not buried at Glastonbury there is no reason why he could not have been born there and Hanson locates the place of his birth on the banks of the Brue.[23] In *The Two Patricks* T. F. O'Rahilly goes further and suggests that St Patrick, apostle to the Irish, might have returned to Glastonbury after his missionary activities,[24] a point which the Irish medievalist, James Carney, is also willing to consider: 'There seems to be at least a possibility that Patrick, tired and ill at the end of his arduous mission, felt released from his vow not to leave Ireland, returned to Britain, and died at the monastery from which he had come, which, if this be so, may perhaps be identified as the monastery of Glastonbury.'[25] As tempting as these speculations may be, they ultimately seem to have no basis in recorded historical fact. St Patrick's own words, moreover, must ring in our ears and stand as a stumbling block to a convinced belief that he really did end his days as Glastonbury's abbot: 'even if I wished to go to Britain I am bound by the Spirit, who gives evidence against me if I do this, telling me that I shall be guilty; and I am afraid of losing the labour which I have begun – nay, not I, but Christ the Lord who bade me come here and stay with them [the Irish] for the rest of my life.'[26]

According to Irish tradition, St Patrick gave the name Benignus (Benén) to a certain man whom he baptized: at this time he also predicted that Benignus would be the heir to his kingdom. At some point in the very late tenth or early eleventh century Benignus' name entered Glastonbury house-tradition, so it seems, through the following piece of mistaken etymology. The name Beonna was relatively common in England and appears in a variety of Anglo-Saxon records. In particular, it seems that a holy man called Beonna was commemorated in a monument at Meare. When the Irish pilgrims saw the memorial, they assumed that the reference was to their own St Benignus who would, it seemed quite logical, have followed St Patrick into exile.

Over the years a number of local stories about this saint developed and in 1091 his relics were translated with great pomp from Meare to the main church at Glastonbury and placed in a beautiful reliquary which had been given to the abbot Aethelweard by King Harthacnut. The translation was

St Benignus

---

[23] *St Patrick. His Origins and Career* (Oxford, 1968), pp. 157–58.
[24] *The Two Patricks* (Dublin, 1942), p. 33.
[25] *The Problem of St Patrick* (Dublin, 1961), pp. 121–2.
[26] Ludwig Bieler, ed. and trans., *The Works of St Patrick* (Westminster, Md., 1953), p. 35.

accompanied by a variety of miracles which took place at a location about halfway between the monastery and the river from Meare. To commemorate the event, a church was built at the site and dedicated to the saint. It was replaced by the present church, now called St Benedict's, at the turn of the sixteenth century. The relics themselves were placed in a shrine before the High Altar at St Mary's, close to those of St Benignus' fellow countrymen, St Patrick and St Indract.

By the time when William of Malmesbury visited Glastonbury in the 1120s, a fully fledged cult of St Benignus had developed which William recorded in a now lost *Life*; traces of this survive in John of Glastonbury's chronicle.[27] Here we learn that after seven years as bishop in Ireland Benignus took a vow to go on a pilgrimage; he arrived at Glastonbury in 462 [sic]. St Patrick, who had preceded him by almost thirty years, told him that he must continue on his pilgrimage until his staff put out branches and flowered; then he would know that he had arrived at the appointed place for his habitation. Accompanied by a boy, Pincius, he trudged through deep forests and boggy salt marshes until he came to a little solitary island: here, at Meare, the staff suddenly took root and soon grew into a tree, a tree which continued to thrive for many centuries as a testimony to the miracle. When Benignus settled at Meare the place lacked one major prerequisite for human settlement: there was no drinking water. Poor Pincius, therefore, had to walk almost three miles each day, often assailed by evil spirits, to fetch fresh water for himself and his master. Fortunately, Benignus soon had a divine vision and gave Pincius his staff – presumably a new one – and directed him to a bed of rushes nearby. At this place, so he ordered, Pincius was to strike a blow with the staff. The boy obeyed the instructions and a spring burst forth: ever afterwards, the water was clear and plentiful – as were fish and other delicacies, a fact which would prompt subsequent abbots to establish a fishery at Meare.

After St Patrick died, the monks insisted that Benignus become abbot, which he agreed to do only on condition that he be permitted to spend much of his time in his hermitage at Meare. On one of his evening visits to the brothers at Glastonbury he met and was tempted by the devil whom he, in turn, attacked with his trusty staff and pushed into a nearby ditch which, ever afterwards, emitted a foul-smelling slime. Slightly later, when the river overflowed and his path to Glastonbury was flooded, Benignus became ill and could no longer leave his cell. After enduring great agony and dreadful struggles he died in a state of blissful grace and was buried in

---

[27] On St Benignus see my edition of John of Glastonbury, pp. xxxviii–xxxix.

the oratory at Meare, to await his later glorious translation. During the later middle ages the festival of his death was celebrated at Glastonbury on 3 November, and all his relics, including his miracle-working staff, were catalogued in the relic lists. In 1323 the church at Meare was consecrated in honour of the Blessed Virgin Mary, All Saints and especially St Benignus and even as late as the sixteenth century it seems to have carried a dedication to St 'Bennynge'.

Abbot's fish house at Meare. This late medieval building includes a dwelling for the abbot's fisherman and store rooms.

When he visited Glastonbury William of Malmesbury discovered enough information about St Indract's local cult to warrant a *Life* of this saint.[28] Like William's other Irish/ Glastonbury *Lives*, this one has been lost and our information on Indract at Glastonbury comes from an anonymous Latin *passio*, based on a now lost Old English *Life*, and from the brief account given by John of Glastonbury in his chronicle, which he in turn based on William's version.

St Indract

John places Indract's martyrdom in the reign of King Ine (688–726) and tells the following story. Indract, the son of an Irish king, vows to make a pilgrimage to Rome. This accomplished, he decides to return to Ireland following a route

[28] See Michael Lapidge, 'The Cult of St Indract at Glastonbury', in Dorothy Whitelock, Rosamond McKitterick and David N. Dumville, eds., *Ireland in Early Medieval Europe: Studies in Memory of Kathleen Hughes* (Cambridge, 1982), pp. 179–212.

which will take him to Glastonbury where he can venerate the relics of St Patrick. After a short stay in Glastonbury he and his seven loyal companions (nine according to the *passio*) set out for the coast, but decide to spend the first night at Shapwick ('Hwisc' in the *passio*). King Ine, as it happens, is staying at South Petherton and the members of his entourage have been billeted elsewhere in the vicinity. Among Ine's retainers are certain wicked men who are overcome by greed when they see the Irish pilgrims arrive at Shapwick with stuffed purses and staves with shiny tips. (Little do the villains guess that the staves have brass tips and that the purses are stuffed not with gold but with the seed of a local celery which the pilgrims have picked to take home for its medicinal value.) The bandits, led by one Huna, craftily invite the Irishmen to be their guests, then murder them in their sleep and snatch up the supposed plunder. When they discover their mistake they mutilate the bodies in enraged frustration and leave them strewn about in wild disarray.

Meanwhile, King Ine, who has gone out to admire the clear evening sky, sees a pillar of bright light rising in the distance. On the two following nights the same phenomenon occurs in the sky and so Ine decides to investigate the spot whence the light originates. There he comes upon the foul carnage and, equally horrible, the criminals have been overcome with madness and are attempting to devour each other's flesh like crazed beasts. King Ine, appalled by the spectacle, brings the bodies of Indract and his companions back to Glastonbury with great solemnity and has Indract laid in a shrine on the left side of the altar and his fellow martyrs placed under the floor of the basilica.

The anonymous Latin writer adds a variety of other details about Indract's cult which do not appear in John's version and which presumably were absent from William of Malmesbury as well. In particular, he describes a number of miracles associated with the saint. For example, he tells of a rich man and his wife who came to pray at Indract's shrine and brought their little son called Guthlac with them. While the parents, tired from their long journey, dozed in the church, the saint appeared to the boy and instructed him how to read and sing psalms. When they awoke the parents were amazed by this miracle and pledged the boy to a life of religion, leaving him to be instructed by the local clergy. As might be expected after such an auspicious start, Guthlac showed himself to be a dedicated scholar and holy individual, and ultimately became abbot of the monastery.

The early Glastonbury liturgical kalendars do not list Indract's name and he first turns up in the Glastonbury context in a text written at Winchester dating from the second quarter of the eleventh century. The actual name Indractus is almost certainly a latinized form of the relatively common Irish name Indrechtach. Irish texts record, moreover, that on 12 March 854 one Indrechtach, abbot of Iona, was martyred among the English while on a trip to Rome. It is quite possible that the martyrdom did occur near Glastonbury, in which case an oral tradition of the catastrophe may have persisted at Glastonbury until the tenth century when a local hagiographer must have set about trying to reconstruct a suitable *Life*. Having only the vaguest of stories he created his own *mise en scène* and chose the reign of King Ine as the historical framework simply because he knew that Ine was a great benefactor to Glastonbury.

St Brigit

St Brigit's name appears under 1 February in the two tenth-century liturgical calendars which survive from Glastonbury. By the time William of Malmesbury visited the community St Brigit's cult was well established and William accepted unquestioningly the house-tradition that she had made a pilgrimage to Glastonbury in 488, that she stayed for some time on the nearby island of Beckery and that she left various objects behind when she ultimately returned to Ireland: a wallet, a collar, a bell and assorted weaving implements.[29]

Relief on St Michael's tower, possibly representing St Brigit milking.

Glastonbury's own records state that there had been a church at Beckery dedicated to St Mary Magdalene previous to St Brigit's visit, and this was later rededicated to Brigit. The chapel had a small opening on the south side and it was rumoured that anyone who squeezed through this opening would be forgiven his sins. King Arthur himself, so some romances relate, had a strange adventure at this chapel.[30] On one occasion when he was staying with a group of nuns at Wearyall, Arthur had a recurring dream admonishing him to arise and go to the Chapel of St Mary Magdalene. The third night Arthur's squire also dreamt about the chapel, which he thought he entered and from which he stole a rich and ornate candlestick. As he was leaving the chapel he received a mortal blow in revenge for the theft. At this point the squire awoke, screaming in pain, and discovered amazingly that both the wound and the candlestick were real. The squire died and the candlestick was given to either St Paul's or Westminster in memory of the strange event. Arthur himself understood this as a sign that he should visit the chapel alone, which he then

---

[29] See John L. Robinson, 'St Brigid and Glastonbury', *Jnl. of the Royal Society of Antiquaries of Ireland* 83 (1953), 97–99. Sharpe points out that St Brigit was most likely a euhemerized deity whose cult first began in the sixth century.

[30] See my edition of John of Glastonbury, pp. 77–79.

did, although with some trepidation. There he witnessed a literal re-enactment of the miracle of the mass, in which the Virgin herself offered up her Infant Son to the priest for the sacrifice. After the completion of the Office the Virgin presented King Arthur with a crystal cross in commemoration of the adventure. The king, in turn, changed his arms in token of the adventure and made them green with a silver cross; on the right arm of the cross he placed an image of the Mother and Child. Ultimately, the same arms were adopted by Glastonbury Abbey itself.

Excavations do, in fact, confirm that a chapel did exist at Beckery in the Middle Ages: there was an outer building dating from the fourteenth century, enclosing a similar chapel of late Saxon or early medieval date, which may even have been built by St Dunstan.[31] Charters indicate that by the tenth century, that is by the time of St Dunstan, the accepted etymology for Beckery was Becc Eriu = Parua Hibernia (i.e., Little Ireland), although modern scholars think that the real derivation is from 'beocere' = beekeeper and 'ieg' = island.[32] Interestingly, Brigit's bell (made specifically for her by St Gildas, according to some accounts) resurfaced briefly in the twentieth century, when it appeared among the collections of Miss Alice Buckton, the owner of Chalice Well. Like Arthur's sword, however, it seems to have disappeared beneath the waters with the passing of its custodian. Two stone carvings illustrating Brigit in her traditional role as milkmaid survive at Glastonbury, one in the doorway of St Mary's Church and the other on the tower of St Michael's on the Tor.

One last early Irish saint completes the Irish roster in the Glastonbury kalendar: St Columba, or as the Irish call him, Colum Cille. St Columba (521–597) was born in Ireland, but left with twelve companions in 563 to establish a foundation at Iona, which would become a major centre for future missionary activity. By William of Malmesbury's reckoning Columba came to Glastonbury during the course of his wanderings, attracted by its fame as the former dwelling place of his compatriots Patrick and Brigit and arrived in 504 – an impossible date since it anticipates his birth by almost 20 years.

In the *Life* of St David, written by the Welsh scholar Rhygyfarch around 1090, it is stated that Glastonbury was the first of twelve monasteries to be founded by St David (d. 589 or 601). From the Glastonbury point of view, this account –

King Arthur's arms.

St Columba

St David

---

[31] See P. Rahtz and S. Hirst, *Beckery Chapel, Glastonbury, 1967–8* (Glastonbury, 1974).
[32] 'St Patrick at Glastonbury', p. 81.

flattering though it may have been in other respects – contained one serious flaw. St David, it is clear, could not have founded a church at Glastonbury in the sixth century when there had already been a Christian foundation there for many generations before his birth. William of Malmesbury pointed out this problem and suggested what amounted to a compromise position: St David must have originally come to Glastonbury to rededicate the Old Church, which had fallen into collapse during the dark days of the early sixth century. The night before the rededication ceremony David was vouchsafed a vision: Our Lord appeared to him and told him that He himself had long ago dedicated the Old Church and that it would be a profanity to repeat the act. As a sign Our Lord pierced the saint's hand, a wound which miraculously healed itself during the consecration of the mass on the following day.[33] After this divine intervention St David decided to build a second smaller chapel which would function as a kind of a chancel at the eastern end of the Old Church. The point of connection of these two chapels, according to later Glastonbury tradition, had some sort of arcane significance: 'in order that it might always be known where the chapels were joined together, a pyramid on the exterior to the north, a raised step inside, and the southern end divide them along a line; on this line, according to certain of the ancients, St Joseph lies buried with a great multitude of saints.'[34]

In Welsh hagiographical tradition it was recounted that St David had received a wonderful altar stone, commonly called 'the sapphire', from the Patriarch of Jerusalem and that he brought it back to Wales with him. The Glastonbury community, on the other hand, claimed that St David had presented this jewel to them, that it was later hidden during the unsettled early Saxon times, and that in the twelfth century the shrewd Abbot Henry of Blois discovered it during the course of renovations. In the fourteenth century Abbot Walter de Monington had the stone richly decorated and it was then hung aloft in the church where it remained until the depredations of Henry VIII's agents: 'Item, delyvered more unto his maiestie ... a Super altare, garnished with silver and gilte and parte golde, called, the greate Saphire of Glasconberye.'[35]

In the later middle ages Glastonbury Abbey also laid claim to the majority of St David's physical remains. It could hardly

Figure of a bishop with a mitre and maniple on an ancient cross at Barton St David. Said to represent St David.

[33] In 1908 Frederick Bligh Bond found in the abbey ruins a pilgrim's medallion of baked clay which seems to represent St David's pierced hand.
[34] See John A. Goodall, 'The Glastonbury Abbey Memorial Plate Reconsidered', *The Antiquaries Journal* 66 (1986), 364–67.
[35] See W. Dugdale, *Monasticon Anglicanum*, ed. J. Caley, H. Ellis and B. Bondinel, 6 vols. in 8 pts. (London, 1817–30), 1.65.

be disputed, the Glastonbury writers pointed out, that the whole of the Ross Valley including the church at St Davids had been devastated by English invasions during the tenth century. At this time of chaos a noble matron, called Aelswitha, acquired the relics and brought them to Glastonbury for safekeeping, where they ever afterwards formed part of the Glastonbury collection. The Welsh, of course, were not convinced that the bones of their patron saint had deserted them. They continued to display their own collection of relics at St Davids Cathedral as the genuine remains: these were so widely venerated that Pope Calixtus II decreed in 1120 that two journeys to St David's shrine in Menevia should be regarded as the equivalent to one to Rome.

III. ANGLO-SAXON SAINTS

St Neot

The famous story of how King Alfred burned the cakes at Athelney first occurs in the earliest *Life* of St Neot.[36] Neot, according to hagiographical tradition, was born of royal stock and was a close relation of King Alfred. Even as a young child he loved learning and was drawn to religion. As soon as he could, therefore, Neot took his vows and became a monk at Glastonbury. Soon afterwards he was ordained as a priest and quickly provided a model for the rest of the community: 'he possessed charity and was humble towards all, mild, affable, serene of countenance, peaceable in the probity of his morals, and excellent from his infancy in all chastity.' Apparently Neot was a particularly short man – 'in littleness of stature another Zacchaeus', as one of his biographers aptly puts it – and always carried with him a small iron stool, much like a modern trivet, on which to stand while saying mass. On one occasion when Neot was acting as sacristan, an important visitor arrived unexpectedly at the outer gate of the monastery and began knocking imperiously at the door. Poor Neot, who had misplaced his stool, became flustered because he was unable to reach the lock with his key. Just at this moment, as he uttered a frantic prayer, the lock suddenly began to lower itself and did not stop until it was at a level convenient for the saint to insert his key and open the door. In the later middle ages the stool was displayed at Glastonbury as a reminder of the happy outcome of this adventure.

As Neot's fame increased, so too did his desire to escape from worldly interruptions and to lead a solitary life. Ulti-

[36] See M. Lapidge in D. Dumville and M. Lapidge, *The Annals of St Neots with the Vita Prima Sancti Neoti*, The Anglo-Saxon Chronicle: A Collaborative Editon 17 (Woodbridge, 1985).

The Abbey ruins in 1795 by Thomas Hearne (City of Birmingham Art Gallery).
Overleaf. The Abbey Ruins (photo Kevin Redpath).

mately he was instructed by a vision to leave Glastonbury and to retire to a deserted place, later to be named Neotestoc, near Bodmin Moor in the wilds of Cornwall. Here he lived first as an anchorite and then as the abbot of a small religious community. He acted as counsellor to his kinsman Alfred, whom he persuaded to revive the English school at Rome. Neot himself went on a pilgrimage to Rome on behalf of Alfred, a deed which helped secure the latter's victory over the Danes. He died in the 870s and his body was later transferred from Cornwall to St Neots in Cambridgeshire, where the antiquary John Leland saw his relics as late as the 1530s: noting, in particular, his comb 'made of a little bone of two fingers' width, into which were inserted small fishes' teeth, the whole having the appearance of a pike's jaw.' At Glastonbury as elsewhere, the festival of St Neot's death was celebrated on 31 July.

Glastonbury Abbey was very much at the centre of the great English tenth-century monastic reform movement, primarily through the efforts of St Dunstan, who found on the site a derelict royal vill, sadly fallen from its former glory, and left a major monastic establishment – thus fulfilling the prophetic dream of his earliest youth in which he had a vision of an old man in white leading him through numerous buildings of a beautiful reconstructed monastery.[37]

St Dunstan

Dunstan, the scion of a wealthy family, was born around 910 in the vicinity of Glastonbury itself, probably at Baltons-borough.[38] From earliest youth, his first biographer (who may even have been personally acquainted with him) relates, Dunstan was slender, good-looking and refined of feature. As a boy he had thin but beautiful hair, which would recede in his early manhood, and throughout his life he was attractive to (and attracted by) numerous women. A gentle child, he exerted an almost eerie charm over animals and showed a natural aptitude for books and music, excelling in particular at harp-playing in his father's hall.

Soon it became clear to Dunstan's parents that he should be sent to study at the Glastonbury 'school' which by all accounts had a fine collection of books, many brought by visiting Irish

Seal of St Dunstan.

[37] Paul Ashdown, who has been working on Dunstan materials at Baltonsborough, argues that the very fact that Glastonbury continued its role in educating the nobility throughout the early tenth century indicates that it was not as decayed as some of the later sources maintain.

[38] At Baltonsborough itself Dunstan's Dyke – that is, the artificial course of the Southwood Stream which takes it into the River Brue at Catsham – still survives. This name occurs in early bounds of the Twelve Hides, as does a reference to Wulfgar the Bearded, keeper of Wallyer's Bridge in Dunstan's time. The present church, probably dating from the early fifteenth century, is dedicated to St Dunstan.

The Abbot's Kitchen (photo Kevin Redpath).

pilgrims. Dunstan was an adoring son – as a much later dream about his parents' presence among a company of angelic spirits would indicate – but in spite of homesickness he soon adjusted to his new life of study and meditation. He over-applied himself to his books, however, and seems to have had some sort of crisis and breakdown; chased by imaginary hounds he scaled the walls of the church and sought safety in the sacred precinct. After he recovered he went to join his uncle Athelm, a former monk of Glastonbury who had become the first bishop of Wells and who would finally be archbishop of Canterbury. The latter recommended Dunstan to King Aethelstan and he appeared at court. Not surprisingly, Aethelstan was captivated by the brilliant young man and equally predictably many of the other courtiers were wildly jealous. After a short period his enemies managed to drive him from the court and as he left they attacked him and beat him. Battered and miserable he made his way to the residence of his kinsman, Aelfheah the Bald, bishop of Winchester, who tried to persuade him to forsake the world and become a monk. Dunstan, however, was not ready for this step, especially since he still felt strongly drawn towards a beautiful young woman whom he thought he might wish to marry. After a sudden attack of illness, though, followed by an escape from a falling stone and the death of his dear Glastonbury friend Wulfrid (who immediately appeared to him in a dream and provided him with prophetic signs about his future career) he at last capitulated and decided to take his vows of religion.

Aelfheah, who like many holy men of his time had the gift of foresight, was called upon to ordain Dunstan, Aethelwold and another individual all at the same time. Aelfheah was greatly moved by the ceremony and predicted that one of the three would become archbishop of Canterbury, one bishop of Winchester, but the third would come to a wretched end through the temptations of worldly pleasure. The outcome was, as might be expected, as he had anticipated. When Dunstan returned to Glastonbury after his ordination he quickly established himself as the spiritual guide to the rich and holy widow Aethelfleda who had built a residence to the west of the church. Aethelfleda spent her wealth on works of charity and in the entertainment of visiting pilgrims. One of these latter was King Aethelstan himself, who on the day before his appearance sent scouts ahead to check on 'local arrangements'. The scouts approved of Aethelfleda's plans, although they were slightly worried about a possible shortage of mead. Aethelfleda implored the Virgin that she might not be disgraced in this matter, and on the next day an almost unending succession of cupbearers filled horn after horn at the cask without it ever drying up.

With Aethelfleda's fortune at his disposal Dunstan was able to widen his sphere of influence and he gathered a large group of pupils around him, teaching them the arts of reading, copying and illustrating manuscripts, harping and embroidery. Dunstan himself excelled at all these skills and up to the time of the Dissolution Glastonbury possessed manuscripts written in his hand as well as altar cloths, crosses, thuribles, phials, chasubles and vestments reportedly of his workmanship.

Osbern, Dunstan's twelfth-century biographer, visited the saint's habitation at Glastonbury, which had been preserved as a kind of relic, and gives an eyewitness account of its admirable simplicity:

> Adjoining the church [St Dunstan] built a cell with his own hands; it is a lean-to or a sort of den … it is more like a tomb than a human dwelling. Let me record what I myself saw, that … the length of his cell is not more than five feet and its breadth two and a half feet. Moreover, the height equals the stature of a man if he were to stand in the dug-out earth; otherwise it would not reach even to his chest. .. So it is clear that he never lay down to sleep and always stood to pray. What was a door to him who entered, became a wall to him who had entered. For indeed in such a small building it was impossible for a door to be made except of the whole side. There is a small window in the middle of the little door through which light shone on the labourer.

It was in this humble workshop that Dunstan was supposed to have had his famous confrontation with the devil. One of the most admirable characteristics of this saint was that he found it difficult to renounce the world and lead a life of cloistered virtue. He was a lover of all forms of beauty and found celibacy in particular a considerable penance. The devil, knowing this, appeared one day at the little window in Dunstan's hut and showed a friendly interest in his work at the smithy. The sun was about to set and Dunstan, worn out from his labours, seemed ready to indulge in conversation as he worked. The devil quickly steered the talk to the subject of women and set about distracting the saint with ribald stories. Dunstan, who had already seen through the fiend's disguise, feigned an interest as he heated his tongs over the forge. Suddenly he seized the red-hot instrument, turned round with a swift movement and twisted the devil's nose. Having taken on human form, the latter was susceptible to human sensations and fled from the cell, shrieking 'O what has that baldheaded villain done? What has that baldheaded villain done?'[39]

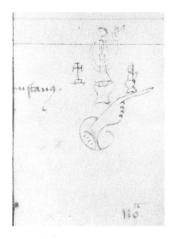

Line drawing of objects made by St Dunstan and still in the Glastonbury collections in the late fourteenth century. Trinity College, Cambridge, MS R.5.16 (711), p. 54.

Stained glass window representing St Dunstan in Duke Humfrey Library, Bodleian Library, Oxford.

---

[39] In his fine novel *Fifth Business* Robertson Davies uses the Dunstan theme; his hero tweaks the nose of a most charming twentieth-century female temptress.

After Aethelstan's death the new king, Edmund, asked Dunstan to come to court as his counsellor, and since Aethelfleda had just died Dunstan decided to accept the invitation. Sadly, history seemed to repeat itself. Dunstan found the life at court lax, even dissolute, and was strict with the courtiers, who in turn managed to prejudice the king against him. Soon he was dismissed and prepared to leave the court, located at Cheddar at that particular time. Edmund, meantime, was taking part in a hunt at Cheddar Gorge. Separated from his group he pursued a wild stag through the hills. The terrified beast plunged over the cliff and the frenzied hounds followed him. Edmund was unable to rein his horse in and it looked as if he too was going to fall to a certain death. Examining his conscience he realized that he had sinned against Dunstan and swore to God that if he were spared he would make amends. As he took this resolution the horse suddenly pulled short, poised at the cliff edge, now as gentle as a lamb. The chastened king sought Dunstan out and without saying a word took him to Glastonbury. There he proclaimed him abbot – fortunately there was a vacancy at the time – and promised rich gifts to the monastery. Ever afterwards, too, he showered Dunstan and his monastery with privileges and lands. After his death, moreover, his body was brought to Glastonbury and buried there.

Dunstan showed himself to be a superb abbot; his biographer describes his daily routine as he walked staff in hand from cell to cell, inspected the kitchen arrangements personally, superintended new buildings, got up at dawn to correct manuscripts and engaged in the offices faithfully, his eyes often bathed in tears. In a period of harsh discipline Dunstan was famous for his gentleness as a teacher and for his sympathy to young people. Almost a century after his death, so Osbern relates, it was the custom at Canterbury to give all the boys an annual beating at Christmas, not for specific faults but for their general improvement. On one occasion the lads, remembering Dunstan's reputation for kindness, besought his aid by seeking refuge in the church and the masters were immediately overcome by a deep sleep, from which they did not awake until the holidays had begun, at which point the period allowed for beating had passed.

When Edmund died his brother Eadred became king and like Edmund showed marked favour towards Dunstan and Glastonbury. The next king, Eadwig, was crowned in 955, and according to Dunstan's earliest biographer behaved abominably on the very day of his coronation – leaving the solemn feast to amuse himself with a noblewoman and her daughter (though he subsequently married the latter). Dunstan and his kinsman, the bishop of Lichfield, went to summon the recalcitrant king and an ugly scene, for which Eadwig never forgave Dunstan, ensued. Soon afterwards Dunstan was deprived of all his ranks and property and sent into exile. A false abbot, Aelfsige, was inflicted on the Glastonbury community while Dunstan took refuge first with Arnulf, Count of Flanders, and then at the monastery of St Peter at Ghent (where he was able to observe at first hand the innovations of the new continental monasticism).

Within two years of his accession Eadwig had lost Mercia and Northumbria to his younger brother Edgar and on his death in 959 Edgar was immediately accepted as king in Wessex as well. Dunstan had been at Glastonbury when Edgar was born at the nearby hamlet subsequently to be named Edgarley and heard a voice thunder forth from heaven: 'Peace upon the church of the English in the time of the boy who is now born and of our Dunstan.' Dunstan was recalled from abroad in 957 by Edgar and became chief advisor to the king. Soon he was made bishop of Worcester, then bishop of London and finally archbishop of Canterbury.

Dunstan and Edgar often met together at their favoured monastery of Glastonbury. On one occasion the two men were sitting together in the refectory when suddenly the image of the crucifix above them shook so violently that the crown of thorns fell to the table. After they recovered from their shock Dunstan turned to the king and asked in a severe voice what he had been thinking. Thoroughly abashed, Edgar confessed that he had been planning to move the monks elsewhere and to set up a congregation of nuns on the site. He repented at once of this nefarious scheme and by way of amendment increased his already great generosity to the monastery, giving further lands, a valuable cross for the altar, huge bells and many relics. After his death he was buried at Glastonbury in the chapter at the door of the church.

Dunstan himself outlived Edgar and continued to foster and encourage the whole English church. He survived through the reign of the unfortunate Edward and into the times of Aethelred, about whom he had predicted when he baptized him: 'By God and his Mother, this one will be a knavish sort.' Dunstan's final illness struck on Ascension Sunday, 988, but he lingered on until the morning of 19 May when he died immediately after receiving Viaticum at a Mass celebrated by his bedside. His last words came from the Psalms: 'The merciful and gracious Lord hath made a remembrance of His marvellous works: He hath given food to them that fear Him.' Although he was undoubtedly buried at Christ Church, Canterbury, later Glastonbury monks asserted that they had rescued his relics from Canterbury in the early eleventh century at the time of the Danish invasions of Kent. Bones being hard to identify, the dispute was never satisfactorily resolved and flared up at periodic intervals for the next five hundred years.

BL, MS Cotton Tiberius A.III, fol.2v: Aethelwold, Edgar and Dunstan. From a mid eleventh-century Christ Church Canterbury, copy of the Regularis Concordia.

The name of St Aethelwold is closely linked with that of St Dunstan.[40] Aethelwold was born only a year or two after Dunstan, probably of royal stock as his name suggests, and spent his early years in Winchester. Like Dunstan he was sent as a young man to the court of Aethelstan and the two young men – bookish and pious both – were ordained together by Dunstan's kinsman Aelfheah the Bald. Aethelwold remained with Aelfheah until Aethelstan's death, when he travelled to Glastonbury, became a monk and served as an apprentice to Dunstan. Under Dunstan's tutelage Aethelwold learned about manuscript production and became aware of the necessity of an ample collection of books in the monastic life. It is no coincidence, therefore, that in his later foundations books formed an important part of the basic materials supplied to each new monastery. Like Dunstan, Aethelwold loved music and at Glastonbury he became an authority on the chant. Aethelwold's skill at illumination became apparent while he was at Glastonbury and during his subsequent career a whole new English style of illumination associated with his school at Winchester would evolve.

In spite of his artistic sensibility, however, Aethelwold was austere in temperament and manner of living. For a time he served as cook to the other brothers – tending the garden with his own hands and even waiting on the rest of the community at meal times – but he himself was rigorous in fasting and ate meat only once every three months. Aethelwold never slept after Matins and did not tolerate sloth in others. When he was made prior he was strict with the other monks, and insisted on full observance of the Rule of St Benedict (which he would later translate into standard Old English for the benefit of those not adept in Latin).

After a few years at Glastonbury Aethelwold felt that his apprenticeship was complete; it was time for him to go out and serve in the field. His first plan was to travel across the Channel to Fleury, but the queen mother, Edith, refused to permit the loss of such a holy man to the English church. As an alternative he was offered the derelict monastery at Abingdon and – accompanied by three other monks, Osgar, Foldbricht, and Frithegar – he arrived there around 956. King

---

[40] For Aethelwold at Glastonbury see, in particular, J. Armitage Robinson, *The Times of St Dunstan* (Oxford, 1923), pp. 105–08.

Eadred pledged full support to this new enterprise and specifically provided much needed land and buildings. As a restorer of abandoned monasteries Aethelwold found his metier and after Abingdon came a variety of other sites: Milton, New Minster and Nunnaminster in Winchester, Peterborough, Ely and Thorney.

As Dunstan's loyalty seems always to have remained with Glastonbury, so too Aethelwold loved Winchester, the place of his birth. After he became bishop of Winchester in 963 he removed the slack and worldly secular clerks from the church and established the first English monastic cathedral. Soon this became a flourishing intellectual and artistic centre. And, as Dunstan and Glastonbury were pivotal to the first phase of the tenth century reform movement, so too Aethelwold and his school at Winchester seem to have been crucial to later developments.

Aethelwold's own last years were plagued by ill health, but, undaunted, he spared neither himself nor his monks. Just before his death in 984 he was visited and counselled by St Dunstan, his old mentor and the man against whom he would be judged by posterity. More rigid in character than Dunstan, Aethelwold appeals less to modern sensibilities. His energy, however, was so great that the scribe of his *Benedictional* calls him a 'son of thunder'. This energy was well channeled and his accomplishments, both administrative and artistic, were many. In future generations the monks at Glastonbury would be proud of him and of his work, but he was never held in the same idealized veneration as Dunstan and the Glastonbury community never seems to have been tempted, for example, to rescue his bones from their resting place at Winchester.

5
Relics

For in his male he hadde a pilwe-beer
Which that he seyde was Oure Lady veyl ...
And in a glas he hadde pigges bones.

Chaucer's description of the unscrupulous and corrupt Pardoner who makes unsuspecting simple folk gulls by selling them his false and valueless relics has a particularly strong resonance for modern readers, who find the medieval cult of relics naively superstitious and almost impossible to respect.[1] Our position is entirely nominalist; we believe in the literal facts of reality, not in hidden or symbolic associative qualities. Nevertheless, almost all cultures – primitive or sophisticated – share a tendency to invest the physical remains of holy personages with some kind of magical power. In our own times, for example, even communist China commemorates the enshrined body of its patron saint, Mao Tse-tung, in the People's Square of Beijing. During the middle ages the cult of relics was ubiquitous in Europe; indeed, it was decreed at the Council of Nicaea in 787 that no church could be consecrated unless it possessed relics of some sort. Corporeal remains of proven saints were a numinous link with a more heroic age, a higher than human point towards which to yearn in a great chain of being which stretched from the lowest sphere in physical creation to heaven itself.

Relics showed their sanctity in a variety of ways: typically a saint's body would remain uncorrupted in its tomb over a long period of time. Other relics were able to communicate their wishes and desires. For example, the Holy Cross of Waltham, which was found at Montacute in the eleventh century, was able to prevent a team of oxen from moving to any place except Waltham where the cross wished to be enshrined. Almost by definition, an important relic was capable of working miracles: it inspired faith, cured the sick, and gave guidance to the spiritually afflicted. One might even describe relics as the senior consultants of medieval medical practice. In another sense, too, the pedantic question we would automatically ask about specific historical authenticity did not enter

[1] Perhaps the most helpful modern book on medieval attitudes to relics is by Patrick J. Geary, *Furta Sacra: Thefts of Relics in the Central Middle Ages* (Princeton, 1981).

into the matter. If a relic worked – if it inspired faith and generated miracles – then it was by definition 'real', no matter what its material origin was. Truth, as it were, took precedence over mere fact. Bloody Johnny Geard, the miracle-working mayor of Glastonbury in *A Glastonbury Romance* explains: 'any lie as long as a multitude of souls believes it and presses that belief to the cracking point, creates new life, while the slavery of what is called truth drags us down to death and to the dead! Lies, magic, illusion – these are the names we give to the ripples on the water of our experience when the Spirit of Life blows upon it.'

Not every miracle, however, was naively acknowledged as legitimate. In the fifteenth century Humfrey, Duke of Gloucester, saw a man, ostensibly blind from birth, who was suddenly granted vision at the shrine of St Alban. Duke Humfrey came forward and asked him to name the colour of his gown and the colours of other individuals' clothing. The man glibly replied with the correct answers, a feat which he would have been incapable of achieving if he had never before seen specific colours to learn their names. He was, therefore, committed to the stocks as a punishment for his fraudulent behaviour.

William of Malmesbury tells us that Glastonbury's fabulous collection of relics made it a 'heavenly sanctuary on earth'. There were many treasures from the Biblical era: a large number of remains associated with the Old Testament, such as parts of Moses' and Aaron's rods, manna, a fragment of Isaiah's tomb, and parts of Daniel's body; many relics from Jesus' mission on earth; items related to the Virgin Mary, including a small portion of her milk; bones from St John the Baptist; bones, teeth and clothing from the Apostles; numerous remains from the Holy Martyrs and Confessors, beginning right with St Stephen protomartyr and moving forward well out of the apostolic age into relatively modern times. Within the church at Glastonbury there would have been a great variety of feretories (and the term describes both the chapel in which a saint was venerated and the ceremonial coffin containing his bones, set on the pedestal or base of the shrine). The contents of each feretory were carefully tabulated in the relic lists: we know precisely which bones were attributed to the feretory of St Dunstan, St Patrick, King Edgar, St Benignus, St Urban, the Holy Virgins, St Vincent and St Apollinaris, St Indract, St Hilda, St David, St Gildas and so forth. A particularly precious small feretory was carried by the monks during their solemn processions on Rogation days: it contained a large collection of relics associated with Our Lord himself. We have no surviving description of the most important feretories at Glastonbury, but they would have been comparable to St Cuthbert's shrine at Durham which was

> exalted with the most curious workmanship, of fine and costly green marble all limned [painted] and gilt with gold; having four seats or places, convenient underneath the shrine, for the pilgrims or lame men, setting on their knees to lean and rest on, in the time of their devout offerings and fervent prayers ... The cover of the shrine being wainscot ... to which six very fine sounding bells were fastened which stirred all men's hearts, that were in the church to repair unto it. On either side of the said cover were painted four lively images, curiously wrought and miraculous to all beholders thereof. Also within the feretory ... were almeries [recesses], varnished and finely painted and gilt over with fine little images, for the relics belonging to St Cuthbert to lie in; all the costly reliques and jewels that hung about within the said feretory upon the irons being accounted the most sumptuous and rich jewels in the land.[2]

In the area of Biblical remains there seems to have been little cause for dispute among English ecclesiastical establishments. That there was a profusion of Biblical relics throughout England and Europe was acknowledged, but then authorities held that relics had the power of miraculous self-multiplication. Glastonbury Abbey might claim to outstrip many of its competitors in terms of quantity, but no single church asserted exclusive possession of what might be termed the common Judeo-Christian heritage. In the area of local saints, however, violent diagreements could – and did – easily erupt. When an individual church possessed its own saintly patron or founder this personage would be the focus for special veneration; his relics would be treated with particular reverence and viewed with a strong sense of territoriality. In this regard Glastonbury stood in an anomalous position, since on one hand it maintained that Joseph of Arimathea was its founder, but on the other nobody knew for certain where his remains were located. As early as the mid-fourteenth century John of Glastonbury's chronicle suggested that Joseph was buried somewhere in the Glastonbury area and Melkin's prophecy promised great miracles when the burial site was uncovered. In 1345 Edward III or his chancellor gave a royal writ to John Blome of London to search for the body and in the late fourteenth century an anonymous East Anglian chronicler stated that the tomb had actually been found at Glastonbury in 1367. As it happens, however, this report was inaccurate and the monks never did discover the burial site – as

[2] See David Knowles, *Bare Ruined Choirs. The Dissolution of the English Monasteries* (Cambridge, 1976), p. 49.

one William Good, a former acolyte, testified after the time of the Dissolution:

> The monks never knew for certain the place of this saint's burial or pointed it out. They said the body was hidden most carefully, either there [in Glastonbury's cemetery] or on a hill near Montacute called Hamden Hill, and that when his body should be found, the whole world should wend their way thither on account of the number and wondrous nature of the miracles worked there.[3]

A variety of other post-Dissolution writers also confirm the tradition associating Joseph's burial with the Montacute area. That Montacute was suggested as a possible location for Joseph's burial seems at first somewhat bizarre when Glastonbury's own cemetery would appear so much more obvious a place; but, in fact, the monks seem to have been genuinely confused about the burial. They assumed that Joseph was buried somewhere in the vicinity but there were no appropriate clues within the cemetery itself; Arthur's tomb obviously occupied the place of greatest honour and there were no other unidentified prominent burial sites. Montacute was nearby, was dominated by a great hill, had a long association with Glastonbury and was famous because the Holy Cross of Waltham had been discovered there around 1035. How and why did this relic get to this location, one might ask. Could it be because Joseph had landed at Montacute Hill before he came to Glastonbury and left the cross there? Or might he be buried at Montacute and, if so, might the cross be a sign of his presence? Joseph's name, moreover, was associated with holy crosses since at St Pauls in London there was another famous cross, the *Crux borealis*, standing on a beam spanning the north transept, which was said to be carved by the saint himself.

No matter what his putative place of burial, Joseph's chief shrine was at Glastonbury and it was here that pilgrims flocked to be healed from a variety of illnesses:

> And syth god there hath shewed many a myrakyl ...
> Ye pylgrymes all, gyue your attendaunce
> Saynt ioseph there to serue with humble affectyon,
> At Glastenbury for to do hym reuerence ...

In the early sixteenth century, in particular, a number of

---

[3] On Good and the place of Joseph's burial see my 'The Discovery of the Holy Cross of Waltham at Montacute, the Excavation of Arthur's Grave at Glastonbury Abbey, and Joseph of Arimathea's Burial', *Arthurian Literature* 4 (1985), 64–69. My theories concerning the choice of Montacute as the probable burial place for Joseph are, of course, entirely speculative and there is no documentary evidence supporting the linkings I suggest.

Cup found in the ruins of Glastonbury Abbey, said to be made of wood from the flowering thorn.

The tomb of King Arthur, marginal illustration to Lydgate's Fall of Princes. *BL, MS Harleian 1766, fol.291r.*

miracles were attributed to St Joseph's shrine. Through his agency two young women from Doulting were cured of the plague. A child from Wells was raised from the dead, the vicar of Wells was cured of lameness, and John Gyldon of Milborne Port recovered from total paralysis.[4]

The story of the Holy Grail is closely linked to Joseph and his appearance in medieval Arthurian romances. The Grail itself certainly could never qualify as a Christian relic and seems heterodox, if not downright pagan, in origin. At Glastonbury, however, the nebulous Grail of French romance was quite thoroughly demythologized. According to Melkin, Joseph brought with him not a miraculous platter or cup but two cruets (that is, tall jugs with stoppers like those used at Communion) containing the blood and sweat of Jesus – and very respectable medieval commentators such as Robert Grosseteste had confirmed that Joseph, standing as he did at the foot of the Cross, would have been amply sprinkled by the Holy Blood.

In a certain sense, too, Arthur's bones could be seen as Glastonbury relics. They clearly fulfilled a number of the functions normally associated with relics: they attracted pilgrims, enhanced the prestige of the monastery and generated devotion. Like relics they were treated with great respect and were transferred to their resting place in front of the High Altar during a state visit by Edward I, an event described in specifically religious terminology: 'the Lord King enclosed the king's bones in their chest, wrapped in a precious pall, while her ladyship the Queen did the same for the queen's bones. They marked them with their seals and directed the tomb to be placed speedily before the High Altar, while the heads and knee-joints of both were kept out for the people's devotion.' This elaborate tomb became a kind of shrine; in his preface to Sir Thomas Malory's *Morte Darthur* William Caxton, for example, refers to it as a key piece of evidence establishing Arthur's historical reality: 'First, ye may see his sepulture in the monastery of Glastonbury ... where his body was buried, and after founden and translated into the said monastery.' Among the treasured items kept among the relic collections of the late middle ages, moreover, was a crystal cross which the Virgin Mary miraculously presented to King Arthur after his adventure at the Chapel of St Mary Magdalene of Beckery.

When the monks first claimed that they had found King Arthur's remains there was a certain amount of scepticism, even open hostility, among the Celts who still saw Arthur as 'the once and future king' and who were patiently awaiting his return. In the area of more conventional saints, too, Glaston-

4 See the verse *Lyfe* of Joseph, pp. 44–49.

bury made some flamboyant assertions, assertions which were met by shocked disbelief in various quarters. Glastonbury had a major collection of relics associated with Irish saints of whom St Patrick is perhaps the most prominent example. According to John of Glastonbury St Patrick died at Glastonbury in 472 and his relics were housed in a position of great honour at the right side of the High Altar. After the fire of 1184 they were once again placed by the altar in a stone pyramid which was covered in gold and silver. The later relic lists firmly assert that all Patrick's remains were contained in his shrine. According to St Patrick's Charter, moreover, St Patrick obtained twelve years of indulgence for those pilgrims piously visiting his shrine at Glastonbury. Nor was Patrick the only Irish saint whose relics were claimed. All the putative remains of St Benignus, with the exception of his head and teeth which were encased separately, were found in his feretory. St Indract was buried to the left of the High Altar. The relic lists and chronicles tell us, moreover, that although St Brigit did not die at Glastonbury she did spend time at the chapel dedicated to St Mary Magdalene at Beckery and left her wallet, collar, bell and weaving implements there. In terms of relics, then, Glastonbury had a corner, as it were, on the Irish market. The relics, too, succeeded on a material as well as a spiritual plane, since they brought Irish pilgrims to Glastonbury throughout the middle ages.

As is St Patrick to the Irish, so is St David to the Welsh. In medieval Welsh tradition it was accepted that St David had built a church at Glastonbury, but it was also well documented that the saint died and was buried in Wales. Glastonbury writers, nevertheless, claimed that during the tenth-century period of devastations in Wales a noble matron called Aelswitha obtained the relics and carried them back to Glastonbury. Other religious men, moreover, brought many other bodies of Welsh saints and relics to Glastonbury at the same time.

To claim to have rescued relics from a dangerous or unworthy spot was a widespread practice in the Middle Ages. In fact, in the most extreme form these acts were known as *furta sacra*, holy thefts, and there were even professional dealers in stolen relics. Since relics are by nature hard to identify and traditions can easily be confused and texts rewritten, there are many examples of two places laying claim to the same relics. Glastonbury was, however, an unusually active subscriber to what might be described as a *furta sacra* revisionism. In the case of St Dunstan – in many ways an English equivalent of St David – a long and acrimonious dispute with Christ Church, Canterbury arose. The monks of Glastonbury maintained that during the early eleventh century they had rescued St Dunstan's bones from Canterbury when it was sacked by the Danes. A delegation of four monks had arrived at an abandoned Canterbury and identified Dunstan's bones by a ring on his finger. As they solemnly brought the relics back to Glastonbury marvellous wonders took place – bells, for example, rang by no human agency when the entourage reached Havyatt – and this, they felt, attested to the saint's pleasure at the removal. Once they got back to Glastonbury, however, the monks feared the wrath of their Canterbury colleagues, so two especially chosen monks placed the bones in a wooden casket suitably inscribed with Dunstan's initials and hid it in the main church near the holy water. Almost two centuries later the great fire occurred and at this time the remains were at last revealed to the community at large and publicly displayed.

As might be expected, the monks at Christ Church, Canterbury were not convinced by the Glastonbury story: Eadmer of Canterbury (c.1060–c.1130) bitingly observed: 'I was not a little confounded to hear such a foolish and even laughable story, especially as it is said to have been invented by Englishmen. Alas, why did you not consult some foreigner – one of those experienced and knowledgeable men from beyond the sea, who would have invented some likely lie on such an important matter!'[5] In the early sixteenth century Richard Beere gave increased prominence to the Dunstan shrine, and perhaps even planned the Edgar Chapel at the east end of the church as a suitable memorial to this great saint; as a result pilgrims began to come to Glastonbury in greater numbers in order to see Dunstan's relics. By 1508, the archbishop of Canterbury, William Warham, felt that the matter had gone too far. He wrote to Beere and explained that a search had been carried out at Canterbury: the traditional coffin of St Dunstan was opened and the bones of a man fully clothed in pontifical vestments were found along with a leaden plate inscribed *Hic requiescit Sanctus Dunstanus Archiepiscopus*. Beere therefore, he suggested, should produce contrary and more powerful evidence or the monks of Glastonbury should refrain from their scandalous assertions. Beere responded forthwith. He acknowledged that he had removed the shrine of St Dunstan to a more conspicous place in the abbey church. He was willing, moreover, to concede that the Glastonbury shrine might not contain all the saint's bones; some smaller ones might at some time have been taken back to Canterbury where Warham could have recently seen them. For his part, though, Beere goes on, he would be unwilling to prevent the

Line drawing of the shrine of St Dunstan as it was in the early fourteenth century. Trinity College, Cambridge, MS R.5.16 (711), p. 211.

[5] See George Garnett's review of Marjorie Chibnell, *Anglo-Norman England 1066–1166*, in *Journal of Ecclesiastical History* 38 (1987), 285.

pious from venerating St Dunstan at Glastonbury and he would counsel the Canterbury community not to publicize their so-called relics until they could be sure that they were not counterfeits. Finally, he pointed out, he would be of course most pleased to come to see Warham to represent his own case but unfortunately his health (which all indications suggest was excellent) at the moment did not permit the contemplation of such a trip. Warham was, as can be imagined, apoplectic. In his next letter, he informed Beere that (a) there was no proof whatsoever that Glastonbury monks ever got the true relics from Canterbury and (b) in the remote case that they did, then these were stolen goods and should be returned to the rightful owners. Moreover, he himself had seen relics at Canterbury, which he was sure were the true ones, and Beere should remember that it is impious and a sin to promote false relics. The very suggestion that Canterbury should give place to Glastonbury and suppress its own Dunstan relics was altogether preposterous. Beere, the letter concludes, was commanded to make an appearance before him with the so-called Glastonbury relics before All Saints Day at the latest. The abbot of Glastonbury, who was clearly a courageous and determined as well as an audacious man, simply ignored the letter and St Dunstan's shrine occupied its new and conspicuous location for the rest of the history of the monastery – the monks celebrated 19 May as the feast of Dunstan's death and 21 October as the feast of his ordination as bishop.

One region in England possessed a large collection of indigenous saints whose relics might be especially treasured: this was Northumbria where very early Christian settlements had flourished. Once again, Glastonbury made a bid for the remains and even as reliable and early a source as the eleventh-century *Old English Martyrology* reports that Glastonbury possessed the relics of the great St Aidan, bishop of Lindisfarne. Some modern scholars, moreover, accept this claim as a valid one, while other more pragmatic individuals, following the eminent Anglo-Saxonist Charles Plummer, scoffingly hold that 'The assertion that the relics of Aidan ... were translated to Glastonbury ... is simply an instance of that huge system of monastic lying in which Glastonbury had a bad pre-eminence.'[6]

There were two traditions about how the northern relics – which also included the remains of Ceolfrith, Benedict Biscop,

[6] Quoted by James Cross, 'A Lost Life of Hilda of Whitby: the Evidence of the Old English Martyrology', *Acta* 6 (1982 [for 1979]), 28. Presumably Cross himself accepts Plummer's judgement. For a more recent discussion of the Northumbrian saints and St Hilda in particular, as well as of the tradition concerning Abbot Tyccea, see Christine E. Fell, 'Hild, abbess of Streonaeshalch', *Hagiography and Medieval Literature: a Symposium* (Odense, 1981), pp. 88–9.

Eosterwine, Hwaetberht and Selfrith, abbots of Wearmouth, the Venerable Bede, Hebba, Begu, Boisil, Hilda abbess of Whitby and St Paulinus, appointed archbishop of York by St Augustine himself – came to Glastonbury. One story held that they were brought by a northern abbot, Tyccea by name, who migrated to the south during the eighth century invasion of the East coast and then became abbot of Glastonbury. Another tradition was that King Edmund gave them to the monastery in the tenth century.

There were many, many other relics associated with less distinguished or controversial figures in the Glastonbury collection: the bodies of local English saints like Gildas and Guthlac; European relics from figures such as St Apollinaris and St Urban; relics from most major Biblical figures and also from many personages who we now consider to have been apocryphal rather than real. Ultimately, those of us who live in a post-medieval world must feel a curiosity about the genuineness of the relics. Concerning this question several points can be made. There is no doubt, for example, that Glastonbury was fortunate in having great patrons who were well-known relic collectors: King Aethelstan, King Edmund the Elder, King Edgar, Henry of Blois and other abbots as well as many nobles and highly placed ecclesiastics. When Seffrid Pelochin was abbot of Glastonbury in the early twelfth century, for example, he went on a mission to Rome and saw the relics of St Nympha of Palermo translated to the church of St Chrysogonus in Rome. Two years later John of Cremona, cardinal of St Chrysogonus, came to England as papal legate and seems to have presented some of the relics to Seffrid, who in turn gave them to the monastic collection.[7] In similar kinds of circumstances altogether improbable relics fetched up again and again at Glastonbury. As a rich monastery Glastonbury could afford to buy relics and many of its abbots actively solicited the prestige and fame which a major collection of relics would bring with it. By the fourteenth century John of Glastonbury could proudly boast 'The stone pavement, the sides of the altar, and the altar itself are so loaded, above and below, with relics packed together that there is no path through the church, cemetery or cemetery chapel which is free from the ashes of the blessed.' The monastery did, moreover, lie in a relatively safe area; it was not badly disturbed by the various invasions which occurred in many other parts of Britain in Anglo-Saxon times and afterwards. Since it was viewed as a holy spot by the Welsh and Irish as well as the English it would have been a

[7] See Denis Bethell, 'The Making of a Twelfth-Century Relic Collection', G.J. Cuming and Derek Baker, eds., *Studies in Church History* 8 (Cambridge, 1972), 61–72.

logical place to bring treasures during times of threat and it would have been able to guard these objects in a long and unbroken continuity. Glastonbury was, indeed, a place where a fusing of English and Celtic cultures did take place over many centuries and the multitude of relics was a visible sign of the this process.

Relics brought in income as well as inspiring piety and promoting miracles: in 1350, during plague time, the shrine of St Thomas at Canterbury received £700 in offerings. Those who were sick and had specific needs went on pilgrimage to particular shrines – two of the chief of which in England were Glastonbury and Canterbury – but pilgrimage, as Chaucer's Parson pointed out, also had a more general function. Theologians envisaged it as a form of penance and self-mortification. Pilgrimage also symbolised the journey of Everyman. Through pilgrimage one could transform the linear human progress towards death and disintegration into a circular eternal journey where the heavenly New Jerusalem was the ultimate goal. By the end of the middle ages, however, pilgrimages had, for the most part, become an excuse for worldly travel. It is no coincidence that Chaucer's pilgrims chose to travel in the spring time rather than in winter and Glastonbury's 'George and Pilgrims' has, of course, always been a comfortable, even opulent, hostelry. The protagonist of *Piers Plowman* has a vision of a pilgrimage such as it would have been experienced by those travelling to Glastonbury during the fifteenth and sixteenth centuries:

One of the stations visited by pilgrims during their tour of Glastonbury Abbey. Situated on the south wall of the Lady Chapel and dating from the thirteenth century.

> And I saw pilgrims and palmers banding together to visit the shrines at Rome and Compostella. They went on their way full of clever talk, and took leave to tell fibs about it for the rest of their lives. And some I heard spinning such yarns of the shrines they had visited, you could tell by the way they talked that their tongues were more tuned to lying than telling the truth, no matter what tale they told.

Not all pilgrims, of course, were pleasure-seeking; but devotional life at the end of the Middle Ages had become in many cases corrupt and hollow, in others frenetic, almost decadent. There was, as Johann Huizinga puts it in *The Waning of the Middle Ages*, 'a mingled smell of blood and roses'. Reformers inevitably reacted against these excesses. Around 1514, for example, Erasmus visited Canterbury in the company of the learned humanist scholar John Colet. Colet was horrified when a reputed arm of St George with dry blood and flesh still on it was offered for his adoration. He also refused to accept a fragment of dirty linen which had reportedly been used by Becket 'to wipe the perspiration from his face or his neck, the runnings from his nose, or such other superfluities from which the human frame is not free.' The end was clearly near. Relics depend on faith; they have no extrinsic value and their power derives from the viewer's response to them. Even the miracles they generate – as in the case of Bishop Berkeley's suppositious tree falling in the forest, the sound of which only exists if there is somebody to hear it – need a sympathetic audience to establish that they really happened. Of all parts of Glastonbury's structure, then, the relic collection was psychologically most dependent on the smooth running of the monastery in an unbroken rhythm of devotion. When Henry's agents smashed the pagan images, as they called them, and undermined the trust the pious had put in their efficacy, they managed to destroy a whole metaphysical system in which relics functioned as meaningful links with the immortal world. Much superstition was no doubt overcome at the Reformation but it was done at a great psychological cost. Protestant man became considerably more alone in the world than were his Catholic predecessors, who had their tangible links with eternity.

Very few Glastonbury relics survived the Dissolution. In the 1580s, however, a certain Fr. Weston visited a former servant of the monastery who had saved one of the nails with which the Lord had been attached to the Cross and which had been brought by Joseph of Arimathea, so it was said, to England.[8] By the time Weston met the old man the nail had been taken from him by the Protestant authorities, but he still had the case with the impress of the nail; using this Weston could deduce that the nail itself had been 'one foot long and the thickness of a finger in the upper part: the head was not indeed broad, but the lower part was somewhat broader than the other part of it, rising gradually to a point, divided by four or five corners.' At Stanbrook, near Worcester, another relic, which is said to have come from Glastonbury, still survives: this is a thorn from the crown put on the Lord's head at the time of the Crucifixion. John of Glastonbury certainly states that such a relic was at Glastonbury in his time, but the sequence of events which brought it to Stanbrook is not altogether clear. What is known is that the relic and the reliquary were given separately to the Altar of Our Lady of Power in the Chapel of the Holy Rosary in London in the seventeenth century, the former by a Benedictine priest, Peter Warnford (d. 1657), the latter by one Augustine Stocker. Both men came from West Country families, and presumably, therefore, the relics were handed

Reliquary of Crown of Thorns from Glastonbury. Now at Stanbrook Abbey.

[8] On this episode see Dom Aelred Watkin, 'Last Glimpses of Glastonbury', *The Downside Review* 67 (1947), 83–86.

down to them in a direct succession from generation to generation. In the modern Glastonbury museum there is (or has been until very recently) a small Tudor reliquary containing a fragment of bone said to belong to St Paulinus and to have been given to the monastery by St Augustine.

6

The Library[1]

Decorated initial from Oxford, Queen's College MS 304, fol.49r, an early fifteenth-century manuscript owned by the Glastonbury monk John Merylynch. It shows a tonsured figure clad in a brown sleeveless habit over a black robe, reading a book, on a bed with a fringed canopy and a cover of rich red material embroidered with gold.

In his brilliant evocation of fourteenth-century monastic life, *The Name of the Rose*, Umberto Eco has his rather sententious abbot construct a series of platitudinous oxymorons: 'Monasterium sine libris est sicut civitas sine opibus, castrum sine numeris, coquina sine suppellectili, mensa sine cibis, hortus sine herbis, pratum sine floribus, arbor sine foliis ...' (a monastery without books is like a state without power, a fortress without troops, a kitchen without equipment, a meal without food, a garden without plants, a meadow without flowers, a tree without leaves ...). Especially after the mid-thirteenth century, when scholarship came to be seen as a strongly viable alternative to manual labour among the Benedictines and when a fair number of monks attended university as a matter of course, reading and study became a prescribed part of the daily ritual. Naturally, the monk-scholars directed themselves primarily towards an examination of holy scripture, and during the course of the middle ages a complicated system of Biblical exegesis evolved. Ultimately, this system came to permeate all aspects of thought, affecting even the physical layout of books, with the result that in many manuscripts the actual text forms only a small section in the centre of the page and commentaries surround it on all sides. In the most complex version of the exegetical method, the Old and New Testaments – and, by extension, all other books as well – were interpreted on four levels: a literal, a spiritual (or allegorical), a moral (or tropological), and an anagogical (or eschatological) level. As a very simple example of this principle, we might take – in the manner of St John Cassian – the word Jerusalem: on a literal level it is the city in Israel, on an allegorical level it represents the Church on Earth, on a tropological level it stands for the soul of man, and on an anagogical level it becomes the heavenly City of God. In this equation, as the Venerable Bede makes clear, the movement is from the letter to

[1] On the Glastonbury library and its contents see Thomas W. Williams, *Somerset Mediaeval Libraries* (Bristol, 1897), pp. 45–98.

the spirit, from appearance to reality: 'If we seek to follow the letter of Scripture only ... what shall we find to correct our sins, to console or instruct us, when we open the book of the blessed Samuel and read that Elcana had two wives, we especially, who are celibate ecclesiastics, if we do not know how to draw out the allegorical meaning of sayings like these, which revives us inwardly, correcting, teaching, consoling?'

In the most general sense, this hermeneutic frame of mind suggests that all the world is a kind of ephemeral stage, the players themselves insubstantial shadows whose true function is to point in the direction of a greater hidden reality. All facets of the world, then, are ultimately symbolic and in need of interpretation. Meaning lies deep below the surface and can be acquired only through keys. Books, of course, are the repositories for the codes of interpretation and therefore have immense power. Richard of Bury's fourteenth-century *Philobiblon* (the title *Lover of Books* is in itself significant) waxes lyrical on the topic: 'In books I find the dead as if they were alive; in books I foresee things to come; in books warlike affairs are set forth; from books come forth the laws of peace. All things are corrupted and decay in time; Saturn ceases not to devour the children he generates: all the glory of the world would be buried in oblivion, unless God had provided mortals with the remedy of books.'[2]

Power, of course, involves the possibility of evil. The secrets revealed by the Word can destroy if misapplied; Faustus, the legends make clear, would have been in no danger without his books. In the monasteries, therefore, the library areas appear to have been closely guarded and not open to everyone. As Eco's abbot explains: 'not all truths are for all ears, not all falsehoods can be recognized as such by a pious soul; and the monks, finally, are in the scriptorium to carry out a precise task, which requires them to read certain volumes and not others, and not to pursue every foolish curiosity that seizes them, whether through weakness of intellect or through diabolical promptings.' Eco, in fact, takes the arcane aspect of books and learning to its limit; in his monastery the library is housed in a separate building, the aedificium, which is constructed in the shape of a labyrinth, itself a highly esoteric symbol capable of a whole range of interpretations, as readers of Jorge Luis Borges well know. Only by delving deep into areas of mysterious knowledge and dangerous secrets can Eco's library be made to yield its mysteries, which appropriately concern a lost book from antiquity.

At Glastonbury, in contrast to the imaginary location

[2] trans. Andrew Fleming West (New York, 1945), p. 12.

conjured up by Adso of Melk, the books, although contained in a regulated area, would not have been housed in a separate room until very late in the middle ages. Some books would have been kept in the sacristy or treasury – we know that two valuable and ornate Gospel books, for example, were stored with the reliquaries because relics formed part of their bindings. Bibles and other especially valuable liturgical books which were meant for display in the church would be chained to their places in the manner of surviving examples in the Merton College library at Oxford. Other books, especially lives of the saints, would have been left in the refectory, where they could be used for public reading during meals. The greater part of the collection, however, would have been stored in long cupboards fastened to the cloister wall – probably the wall nearest the church. On the other side from the cupboards there would have been tall glazed windows with carrels and desks. Here, the monks would store individual books which they could read in the strong light of their southern exposure or copy with the writing equipment and vellum at their desks. Each monk would almost certainly have read aloud, savouring the details of each passage and admiring rhetorical tropes and figures; for modern tastes the resulting hubbub would constitute an intolerable distraction. No description survives of the library area at Glastonbury, but it would have been similar to Durham Priory, where there is a written record of the 'great almeries [or Cupboard] of waynscott all full of bookes [with great store of antient Manuscript to help them in ther studdy], wherein dyd lye as well the old auncyent written Docters of the church as other prophane authors, with dyuerse other holie mens woork, so that eueryone dyd studye what Docter pleased them best, hauinge the librarie at all tymes to go studie in besydes there Carrell.'[3]

At any given time a certain number of the monks would be involved in writing books. They might be at work on a Biblical commentary, on a collection of sermons or saints' lives, a history of their monastery, or more practically a survey of monastic estates and names of tenants. Even more time would have been spent copying other people's books. A number of books, especially service books, inevitably became worn out with constant handling and needed to be replaced regularly. A variety of texts would have been borrowed from other monasteries to be copied and in the period previous to the invention of the printing press, of course, there was nothing even remotely resembling an equivalent of copyright laws, the very concept of which might seem ridiculous to the medieval scholar. Other texts would need annotation and sometimes the

Oxford, Queen's College MS 304, fol.58r. Monk sitting on a pink carved desk with a wooden canopy over his head and reaching to take a book from an open cupboard.

---

[3] See the *Rites of Durham* (Surtees Society 107; 1903), p. 38.

annotations themselves came to stand as separate works. Some works, like William of Malmesbury's *The Early History of Glastonbury*, had to be brought up to date from time to time in the light of modern findings, and medieval scribes had no qualms about correcting their sources. The reproduction work of the scriptorium, then, could not have been replaced by any technological equivalent of printing press or xerox machine; copying was a far more creative, imaginative, exercise than it has since come to be. All this activity, moreover, was seen in an allegorical light: 'The parchment on which we write [for the Lord] is a pure conscience, whereon all our good works are noted by the pen of memory ... The knife wherewith it is scraped is the fear of God ... The pumice wherewith it is made smooth is the discipline of heavenly desires ...'[4]

It is hard to know now exactly how many books were at Glastonbury Abbey at any specific time. Fortunately, however, a remarkably thorough catalogue dating from 1247/48 has survived. This list, which gives the titles of nearly 500 texts, also includes in a number of cases references to the relative age and condition of the book. Using it and various other bits of evidence, we can speculate about the growth of the library. When consulting medieval catalogues, nevertheless, it is necessary to remember that several texts, sometimes of wildly disparate age and topic, could often be bound together as one volume and cataloguers did not always list all the contents. Medieval catalogues, moreover, were rarely designed to be complete and each one covered only a specific storage area. Other books in different locations were simply not listed. There were probably, in other words, significantly more works in the library than the catalogues suggest. We know, for example, that Glastonbury had a number of Arthurian romances, but these do not turn up in the library lists.

By the fourteenth century the monks themselves had a tradition concerning their earliest volume: in St Patrick's Charter (itself a thirteenth-century forgery) it is narrated that in an old oratory on the top of the Tor St Patrick found a badly damaged volume containing the Acts of the Apostles and the *gesta* (that is acts and deeds) of St Phagan and St Deruvian, a volume presumably dating from the second century when the missionaries described by William of Malmesbury arrived at Glastonbury. Needless to say, no book remotely answering this description appears in surviving records. There is no reason, however, why we should doubt the presence of Bibles from the very early period, even if none have survived;

---

[4] Quoted in translation from a twelfth-century Latin sermon by G. S. Ivy, 'The Bibliography of the Manuscript Book', in Francis Wormald and C. E. Wright, eds., *The English Library before 1700* (London, 1958), pp. 33–4.

post-Conquest writers tell us that as early as the eighth century King Ine provided an ornate cover – containing twenty pounds of silver and sixty pounds of gold – for a book of the Evangelists.

In some ways the man who really established Glastonbury as an important literary centre was St Dunstan, himself an expert scribe and talented illustrator and a local man. Dunstan was widely read and some of his enemies even accused him of having more interest in heathen poetry than in holy books. He built himself a little private cell for his scholarly work, we are told, near to the great church and he spent his leisure time here, occupied in writing and singing hymns, painting and carving. Under his reforming temperament Glastonbury flourished as an intellectual centre and attracted scholars from as far away as Ireland. MS Hatton 30 in the Bodleian Library, for example, which contains a set of homilies on the Apocalypse attributed to St Augustine, was commissioned by Dunstan personally. Another Bodleian manuscript, Auctarium F.4.32, is a composite work and one section, closely associated with Dunstan's abbacy, is made up of a famous grammatical treatise, Eutyches' *Ars de verbo*. On fol.1 there is an illustration of a little figure kneeling at the foot of Christ: this appears to be a self-portrait by Dunstan.[5]

Even in the early eleventh century, when somewhat of a decline had set in at the monastery, there were still books being acquired or produced locally: Gospel books, collections of sermons and prayers, all richly illustrated in gold, a devotional book, *De laude crucis*, by the famous Biblical commentator Hrabanus Maurus, and a variety of other works of a religious nature.

There seems to have been a wide assortment of material available at pre-Conquest Glastonbury, then, even if only a few items have survived: collections of writings by the Latin church fathers, detailed commentaries on practically every book of the Old and New Testament, homilies, sermons and saints' lives, a Latin English dictionary, an English translation of parts of Orosius' history of the ancient world, many works by the Venerable Bede, collections of writings by Alcuin and pseudo-Alcuin (and all copies of some of these works have now perished, leaving no trace of their contents), a variety of riddle collections and grammatical works, perhaps a version of Gildas' history of the British people, and many others. One of the most dedicated early collectors of books at Glastonbury was Henry of Blois, who before 1171 caused almost fifty

---

[5] See R.W. Hunt, ed., *Saint Dunstan's Classbook from Glastonbury* (Amsterdam, 1961).

Late eighth or early ninth-century fragment from a Glastonbury copy of Isidore of Seville's Etymologies. *Now at Longleat House.*

Wells Cathedral Library. A pre-Conquest copy of The Rule of St Benedict, *possibly with Glastonbury connections.*

books to be transcribed on a whole range of subjects: these included Pliny's *Natural History*, Jerome upon Jeremiah and Isaiah, Origen on the Old Testament, Cyprian's works, a 'Liber dictus Paradisus', seven volumes of the passions of the saints for the cycle of the whole year, a lapidary, books of rhetoric, Quintilian, Isidore of Seville's *Etymologies*, and St Anselm's *Cur Deus Homo*. In his *Didascalion* (i.e., *Book of Instructions*), a text contained in the Glastonbury library, Hugh of St Victor provided a manual for the intellectual direction of those following the *vita regularis*; the recommended titles show just how richly representative the Glastonbury library of the period was.

As in so many other areas, the great fire of 1184 signalled a catastrophic end to the first stage of the library's development, although the 1247/48 catalogue indicates that books must have been so treasured that a number were snatched up by monks, presumably at some risk to life and limb, and rescued from the conflagration. The monks immediately set about replacing lost volumes and within seventy-five years once again had a well rounded, largish collection. At this point they had many Bibles, and volumes of the individual books of the Bible, some so old that they were unreadable; most of the works of St Augustine, some also old but at least readable; works by St Jerome, St Gregory, St Bernard, Origen, Ambrosius, the Sentences of Peter Lombard, decretals, books of rhetoric, writings by Anselm, Athanasius, St John Cassian, Boethius, Cassiodorus, Isidore of Seville, Hugh of St Victor, Hrabanus

Maurus, Peter Comestor, Bede, Alcuin, John of Salisbury, Robert Grosseteste, tracts of the virtues and vices, many lives of the saints, copies of the Rule of St Benedict and commentaries on the Rule, treatises on logic, on civil and canon law, Vergil, Ovid, and Ausonius, Prudentius, Sedulius, Solinus, Rufinus on weights and measures, Alan of Lille's *Anti-claudianus*, Freculph's history, Martinus Polonus, Geoffrey of Monmouth, William of Malmesbury, Henry of Huntingdon, Gerald of Wales, the deeds of King Alexander and King Richard, numerous grammatical texts, various scientific writings and astronomical works, medical texts by Galen, Isaac Judaeus, Constantine the African, Avicenna's *Canon of Medicine*, about half a dozen books in English and several French romances.

Later monks and abbots continued to add to the collection: William Britun, John of Taunton, Walter of Taunton, Adam of Sodbury and especially Walter de Monington, who was collecting at a time when Geoffrey Chaucer first began to visualize his *Canterbury Tales*. Monington was, it seems, an avid reader and bibliophile; over the course of his 33 years as abbot he acquired a total of 99 books.[6] This is an average of three a year and an impressive number when one remembers the extravagant ambition of Chaucer's Clerk to possess a grand total of 20 books. During the mid- and late fourteenth century, however, there was a significant growth in monastic libraries throughout England, probably through the development of a new and faster 'anglicana' book hand, and there are, in fact, examples of other individuals who amassed even more books than Walter de Monington. For the most part Monington assembled a representative kind of collection: theology, philosophy, canon and civil law, medicine, grammar and divine service; but in his choices he showed a somewhat academic bias and included an unusually high percentage of philosophical and even vernacular items. Many of the texts were not written until the late twelfth or early thirteenth century: obviously Monington kept abreast of contemporary developments and wished to bring Glastonbury's library up to date. Several of the more modern books consisted of collections of sermons. The sermon was, of course, a highly popular genre in the period and we need only think of 'The Pardoner's Tale' of the old man and the three rioters to realize just how dramatic this form could be. In the theological area Monington favoured books on the seven cardinal virtues and the seven deadly sins: books of the type the Parson had carefully studied before he told his 'myrie

6 For an annotated edition see James P. Carley and John F. R. Coughlan, 'An Edition of the List of Ninety-nine Books Acquired at Glastonbury Abbey during the Abbacy of Walter de Monington', *Mediaeval Studies* 43 (1981), 498–514.

tale in prose' to 'knit up al this feeste' as the pilgrims rode into Canterbury. In Monington's collection there was also a relatively contemporary book of saints' legends written by Peter Calo; and here we see the source for stories such as the 'Second Nun's Tale' of St Cecilia. The French romances on the *Life* of King William would have been appreciated by the Prioress, who prided herself on her linguistic prowess. Robert Holcot's exegesis of books of the Bible would have been the sort of reading to appeal to the Clerk, and Monington's collection contained ample materials to interest the Sergeant at Law and the Physician too. Indeed, what is striking is how very closely Monington's booklist overlaps with the cultural milieu of *The Canterbury Tales*. In some ways, it provides a gloss on Chaucer's fictional world.

Chaucer's pilgrims expressed a variety of views about learning, but only one individual, the Wife of Bath, actively disliked books, which for her represented the harsh hand of dry authority and male dominance repressing the rich fecundity of human experience. In particular, she set out to destroy the antifeminist volume from which Jankyn, her fifth husband and a scholarly clerk, was accustomed to lecture her. Clerks, Alysoun points out, have a vested interest in downgrading the daughters of Eve: women, if asked, might produce quite different volumes. The pernicious book she abominates stands as a representative collection of standard male, often monkish, authorities: St Jerome's letter against Jovinian, Walter Map's *The letter of Valerius to Rufinus against taking a wife*, Theophrastus' *Book of Marriage*, Tertullian's treatises in favour of chastity, selected examples from the Book of Proverbs, and Ovid's *Art of Love*. Fascinatingly, the Glastonbury library could provide a copy of every treatise used by Jankyn in compiling his volume. His perspective, then, seems based on the evidence of 'sound' authorities rather than on his own personal misogyny.

Jankyn himself reminds us of the scholarly Clerk of Oxenford. During the fourteenth century Glastonbury regularly sent young men who would have had similar intellectual interests to the Clerk to study at Oxford; of the 63 monks admitted by Monington to the monastery, for example, at least nine attended the university. In spite of the antics of some of the young men, who indulged in hunting, swimming, even womanizing, the Glastonbury monks were a serious lot – 'of studie took [they] most cure and moost heede'. For the most part, they made a good show at Oxford and came back intellectually sharp and ready to teach in the local monastic school. They used their Oxford contacts to obtain books to be copied in order to supplement the library collection at

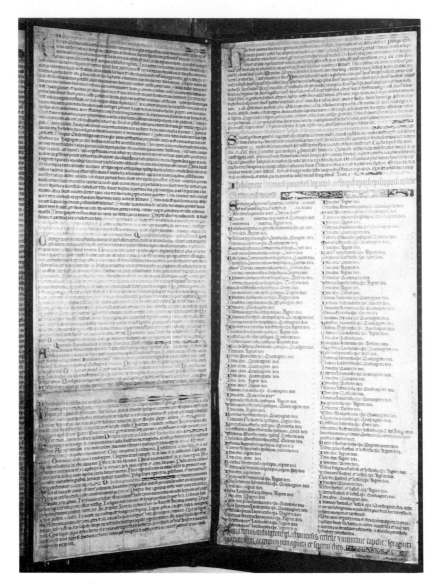

Oxford, Bodleian MS Lat. Hist. a.2 ('The Magna Tabula'), fol.1v–2r.

Glastonbury and they also wrote their own learned tomes: Roger of Ford's *Speculum ecclesiae*, for example, Edmund Stourton's *De nominibus Ihesu et Mariae* or John Merelynch's *De nominibus Mariae et Joannis*. Some, moreover, seem to have become involved in the Wycliffite controversy which was raging at the time and compiled collections of writings on the topic.

The references in John of Glastonbury's chronicle suggest that the Glastonbury library possessed a variety of French romances. In particular, the monks must have had access to *Perlesvaus* and the Vulgate cycle of Arthurian romances, and they interpreted the evangelization aspects of the French Grail story in a manner which flattered their own past. During the late fourteenth century, that is during the abbacy of John Chinnock, Glastonbury stocked its library with a number of copies of John's chronicle. Chinnock also oversaw the production of the *Magna Tabula*. This is an unusually large manuscript of six leaves mounted on a wooden frame measuring 3 ft 8 in × 3 ft 6 in. It is written in an elegant gothic book hand and has beautifully coloured enlarged initials. The text begins with the mission of Joseph of Arimathea to Glastonbury, and continues with excerpts from Melkin's prophecy, St Patrick's Charter, St Dunstan's translation, the excavation of King Arthur's tomb and other signficant events in Glastonbury's early history. The *Magna Tabula* was probably attached to a pillar in the church, where it would be in a prominent position to be read by visiting pilgrims.[7]

Although there is no apparent reference in any of the medieval catalogues surviving from Glastonbury Abbey to alchemical texts, there is a hint in Melkin the Bard's prophecy – dating to the fourteenth century at the latest – that alchemical lore circulated among members of the community. Melkin makes the cryptic statement that when Joseph of Arimathea's body is found neither water nor heavenly dew ('ros caeli') will be lacking to the inhabitants of the noble island of Glastonbury. Taken literally, the prophecy seems to constitute a threat rather than a promise, since there was an adequate source of water at the monastery and since floods were a constant danger even after a system of moor drainage was established. In alchemy, however, 'ros caeli' has an esoteric signficance and this seems to be the hidden meaning here.

Much later, just after the Dissolution, the Elizabethan magus John Dee directed his readers to this interpretation of dew in his complex esoteric work, the *Monas Hieroglyphica*. As tradition has it, moreover, Dee and his notorious companion Edward Kelley discovered the secret of the philosopher's stone at Glastonbury itself. In this context, too, the name of St Dunstan becomes relevant. There seems to have been a medieval tradition associating Dunstan's name with an alchemical text, *De lapide philosophorum*, which survives in Oxford as Corpus Christi College 128. The famous seventeenth-century collector of scientific texts, Elias Ashmole, refers to yet another text (now Oxford MS Ashmole 1382) which he says is a Latin translation of an English original: 'This book I hear was found in the treasury of Glastonbury Abbey at the time of the suppression of the Abbey, the originall copie whereof, I hear,

---

[7] On this and similar tabulae whose 'purpose was to increase the church's prestige and perhaps encourage the visitors to give more generously' see Antonia Gransden, *Historical Writing in England ii: c.1307 to the Early Sixteenth Century* (Ithaca, NY, 1982), p. 495.

remaineth yet written in parchment in a freinds hand whom I knowe.' After a consultation of the Glastonbury/Dunstan opera Ashmole waxed lyrical in his praises of the miraculous powers of the Philosopher's Stone, speculating that it is 'not unlike, but the Wallnut-Tree which anciently grew in Glastenbury Church-yeard, and never put forth Leaves before S. Baranbies Day, yet then was fully loaded with them as also the Hawthorne there, so greatly fam'd for shooting forth Leaves and Flowers at Christmas ... may be [the result of] some experiments made of the ... Stone.'

No single individual knew more about the contents of monastic libraries than John Leland, Henry VIII's unofficial antiquary general, who spent over a dozen years examining book collections throughout England and Wales. On various occasions in his travels, he made notes to himself that if he could not find a text elsewhere he was certain that it would turn up in Glastonbury's monumental collection. When he first visited the monastery he was stunned:

> I was a few years ago at Glastonbury in Somerset, where the most ancient and at the same time most famous monastery in our whole island is located. I had intended, by the favour of Richard Whiting, abbot of that place, to refresh my mind, wearied with a long course of study, when a burning desire to read and learn inflamed me afresh. This desire, too, came upon me more quickly than I thought it would. So I straightway went to the library, which is not open to all, in order to examine most diligently all the relics of most sacred antiquity, of which there is so great a number that it is not easily paralleled anywhere else in Britain. Scarcely had I crossed the threshold when the mere sight of the most ancient books took my mind with an awe or stupor of some kind, and for that reason I stopped in my tracks a little while. Then having paid my respects to the deity of the place, I examined all the bookcases for some days with the greatest interest.[8]

As in Eco's fictional world, the library constitutes a privileged area, not open to just anyone (Leland shrewdly brought a letter of introduction from the king himself), and in entering its precincts Leland was going into a private, even arcane, territory. It took Leland some length of time to go through the collection and he listed in his notebooks over forty titles; these reflect his own interests but also give us some insight into the last days of the library. Most of the books he saw appear to have been of a venerable age, and at least thirty could possibly date from pre-Conquest times. (Five or six of these, moreover, still survive.) A majority of the texts which Leland described

[8] See my 'John Leland and the Contents of English Pre-Dissolution Libraries: Glastonbury Abbey', *Scriptorium* 50 (1986), 107–20.

were historical, but he also noticed some English exegetical works and several vernacular items. A keen Arthurian, he was pleased to see Geoffrey of Monmouth's *Life of Merlin*, but what impressed him most was the Charter of St Patrick, of which he seems to have taken possession, and the garbled fragment of Melkin's prophecy. In the eyes of the monks, too, both of these items would have ranked among the greatest treasures of the library.

As genuine religious vocation declined during the sixteenth century, the more serious of the younger monks at Glastonbury (as elsewhere) became increasingly bookish and correspondingly less pious. Indeed, at the time of the last episcopal visitation in 1538, one of the most common complaints was that the daily liturgical rituals did not permit enough time for individual reading and scholarship. There were also allegations that 'the brethren hath no library nor books to resort unto';[9] this may mean that the collection had already been divided up, although it could simply show that the library was out of bounds to junior monks. Within a year of these complaints, however, the monastery was dissolved and the books dispersed without concern for value or rarity, many to be permanently destroyed. With Leland's contemporary and close friend John Bale, the twentieth-century bibliophile must conclude that

> to destroye all without consyderacyon, is and wyll be unto England for euer, a most horryble infamy among the graue senyours of other nacyons. A great nombre of them which purchased those superstycyouse mansyons [like Glastonbury], reserued of those lybrarye bokes, some to serue theyr iakes, some to scoure theyr candelstyckes, & some to rubbe their bootes. Some they solde to the grossers and sope sellers, & some they sent ouer see to the bokebynders, not in small nombre, but at tymes whole shyppes full, to the wonderynge of the foren nacyons.[10]

Of the massive library, which would have constituted thousands of volumes by this time, only approximately forty volumes are known to survive. Presumably most of the books shared the sad fate of manuscripts all over England; at New College, Oxford, for example, pages from the writings of Duns Scotus floated like falling leaves in every corner of the quadrangle.

Glastonbury Abbey stood longer than most English monas-

---

[9] See Robert W. Dunning, 'Revival at Glastonbury 1530–9', *Studies in Church History* 14 (1977), 215.

[10] John Bale's preface to Leland's 'New Year's Gift'. Printed by Bale as John Leyland. *The Laboryouse Serche for Englandes Antiquitees* (London, 1549; rpt. Amsterdam, 1975), B 1r.

teries and was one of the last few to surrender late in 1539. The monks must have had some warning about what was happening elsewhere in England and they certainly hid a number of their jewels and relics. We can imagine that they might also have smuggled some of the most valuable books out of the library and, as Dom Aelred Watkin suggests, it is not impossible that someday someone will open a false wall in one of the surviving manor houses formerly associated with the monastery and a huge cache of hidden books will tumble forth. At that time, the intellectual and cultural history of Glastonbury Abbey will have to be rewritten.

Graves discovered during excavations of the early cemetery at Glastonbury.

Glastonbury Tor (photo Tom Eveson)
Overleaf. The Abbey ruins from the air (photo Kevin Redpath).

7

The Cemetery

For a variety of reasons, some more or less incomprehensible to the post-Renaissance imagination, the cemetery formed as important and 'vital' a part of the monastic heritage at Glastonbury as the library did. It was in many ways an emotional centre for the community and balanced the library as an intellectual centre. In a civilisation ruled by mass projection as we would now call it, where numinosity clung to the inanimate as well as the animate aspects of the natural world, where at the first view of Jerusalem, say, pilgrims like Margery Kempe routinely 'shrieked as though in labour, cried aloud and wept', the sanctity of Glastonbury's cemetery would provide a constant solace to the monks. The burials represented an unbroken tradition of worship; each new grave increased the total effect. Unlike a modern cemetery, where our thoughts are directed towards death and disintegration, this site struck awe and a sense of God's nearness into the heart of the observer; its numinosity was so powerful that a touch of the sacred soil acted in itself as a kind of intercession at the seat of God.

William of Malmesbury relates that 'no one has brought a hunting bird within the cemetery or led a horse thither and left again without himself or his possessions being harmed. Within living memory everyone about to be tested by ordeal by iron or water who has offered a prayer there has, with one exception, rejoiced in his vindication.' John of Glastonbury is even more passionate when he states that no one dared even expectorate in this holy spot except under dire necessity; if an unredeemed sinner, moreover, happened to be buried in the cemetery horrible voices would be heard and evil apparitions would appear. John also relates the story of one Rainald of Marksbury, who had been taken prisoner in the Holy Land at the time of the Crusades. When his captor, a certain Sultan, realized that Rainald came from Glastonbury he agreed to release him on condition that he bring back a gloveful of soil from the cemetery. Rainald kept his word and returned with

Chalice Well (photo Kevin Redpath)

the soil. As a test, however, he first offered soil from elsewhere; the Sultan immediately recognized the fraud and was enraged. When he was then presented with the legitimate soil he was placated and explained that 'those who live at Glastonbury do not know the virtue which resides in that earth; anyone, however great a sinner among thousands will hardly suffer the pains of hell if he is buried in that location.'

Most modern authorities would agree that in prehistoric times hills were viewed as holy places. There is evidence, moreover, that there were ancient burials in the Glastonbury area, dating from the time of the Lake Villagers or even before. Perhaps a confused folk memory of this fact survives in the allusion in Melkin's prophecy to the Isle of Avalon as a pagan burial site where 'Abbadare, powerful in Saphat, most noble of pagans, took his sleep with 104,000 companions.' The surviving fragment of Melkin is very garbled at this point, however, and contains a whole range of accretions: the actual name Abbadare, for instance, probably entered the tradition late, at the time that is when Rainald or someone similar came back from the East and the Crusades. In this case Saphat is very likely a rendering of Safad, the major Templar fortification in the kingdom of Acre.

Melkin's prophecy also makes reference to what would be, if true, the earliest Christian burial in the cemetery: that of Joseph of Arimathea, who 'lies on a bifurcated line close to the southern corner of the wattled chapel.' There are a number of more or less incomprehensible allusions in this passage. First, Joseph himself is explicitly linked with pagans, an unusual association but one which is also hinted at in the Rainald passage when the Sultan asks Rainald 'whether he knew of an island between two mountains where the noble decurion Joseph of Arimathea rested, who took the prophet Jesus down from the Cross.' Secondly, Joseph is called 'de marmore' which some commentators take to mean that he was originally buried in a marble tomb, the location of which could well have become obscured in the period after the members of the first Christian settlement all died and the site returned to wilderness. Thirdly, the prophecy is enigmatic in the extreme on just where the grave is situated in the cemetery: 'Et iacet in linea bifurcata iuxta meridianum angulum oratorii cratibus preparati.' What this phrase actually means has exercised the ingenuity of generations of scholars. The literal significance of the words *linea bifurcata* 'on a two-forked line' defies interpretation. An ingenious but not altogether satisfactory explanation is that it means that Joseph was buried in a linen shroud; that is, linea = undergarment and bifurcata = divided into two parts. Dom Aelred Watkin raises the possibility that the phrase may be a corruption of *ligno bifurcato*, the sense being that Joseph lies in or under a cross. Even in the middle ages the Glastonbury writers had trouble interpreting the words; John of Glastonbury, for example, understands the reference to be to a dividing line in the original wattled chapel, although he is not clear about its location. Another anonymous late medieval text is somewhat more specific. It describes how St David added a chapel to the east of the original wattled church, and adds that where the two chapels joined, a pyramid in the northern part on the outside and a platform on the inside in the south divided them. According to ancient documents, the text says, Joseph and a great multitude of saints were also buried near this line. Even Melkin, presumably our earliest authority on the topic, admits that the exact spot where Joseph is buried remains a mystery, but he adds that when the tomb is found great miracles will occur. In fact, try as they might, the monks never could discover Joseph's tomb, as William Good testified after the Dissolution. That the monks did not fake an excavation in order to retrieve Joseph's bones stands as a strong argument against the pragmatic nineteenth-century dismissal of Glastonbury Abbey as a forgery factory; it can also be construed as a piece of evidence in favour of the legitimacy of the Arthurian excavation – i.e., the monks probably did not just dig arbitrarily; they really did have some sort of oral or written clue to work from and they did come across legitimate early graves.

Dr Ralegh Radford, who has carefully examined the area, has pinpointed the location of the cemetery for the period of the earliest monastic community, it lay to the south of the post-1184 Lady Chapel. The east wall ran just outside the late extension of the pre-Conquest church, through the south door of the thirteenth-century nave, and the south wall was approximately one hundred feet distant from the Lady Chapel. The entrance, corresponding to St Dunstan's Chapel to the west of the Lady Chapel, was in the west wall. The poetical *Lyfe* of St Joseph gives a description, stating that the famous Glastonbury walnut tree stood:

> in the holy grounde called the semetory; harde by the place where kynge Arthur was founde; south fro Joseph's chapell it is walled in rounde.

Within these enclosed precincts, modern archaeologists have found post-holes belonging to at least four oratories of a wattled type characteristic of the cemeteries of Celtic monasteries such as Clonmacnois in Ireland.

For the community at Glastonbury 1190/91 represented a vindication and a turning point: unknown to all, the cemetery contained the bones of the most important prince in Christendom: Arthur himself, it transpired, was buried at Glastonbury. Soon afterwards several conflicting explanations of what prompted the dig were circulated: indications on the two ancient stone pyramids standing in the cemetery; a monk who wished to be buried between the crosses; Henry II who, it was stated, had heard reports from a Welsh bard that Arthur was buried in this site. Perhaps the most interesting account is the one given by Gerald of Wales not long after the event:

> Now the body of King Arthur, which legend has feigned to have been transferred at his passing, as it were in ghostly form, by spirits to a distant place, and to have been exempt from death, was found in our own days at Glastonbury, deep down in the earth and encoffined in a hollow oak between two stone pyramids erected long ago in the consecrated graveyard, the site being revealed by strange and almost miraculous signs; and it was afterwards transported with honour to the Church and decently consigned to a marble tomb. Now in the grave there was found a cross of lead, placed under a stone and not above it, as is now customary, but fixed on the under side. This cross I myself have seen, for I have felt the letters engraved thereon, which do not project or stand out, but are turned inwards towards the stone. They run as follows: 'Here lies buried the renowned King Arthur, with Guenevere his second wife, in the Isle of Avalon.' Now in regard to this there are many things worthy of note. For he had two wives, the last of whom was buried with him, and her bones were found together with his, but separated from them as thus; two parts of the tomb, to wit, the head, were allotted to the bones of the man, while the remaining third towards the foot contained the bones of a woman in a place apart; and there was found a yellow tress of woman's hair still retaining its colour and freshness; but when a certain monk snatched it and lifted it with greedy hand, it straightway all of it fell into dust. Now whereas there were certain indications in their writings that the body would be found there, and others in the letters engraven on the pyramids, though they were much defaced by their extreme age, and others again were given in visions and relations vouchsafed to good men and religious, yet it was above all King Henry II of England that most clearly informed the monks, as he himself heard from an ancient Welsh bard, a singer of the past, that they would find the body at least sixteen feet beneath the earth, not in tomb of stone, but in a hollow oak. And this is the reason why the body was placed so deep and hidden away, to wit, that it might not by any means be discovered by the Saxons, who occupied the island after his death, whom he had so often in his life defeated and almost utterly destroyed; and for the same reason those letters, witnessing to the truth, that were stamped upon the cross, were turned inwards towards the stone, that they might at that time conceal what the tomb contained, and

John Mortimer,
The discovery of Prince Arthur's Tomb *(c.1767).*
Possibly the only instance of one of the 'history painters' of the period attempting an Arthurian subject.

yet in due time and place might one day reveal the truth. ...
You must also know that the bones of Arthur thus discovered
were so huge that the words of the poet seemed to be fulfilled
... For his shank-bone when placed against that of the tallest
man in that place, and planted in the earth near his foot,
reached, as the Abbot showed us, a good three inches above his
knee. And the skull was so large and capacious as to be a
portent or a prodigy, for the eye-socket was a good palm in
width. Moreover, there were ten wounds or more, all of which
were scarred over, save one larger than the rest, which had
made a great hole.[1]

Modern excavations by Radford of the area between the spots
where the two stone pyramids would have stood reveal that a
large irregular hole had been dug and then filled in after being
open for only a very short time. At the bottom of the hole
there are indications that there had been two or three slab-lined
graves from the very earliest burial period and that these had
been disturbed shortly after the fire of 1184. Arthur's tomb
was discovered only at a great depth, moreover, because in the
tenth century St Dunstan had artificially raised the level of the
cemetery.

Recently, Richard Barber has postulated that Gerald's
account is by no means an eyewitness one as many have
claimed. Citing another less well known text called the
Margam chronicle, he argues that although the monks did
indeed find ancient burials they rather arbitrarily chose to label
them with the names of Arthur, Guenevere and Mordred, the
last of whom was not necessarily evil in Welsh tradition. They
circulated the account of their findings in what we might now
call a kind of newsletter; the reaction to Mordred's name by
those who knew Geoffrey of Monmouth's *History of the Kings
of Britain* rather than Welsh materials, however, was one of
horror and so the story was revised. Gerald of Wales then
became the offical purveyor of the new version.

Other explanations concerning the Arthurian find and its
validity abound, although in recent times there has been some
reaction against the airy dismissal of the whole affair as a
consciously articulated scheme to raise money for the monastery. The cemetery, as *mise en scène* of the whole affair, has an
important role as well. In this context, the devastating fire of
1184 is relevant, but in a psychological rather than a material
manner. After the fire there was a feeling of disorientation and
breakdown of continuity. The buildings had stood as a
powerful symbol of an unbroken tradition of worship, of a
link from generation to generation. The monks now could turn

[1] See the discussion of this passage by Richard Barber, *King Arthur. Hero and Legend*
(Woodbridge, 1986), pp. 132ff.

only to the cemetery as a physical manifestation of their heritage. Unlike buildings, however, bones are not immediately identifiable, especially when upheavals have caused markers to be shifted or even to have disappeared. As the monks began reconstruction work in the mid 1180s they turned up a variety of remains among the ashes and other fragments surfaced too as foundations were dug. This was exciting but also, I suspect, unnerving. The cemetery stood like a hieroglyph, full of meaning if only one could break the code. The hieroglyph metaphor is especially appropriate when one thinks of the two ancient stone pyramids with their partially illegible writing, standing in the cemetery like talismen of treasures waiting to be revealed. That the monks discovered a burial they could associate with King Arthur is not at all surprising; what is remarkable in some ways is the restraint they applied in not excavating the whole cemetery in quest of even more exciting bones.

What were the earliest remains, apart from Joseph's and Arthur's, that the post-conflagration chroniclers attributed to the cemetery? According to John of Glastonbury, King Coel, nowadays most famous in the nursery rhyme, was buried in the cemetery. Glastonbury tradition held that Coel was the son of Arviragus, the king who first gave the Twelve Hides to Joseph. He was, moreover, the father of St Helen, who in turn was the mother of the Roman emperor Constantine. The case of St Patrick is more complex and controversial, since it is still not clear which, if any, St Patrick came to Glastonbury. Nevertheless, the remains of two mausolea dating from the Celtic period have been uncovered in the cemetery and it is possible that these tombs were early associated with Patrick and his disciple Indract.[2]

When we turn to the Saxon period and the stone pyramids between which King Arthur's remains were discovered we move out of the area of speculation and into the realm of recorded fact – or at least we advance in this direction. These pyramids, tall slender carved shafts, flat on top, would have closely resembled the surviving crosses at Bewcastle and Ruthwell. Recent excavations show that one was situated forty feet south of the second bay from the east end of the Lady Chapel, and the other was probably fifteen feet further south, where it may even have functioned, Radford suggests, as a marker for one of the two mausolea. (There may possibly have been a third pyramid in the cemetery dating from the same period, which had the name of Centwine, king of Wessex,

[2] There is, of course, considerable controversy surrounding the (possible) Celtic church at Glastonbury and not all experts agree with Radford's interpretations of the findings in the cemetery.

engraved on it. Centwine was a great benefactor to Glastonbury and ultimately retired to the monastery. His pyramid, if a separate monument, would almost certainly have been a sepulchral rather than a commemorative device.) Unfortunately the first written reference to the pyramids does not occur until the time of William of Malmesbury, who examined them when they were already many centuries old:

> That which is almost wholly unknown would I gladly tell, if I could shape out the truth of it: namely, the meaning of those pyramids which stand a few feet from the Old Church in the cemetery of the monks. The nearer to the church is twenty-six feet high and has five storeys to it. This, though threatening ruin from its extreme age, has yet some memorials of antiquity, which may clearly be read even if they may not fully be understood. For in the topmost storey is an image fashioned in episcopal guise. In the second an image exhibiting royal pomp, and the letters HER, SEXI and BLISYER. In the third indeed the names: WEMCREST, BANTOMP, WINETHEGN. In the fourth: HATE, WULFRED AND EANFLED. In the fifth, which is the lowest, an image and these words: LOGWOR, WESLICAS ET BREGDEN, SWELWES, HWINGENDES, BERN. The other pyramid is eighteen feet high and has four storeys, on which are written these words: HEDDE EPISCOPUS et BREGORED et BEORUUARD. What these signify I do not rashly determine but surmise and suspect that the bones of such as are read outside are placed in stones hollowed within.[3]

The references on the smaller pyramid are relatively easy to pinpoint: Haeddi, the famous bishop of Winchester; Bregored, the last British abbot of Glastonbury; and Beorhtwald, the first Anglo-Saxon abbot. Using William's description of the engraving on the larger monument, Dom Aelred Watkin has made a number of tentative attributions from seventh-century notables: St Birinus, St Wilfrid, Eanfled, queen of Northumbria, Sexburga, queen of Wessex, and Haetla, bishop of Dorchester. Watkin, moreover, thinks the two pyramids were not memorials to individuals buried in the cemetery but rather commemorative of a visit to Glastonbury by St Wilfrid, Queen Eanfled and bishop Haetla as part of a campaign to break Celtic patterns and to make the monastery definitively Roman in practice.

[3] On the pyramids and Watkin's discussion of the names engraved on them see above pp. 102–03. In an unpublished letter to Watkin dated 17 July, 1946, J. R. R. Tolkien provided a linguistic analysis of these names as William reported them. He concluded that 'As far as I can see the forms of the name-lists do not suggest a very early date – unless, and they do rather suggest this to me, we are to assume that the corruption is due in part to a written tradition; in fact that W. of M., though he may have clomben a ladder and squinted for himself, drew also on some written account, the work of some earlier decipherer (and possibly emender and mystifier as well).'

In the generations after William's visit the stone monuments continued to undergo a weathering process and by the time of John Leland they were in a melancholy state:

> Within the burying place which was consecrated at *Aualonia* stand two *Pyramedes* of most auncient buylding, bearing a shew of figures & letters, but the windes, stormes and time which consumeth all thinges, finally envy of man from time to time haue so defaced the notable figures and inscription of auncient workes, that they can scarce be discerned by any neuer so sharpe sight of the eye.[4]

Finally, they were dragged away in the eighteenth century and used, as a contemporary antiquary laments, to make a post in a field or to form a prop for a cottage.

During the Celtic and early-Saxon period the whole monastic site existed very clearly as an integrated entity: the wattled church was a key feature, of course, but it functioned in a landscape of which the cemetery was also an active part. From the time that the larger stone church was built during Ine's reign, however, there was a shift: the most distinguished individuals were now interred in stately monuments which were displayed inside the church rather than in the cemetery itself. Kings such as Edmund the Elder, Edgar and Edmund Ironside were buried in the church as were relics from a great multitude of saints: some of these saints died at Glastonbury, the bones of others were brought much later to the monastery. The abbots themselves were also laid in stately monuments throughout the monastic buildings.

In the tenth century there was a major physical disruption to the cemetery when St Dunstan built a wall on the south side and raised the level of the ground; the cemetery thus 'became like a pleasant meadow isolated from the noise of the passerby, so that it might be said of the saints resting therein, their bodies are buried in peace.' At this time, one assumes that a certain number of stones were covered over and that there was some displacement of tombs. Although St Dunstan seems to have converted the cemetery into a more park-like area monks continued to use it as a burying ground throughout the middle ages and wealthy laymen left the monastery large sums of money in their wills for the privilege of being buried in such a holy location. By the time John of Glastonbury wrote his history the site had become legendary:

> Aside from those named above [as buried in the cemetery], many bishops, dukes, abbots, and other magnates rest there

[4] See Richard Robinson's translation of Leland's 'Assertio Inclytissimi Arturii' in William Edward Mead, ed., *The Famous Historie of Chinon of England by Christopher Middleton* ... (EETS, OS 165; London, 1925), p. 61.

whom I pass over for fear of tedium; and indeed, these men built no whited sepulchres nor constructed lavish monuments, but gloried rather that they could be buried in the humble turf of this holy land. And although their places of burial are not visible, nevertheless, they appear worthy of eternal memory in the sight of the Lord.[5]

In other words, burial in the cemetery was an almost certain guarantee of a place in heaven; a peaceful burial at Glastonbury was the equivalent of a posthumous trial by ordeal. If one were unworthy of salvation, so it seemed to the monks, then there would be some visible sign of rejection – a miracle would indicate the Lord's displeasure with the contamination of such a sanctified place.

Nowadays no visible markers mark the final resting place of so many distinguished and pious individuals; only a slight downward slope in the grass where the south wall ended (landscaped as such by Radford when his excavations were completed) indicates the spot. It is more or less the same as it was when in 1777, the antiquary Revd. J. Whitaker described it:

John Carter's drawing of the gateway with inn beside it, c.1785. BL, MS Addit. 29926, p.39.

> The burying ground is still pointed out by the finger of tradition, stretching along the north side of the church, but now serving as the kitchen-garden to that inn in the town, the White Hart, at the back of which the ruins lie. ... Thus too, vegetables for visitors to the ruins are raised in higher luxury from a soil impregnated with the bodies of monks, bishops, nobles and kings innumerable.[6]

Most abandoned graveyards make us feel melancholy, make us aware of the frailty of human memory. Glastonbury's cemetery has passed even beyond this; the cycle of decay and rebirth is complete. Now this area, the epitome of 'England's green & pleasant Land', has returned to the condition (albeit considerably more carefully tended) where it was when the first Christian settlers arrived. Unlike the library, whose lost secrets continue to tantalize and haunt us, whose destruction is remembered, as the sixteenth-century antiquary John Bale predicted, as a most horrible infamy, the cemetery seems at peace and the ghosts – whose presence even official archaeologists such as Frederick Bligh Bond have felt – are not tormented; their destiny has been fulfilled.

---

[5] Even in the twelfth century, when William of Malmesbury visited Glastonbury, the cemetery was venerated far and wide.

[6] See Whitaker's *Life of St Neot* (London, 1809), p.36.

8

Arthur, Avalon and the Bridge Perilous

I

When he composed his comprehensive *Deeds of the Kings of England* around 1125 William of Malmesbury made a sharp distinction between the Arthur of historical fact and the Arthur of the realms of the imagination. For his part, William opted firmly for the former:

> This is that Arthur of whom the trifling of the Britons talks such nonsense even today: a man clearly worthy not to be dreamed of in fallacious fables, but to be proclaimed in veracious histories, as one who long sustained his tottering country and gave the shattered minds of his fellow citizens an edge for war.

Very little, so William maintained, can be ascertained about this hero. All we can really establish is that he aided Ambrosius Aurelianus in resisting the Saxons and that at the siege of Mount Badon, where he carried the image of the Virgin Mary on his armour, he singlehandedly defeated a vast multitude of the enemy. Unfortunately, the location of his final resting place lies in doubt and this, William laments, has led to foolish rumours about his second coming.

At the other extreme from William's circumspect account come the great cycles of stories which first circulated in oral form in France and Britain and which were written down only in the twelfth century. These constitute the *matière de Bretagne* which, together with the stories of Alexander and Charlemagne, make up the major literary cycles of the High Middle Ages. 'I know not', says the twelfth-century Anglo-Norman chronicler Wace,

> if you have heard tell the marvellous gestes and errant deeds related so often of King Arthur. They have been noised about this mighty realm for so great a space that the truth has turned to fable and an idle song. Such rhymes are neither sheer bare lies, nor gospel truths. They should not be considered either an idiot's tale, or given by inspiration. The minstrel has sung his ballad, the storyteller told over his tale so frequently, little by

little he has decked and painted, till by reason of his embellishment the truth stands hid in the trappings of a tale. Thus to make a delectable tune to your ear, history goes masking as fable.

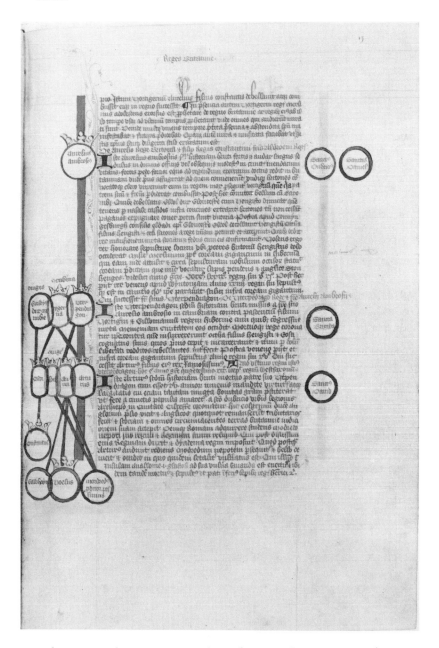

Arthur's genealogy as portrayed in a fourteenth-century manuscript. Oxford, Queen's College MS 304, fol.13r.

It is not through strict history and judicious chronicle, though, but through these 'gestes' and ballads that Arthur came to his pre-eminence among the Nine Worthies.

'Whither,' proudly asks a twelfth-century commentator on Geoffrey of Monmouth's *Prophetiae Merlini*,

> has not flying fame spread and familiarized the name of Arthur the Briton, even as far as the empire of Christendom extends? Who, I say, does not speak of Arthur the Briton, since he is almost better known to the peoples of Asia than to the Britanni [the Welsh and Cornish], as our palmers returning from the East inform us? The Eastern peoples speak of him, as do the Western, though separated by the width of the whole earth. Egypt speaks of him, nor is the Bosphorus silent. Rome, queen of cities, sings his deeds, nor are Arthur's wars unknown to her former rival Carthage. Antioch, Armenia, and Palestine celebrate his acts.

In the writings of Geoffrey himself – who was more or less contemporary with William – we have an unprecedented coupling of history and myth, fact and speculation. The *History of the Kings of Britain*, written c.1138, puts Arthur at the pinnacle of Britain's history. Succeeding to the throne of a kingdom ravaged by Saxon raids, Arthur quickly routs the enemy, achieving his decisive victory at Badon (which Geoffrey identifies as Bath), where he triumphantly slices his way through his opponents with his trusty sword Caliburn (i.e., Excalibur), itself forged in the fabled Isle of Avalon. After subduing the Saxons, Arthur then crushes the Picts and Scots in the North, marries Guenevere and turns his attention to foreign affairs. He conquers Ireland and Iceland in short order and then subdues Norway, Denmark and Gaul. Finally, he confronts the Roman ruler Lucius in Gaul and plans an advance on Rome. At this juncture, alas, he is cruelly betrayed by his wicked nephew Mordred who has usurped the throne at home. Arthur returns to England and defeats Mordred in a battle by the River Camlan in Cornwall, but he himself is mortally wounded during the fracas and is carried off to Avalon:

> It was there we took Arthur after the battle of Camlan where he had been wounded, Barin thus was the steersman because of his knowledge of the seas and the stars of heaven. With him at the tiller of the ship, we arrived there with the prince; and Morgen received us with due honour. She put the king in her chamber on a golden bed, uncovered his wound with her noble hand and looked long at it. At length she said he could be cured if only he stayed with her a long while and accepted her treatment. We therefore happily committed the king to her care and spread our sails to favourable winds on our return journey.

Its proud leader removed, the British resistance collapses and the Saxons at last prevail.

Geoffrey, it is clear, is well aware of the traditional linking of Arthur's demise with Avalon, but whereas he rashly speculates about the modern names of many other Arthurian sites, he is deliberately poetic and imprecise about this particular location:

> The island of Apples, which men call the Fortunate Isle, is so named because it produces all things of itself. The fields there have no need of farmers to plough them, and Nature alone provides all cultivation. Grain and grapes are produced without tending, and apple trees grow in the woods from close-clipped grass. The earth of its own accord brings forth not merely grass but all things in superabundance.

That Geoffrey does not identify Avalon in terms of contemporary geography is particularly appropriate, since Arthur himself is a kind of manifestation of the 'sleeping king' motif throughout early Celtic myth, a man whose final resting place, as William had noted, is full of magical connotations:

> A grave for March, a grave for Gwythur, a grave for Gwgawn of the Red Sword; concealed till Domesday the grave of Arthur.[1]

In the context of a long and proud tradition of Arthur as a mysterious sleeping hero it is easy to see why the discovery of his tomb at Glastonbury generated such speculation and – in some quarters – even disbelief. In his account written approximately forty years after the event the author of the Old French romance *La Mort Artu* makes a heroic struggle to reconcile the *rex quondam rexque futurus* motif with the 1190 discovery: he tells us that after Arthur was mortally wounded by Mordred, Morgan and her ladies came to take him away in their ship. His loyal knight Girflet witnessed the departure and after a period of mourning rode forth to the Black Chapel where he saw a new tomb with the inscription: 'Here lies King Arthur, who by his valor made twelve kingdoms subject to him.' Girflet then met a hermit who told him that the group of ladies brought the body to this most holy chapel for burial. Thus, a real Chapel [as at Glastonbury, where John Hardyng later refers to Arthur's burial in 'the blacke chappel Of our Lady'] becomes conflated with Morgan's traditional Avalon. The author of the *Vera historia de morte Arthuri*, composed in Latin before the end of the thirteenth century, provides a similar conflation of motifs. In this text Arthur's body is taken to be buried in a certain chapel dedicated to the Blessed Virgin Mary, but since the entrance is too narrow to allow entrance

---

[1] On this stanza in *The Black Book of Carmarthen* – as well as conflicting translations and interpretations – see Barber, *King Arthur. Hero and Legend*, pp. 15–16.

the body is left outside. A great storm occurs and mist envelops all; when the air clears the body has disappeared and in its place there is a sealed tomb. Some say that this is where the body resides; others claim that it was mysteriously carried off to an unknown destination during the storm.

In spite of this kind of attempt at reconciliation of conflicting traditions, nevertheless, scepticism about the Glastonbury discovery continued. Almost three centuries after the excavation, for example, Sir Thomas Malory informs us that 'yet some men say in many partys of Inglonde that Kynge Arthur ys nat dede, but had by the wyll of oure Lord Jesu into another place; and men say that he shall come agayne, and shall wynne the Holy Crosse.' Even later, it is reported that when Phillip II of Spain married Mary Tudor in 1554 he swore – presumably somewhat ironically – that he would hand over the kingdom if Arthur were to return. In relatively modern times, too, an ancient rustic is said to have approached antiquaries visiting South Cadbury to enquire querulously: 'Have you come to take the king out?'[2]

The widely held scholarly stance is that the 1190 excavation was a hoax. That curtains may have surrounded the site during the dig (as is reported by the Glastonbury chronicler Adam of Damerham), makes the whole business seem even more suspicious. Glastonbury was in relatively dire straits at this period, as it happens, because of the decimating fire in 1184. Funds were urgently needed to implement large scale rebuilding plans and pilgrims to Arthur's shrine would provide a fine supplemental income for the monastery. That one almost contemporary account makes King Henry II himself the motivating authority for the excavation also fits in with this line of reasoning. The Angevin monarchy had been having a certain amount of trouble with the Welsh and it was feared that they might openly rebel given the right political context – in this case Arthur could easily become a kind of rallying cry. On the other hand, Arthur proved safely dead and buried in English territory would act as a deterrent to potential Celtic nationalism.[3]

[2] J. Armitage Robinson refers to this episode in *Two Glastonbury Legends*, pp. 51–3.
[3] In a letter to Aelred Watkin dated 12.vii.60, Professor Christopher Brooke has speculated on the excavation, erecting – as he puts it – 'a card-house of conjecture.' He points out that Walter Map – to whom the author of the *Queste* and other parts of the Vulgate cycle later, and quite inaccurately, gave credit for the composition of a supposed Latin source book – was indeed a fine romancer and enjoyed falsification for its own sake. 'Map was a Welshman, whose home was in the border country. He was also a courtier who knew Henry II well, and travelled widely in France in his service. He was also a friend of Gerald of Wales; and evidently well-known as a story teller. He would fulfil all the conditions needed for the man who prompted Henry II to tell the monks of Glastonbury to dig Arthur up – a distinctly Map-like jape.' Brooke now feels dubious about his earlier schema, especially since in the *De nugis curialium* Map

The foregoing thesis does not lack merit and may well provide at least a partial explanation for the triumphant success of the dig, which quickly became known in England and abroad and which influenced the whole course of development of the English Grail legends. Nevertheless, other factors, less easy to pin down, seem also to enter into the matter. In particular, why does King Henry II allege that he heard about Arthur's place of burial from a Welsh or Breton bard? Does this detail suggest that the story might have independent origins, that it might have other causes apart from the obvious benefits the find conferred on king and monastery? Is there, in other words, a pre-excavation oral tradition of Glastonbury as an Otherworld, a Celtic paradise or Avalon? In trying to probe this sort of question we move very quickly into a realm of hints and speculations, of possibilities and wishes, non-sequiturs, blind alleys and sometimes even absurdities. All too easily the deceptive Celtic twilight can descend, obscuring clear logic and sharp, crisp powers of deduction.

Although the written form is late, the Welsh *Mabinogion* provides one of the earliest glimpses of the preliterate Celtic Otherworld and its myths. This group of four interconnected stories, extremely garbled in their present form, concerns – so linguists and folklorists now postulate – the prototypical British god 'Maponos', that is, the divine youth. In Branch I the adventures of Pwyll, Prince of Dyfed, are narrated. Pwyll meets Arawn, prince of Annwfn (the Celtic Otherworld) on a sacred mound. The two men agree to change physical form, wives, and kingdoms for a year. At the end of the year Pwyll, disguised as Arawn, contracts to challenge one Hafgan on the ford, but Pwyll must wield only one blow. (As in *Sir Gawain and the Green Knight* magical symbolism seems to be connected with a single stroke.) Pwyll does as he is instructed and sleeps beside Arawn's wife in Annwfn, his face resolutely to the wall, for the next twelve months. He then confronts Hafgan, defeats him because he remembers not to strike him more than once, and at last returns to his own kingdom of Dyfed, where he is henceforth known as Pwyll Head of Annwfn instead of his former title as Pendevig of Dyfed.

In spite of a variety of strange convolutions and seeming confusions of name and character, scholars have unravelled several primitive strands in this story. Most obviously, we have

studiously avoids mentioning Arthur. He still maintains, however, that 'some story of this kind may lie behind these curious events and documents, even if not Map!' In 'The Grave of King Arthur' the eighteenth-century poet and antiquary Thomas Warton gives a suitably 'rationalist' rendition of the speech made by the bard who supposedly told Henry about the burial site: Henry is exhorted to make emends for the fact that Arthur was buried in an unmarked grave and to renew 'the faded tomb, with honour due.'

a variant of the Chastity Test, a motif of immense antiquity, one which forms a basis of certain aspects of the Grail stories and which achieves its literary apotheosis in Gawain's bedroom adventures with Lady Bertilak in *Sir Gawain and the Green Knight*. Through a complex process of reconstruction it is possible, moreover, to detect in Pwyll remnants of the story of the birth of the national hero through the descent of a shape-changing god. In this respect, the story is a Celtic equivalent to the Leda and the Swan tale and distantly prefigures the events surrounding Arthur's own conception. Finally, Pwyll himself, in his role as god-king and tribal wiseman, seems to be a prototype of Pelles, the Fisher King of the Grail stories, whose residence is at the fabled Corbenic and who is wounded in his thigh as a punishment for drawing the sword of David.

In another early Welsh text, *The Spoils of Annwfn*, Arthur himself makes a voyage in his ship Prydwenn to Annwfn to fetch away the magic cauldron of plenty (perhaps a prototype for the Grail) belonging to the chief of Annwfn:

> The cauldron of the Head of Annwfn, what is its custom, dark about its edge with pearl?
> It does not boil a coward's food; it had not been so destined. ...
> And when we went with Arthur, renowned conflict, except for seven, none returned from Caer Feddwid.[4]

In this poem, supposedly composed by the sixth-century bard Taliesin, Annwfn is called among other names Caer Siddi, that is Faery City, and Caer Wydr, that is City of Glass: the latter reminds us of the great importance of the mythical Glassy Isle in Celtic legend.

In some stories the chief of Annwfn is Pwyll, in others he is nameless, and elsewhere he is called Gwynn ap (i.e., son of) Nudd. According to *Culhwch and Olwen*, which deals with a trip to Annwfn, Gwynn's wife Creiddylad (a prototype of Cordelia) is abducted by Gwythyr. Arthur restores her to the house of her father Leir, but decrees that Gwynn and Gwythur will have to fight for her hand every Mayday until Domesday. Long ago, Matthew Arnold noted the symbolic undertones here:

> What is Gwyn the son of Nudd, king of Faerie, the ruler of the Tylwyth Teg, or family of beauty, who til the day of doom fights every first day of May – the great feast of the sun among the Celtic peoples – with Gwythyr for the fair Cordelia, the daughter of Lyr? ... Who is the mystic Arawn, the king of Annwyn, who changed semblance for a year with Pwyll, prince

---

[4] For this translation see John K. Bollard, 'Arthur in the Early Welsh Tradition', in James J. Wilhelm and Laila Zamuelis Gross, eds., *The Romance of Arthur* (New York and London, 1984), pp. 21–23.

of Dyved, and reigned in his place? These are no mediaeval personages; they belong to an older, pagan, mythological world.[5]

Gwynn also appears in the *Life* of St Collen, where he is portrayed as the king of the Otherworld, the entrance to whose realm is found at the summit of Glastonbury Tor. A variation of this motif is found in a fourteenth-century English poem, *A Dispute between a Christian and a Jew*, which describes the magnficent manor of Arthur and the knights of the Round Table; the manor is reached by a path under a hill.

Another son of Nudd, himself a manifestation of the ancient British god Nodons, is Yder. According to the French romance bearing his name, Yder undertakes the courtship of Queen Guenloie. During the course of his adventures he is treacherously wounded by Kay. Once healed of his wounds, he rescues Queen Guenevere from a bear and she announces that she would have preferred him to Arthur as a lover if she had had the choice. Not surprisingly, this provokes Arthur to jealousy and he attempts to kill Yder before the plot is finally resolved. Yder turns up in quite a different context in William of Malmesbury's *The Early History of Glastonbury*. Here King Arthur decorates the young Yder as one of his knights and sends him off to fight giants at the Mount of Frogs in Brent Knoll. Yder conquers the giants but is killed himself in the effort. Arthur feels responsible for his death and gives rich territory to the monastery at Glastonbury as a kind of penance and establishes 24 monks there in Yder's memory.

Yet another cluster of stories concerning the ruler of the Otherworld focuses on the figure of Melwas ('mael' + 'gwas' = prince youth). In Caradog of Llancarfan's *Life* of Gildas Melwas, as king of the Summer region, abducts Queen Guenevere and in retaliation the 'tyrant' Arthur brings all the forces of Devon and Cornwall together to retrieve her. St Gildas, accompanied by the abbot of Glastonbury, obtains her release and peace is restored. Ultimately Caradog's story, as respectable and historically accurate as he tries to make it, derives – like the equivalent Yder episode – from a Celtic form of the Pluto and Persephone myth, a myth which also turns up in the Welsh *Dialogue of Arthur and Gwenhwyfer*, where the same events are described with Melwas, Gwenhwyfer and perhaps Cei (Kay) as the principal participants.[6]

The Melwas/Pluto story also comes into the French Arthurian romances. In Chrétien de Troyes' *Erec and Enide*, for

---

[5] *The Study of Celtic Literature* (London, 1912), p. 51.
[6] For a rather bizarre folklore interpretation of this poem see Mary Williams, 'An Early Ritual Poem in Welsh', *Speculum* 13 (1938), 38–51.

example, the Melwas figure appears briefly, his name rendered as Maheloas. He is described as the lord of the Isle de Voirre (i.e., Glass), where there is never storm, winter's cold or excessive heat, and he attends the wedding of the hero and heroine. In Chrétien's *Lancelot* we have the figure Meleagant, who is characterised as the evil son of Baudemagus, king of the land of Gorre. Meleagant, true to his Melwas prototypical origins, abducts Guenevere and this time it is Lancelot who travels to Gorre, crossing a sword bridge on the last part of his trip and arriving at Meleagant's castle in time to rescue the Queen. Just as Lancelot is about to overcome Meleagant in armed combat Baudemagus asks Guenevere to intercede on behalf of his son. Even after Guenevere persuades Lancelot to spare him, however, Meleagant refuses to admit defeat and Lancelot therefore consents to meet him again in battle for the queen at Arthur's court in one year's time. This combat duly takes place in the presence of Arthur and Guenevere in their residence at Escavalon. The parallels here with Caradog's Melwas story are obvious and suprisingly specific.

If the Celtic Isle of Glass – linguistically analogous with Glastonbury itself – was a winterless Otherworld, an appropriate venue for the British form of the Persephone story in its Arthurian context, so too the Isle of Avalon, the Apple-clustered island, realm of King Avallach, home of nine maidens, chief of whom was Arthur's kinswoman Morgan le Fay, represented the same paradisiacal concept. A variety of factors could have suggested an identification of Avalon with Glastonbury once the latter had been etymologized as the Isle of Glass. To begin with, the Isle of Glass as mythical concept might well suggest the Isle of Apples, almost identical in its attributes. It also seems quite possible that Glastonbury Tor and the island around it had been a sacred enclosure even since prehistoric times and as such might well have been viewed locally as an Avalon, that is holy place. Presumably, too, apple trees grew plenteously in the region then as now. Nor is there any reason to doubt that stories concerning Arthur, who appears early to have been associated with the south west, would have circulated orally at Glastonbury even before Caradog wrote about his sojourn at Glastonbury. If Glastonbury could be identified as Avalon as well as the Isle of Glass, moreover, then the logical consequence would be that Arthur's mortal remains (known to be at Avalon) must be found in the cemetery, itself revered as a magically resonant and holy place. From the viewpoint of the medieval Glastonbury community it would seem altogether logical that this great Christian leader would have venerated the oldest church in his kingdom and wished to be buried there. In this respect the 1190 discovery represents a solution to a complex series of interconnected problems and provides an extremely neat tying up of a whole set of themes.

II

The origin of the name 'Avalon' is still open to dispute and even modern etymologists cannot agree about its ultimate derivation. One fairly obvious possibility is that the name comes from the Celtic Aval = apple; and certainly the apple was a magical fruit in Celtic myth as it was in many other cultures – we need only think of the judgement of Paris, the Apples of the Hesperides or even the Garden of Eden. On the other hand, the character Avallach, father of Morgan, is a very ancient figure in the Celtic pantheon and is portrayed as the King of the Underworld. It seems at least possible, then, that Avalon derives from his name.

There are also several different explanations for the origin of the first element – that is, the Isle of Glass aspect – in Glastonbury. It possibly represents a Welsh personal name, but it could come from glasstan (oak) or glasto (woad). Some scholars have claimed, moreover, that the later, so-called British, name for Glastonbury, that is Iniswitrin – the second element of which Caradog derived from witrin (glass) – may have a completely different origin and come from the proper name Vitrinos.

The late medieval chronicles at Glastonbury create an account which brings together and reconciles most of the forms of the various names. We begin with Glasteing's arrival at the site. Glasteing, it appears, has left the land of his ancestor Cunedda and has migrated south. At Wells he catches sight of a wild sow and pursues her along Sugewey (and here sugga = marsh is ingeniously etymologized as suga = sow). Soon he finds her suckling under an apple tree near the Old Church and decides that this is a sign that he should colonize the place. And since he finds precious apples there he names it Avalon, although he subsequently discovers that the local ruler is called Avalo. Later the Saxon invaders change the name to Iniswitrin, Isle of Glass, or Isle of Glasteing.

Through their synthesis the medieval chroniclers produced a happy marriage, as it were, of all the foundation motifs with the exception of the Vitrinos strand. One modern scholar, Louis H. Gray, has shown himself even more ingenious and has managed as well to assimilate this element and deserves, therefore, the last word on the matter:

As I reconstruct the story, a settlement called Avallonia ... already famous as a British Elysium, intimately associated with the Arthurian cycle, and a renowned centre of Christianity, was occupied, about 500, by a band headed by Vitrinos Glast, who had migrated from Manau Guotodin, the littoral area between the Firth of Forth and the Aln, along the west coast through Glassonby and Glasson to Wells. He gave his own name to Aballonia (Inisvitrin), but the appellation was soon changed from his original name to his nickname, and made to include his followers as well – probably something like *Glastincodunom*. Finally, between 658 and 688, with the Saxon conquest, this name was transformed into its Saxon equivalent Glaestingaburh, whence the present designation Glastonbury.[7]

III

Whether Arthur's tomb was found at Glastonbury because Glastonbury was identified as Avalon or whether Glastonbury was identified as Avalon because tradition suggested that Arthur was buried there, one thing is certain: once the identification was made it was inevitable that Glastonbury/Avalon would be seen as the final destination for the Holy Grail, that mysterious relic of the Crucifixion associated with Joseph of Arimathea and King Arthur's court. The Grail, however, is not the only Arthurian relic closely linked with the region around Avalon. Traditionally Arthur's last gesture before being taken to Avalon was to have his mighty sword Caliburn (itself forged in the Isle of Avalon) hurled from Pomparles Bridge, which was identified as the bridge between Glastonbury and Street as early as the fourteenth century in the English poem *Libeaus Desconnus*. The author of this poem, moreover, locates King Arthur's court at Glastonbury and sends his hero out from the court over Pomparles Bridge to the Chapel Adventurous in Street.

Pomparles turns up in Latin records under the form Pons periculosus as early as 1344, when a charter of Ralph, Baron Stafford is dated 'apud Strete iuxta pontem periculosam'.[8] Such was its fame in the sixteenth century that John Leland made a special point of visiting it and noting his impressions: 'a Bridge of Stone of a 4. Arches communely caullid Pontperlus, wher men fable that Arture cast in his Swerd.' Even after the Dissolution the bridge continued to attract pilgrims and Sir John Harington refers to it in 1591, carefully dissociating himself from popular tales in his analysis:

Engraving of Pomparles Bridge as it was before 1826, from William Phelps, The History and Antiquities of Somersetshire *(1835–39).*

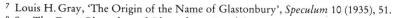

7 Louis H. Gray, 'The Origin of the Name of Glastonbury', *Speculum* 10 (1935), 51.
8 See *The Great Chartulary of Glastonbury*, 3.ccxlvi.

But what manner of death King Arthur himself died, it is doubtfull, and that which they report seems meerly fabulous, namely that he was carried away in a barge from a bridge called Pomperles, neare the said Glassenbury, and so conveyed by unknown persons (or by the Ladie of the Lake) with promise to bring him back againe one day: upon which it seemes the foolish people grounded their vaine saying (King Arthur comes againe).

Most modern readers think of Pomparles and Caliburn/ Excalibur in terms of the epic gesture of the dying king, so powerfully evoked in Tennyson's *Idylls of the King*:

> Thou therefore take my brand Excalibur,
> Which was my pride: for thou rememberest how
> In those old days, one summer noon, an arm
> Rose up from out the bosom of the lake
> Clothed in white samite, mystic, wonderful,
> Holding the sword – and how I row'd across
> And took it, and have worn it, like a king;
> And, wheresoever I am sung or told
> In aftertime, this also shall be known:
> But now delay not: take Excalibur,
> And fling him far into the middle mere …

In no other area of Arthurian romance, then, is there such a striking contrast between the imagined and the 'real'. Centuries of irrigation work have reduced the River Brue to a small and often sluggish stream which is crossed by a paved road and a perfectly undistinguished bridge. At Pomparles, more than at any other single spot, we must be reminded that Avalon is an act of the imagination, that modern Glastonbury is only the casement opening to magical transformations, whose source must come from within the quester himself. 'There was much mud there,' we learn in *A Glastonbury Romance*

and several extraneous objects carrying little association with Excalibur, rested half-buried in this mud, while a pathetically small stream of tawny-coloured water struggled with weakened impetus to deliver itself of such degrading obstacles. John's eyes [and John is the mocker of the whole Arthurian/Glastonbury myth] fell eventually upon a dead cat whose distended belly, almost devoid of fur, presented itself, together with two paws and a shapeless head that was one desperate grin of despair, to the mockery of the sunshine … [Suddenly] he … distinctly saw … literally shearing the sun-lit air with a whiteness like milk, like snow, like birch-bark, like maiden's flesh … an object, resembling a sword, falling into the mud of the river! When it struck the mud it disappeared …

Bedivere throws Arthur's sword Excalibur into the lake: miniature from a fourteenth-century manuscript. BL, MS Addit. 10294, fol.94.

Glastonbury: a sleepy market town whose sheep now provide material for coats instead of parchment for manuscripts. Like

Bethlehem, least of cities among the tribes of Judah, so too this most unlikely of places can still lead us to the land of Avalon, of high adventure, romance and prophecy. Even at the end of the twentieth century, the monastery long since gone, the meres drained, the suburbs spreading, the words of the tenth-century description have a haunting ring:

> There was within the realm of King Aethelstan a certain royal island known locally from ancient times as Glastonbury. It spread wide with numerous inlets, surrounded by lakes, full of fish and by rivers, suitable for human use and what is more important, endowed by God with sacred gifts. In that place at God's command the first neophytes of the Catholic law discovered an ancient church built by no human skill . . .[9]

That ancient church is an inner church, still intact, still beckoning, still promising adventure to those who pay heed to its call. As Powys so confidently assures us:

> The builders of Stonehenge have perished; but there are those who worship its stones still. The builders of Glastonbury have perished; but there are people, yet living among us, whose eyes have seen the Grail.

---

[9] This is found in the *Life* of Dunstan by 'B'.

PART THREE

AFTER THE FALL

Nineteenth-century watercolour view of the interior of the Lady Chapel by Rev. D. T. Powell. BL, MS Addit. 17463, fol.134.

View of west end of nave by Rev. D. T. Powell. BL, MS Addit. 17463, fol.132v–133.

9

Antiquaries and Archaeologists

John Leland is an extraordinary witness to the latter-day fortunes of Glastonbury Abbey, since he records his impressions both before and after Henry VIII's dissolution of the English monasteries. On his visit in 1533 Leland is ecstatic in his praises of the library and of Abbot Whiting, yet in 1542 he can give a curiously dispassionate account of the town, not even casting a nostalgic glance at the disbanded community and disintegrating buildings:

> There is a market kept in Glessenbyry every weke on the Wensday. Ther be 2 paroche chirchis yn Glessenbyri, S. John Baptiste on the north side of the principal streat of the toune. This is a vary fair and lightsum chirch: and the est part of it is very elegant and isled.

Elsewhere in his notebooks Leland describes the monuments and inscriptions which were formerly found in the interior of the monastic church: tombs and epitaphs of famous knights and powerful abbots, Peter Lightfoot's impressive mechanical clock, and most conspicuously:

> In Presbytero
> Edmundus Senior in bor. parte.
> Edmundus Irenside in merid. parte.
> Arcturus in medio.

Leland's offhand, almost cavalier, attitude to the sudden and violent destruction of Glastonbury contrasts remarkably with the shocked, but self-justifyingly protestant, response of the magus John Dee to the ruins in the years just after the Dissolution:

> O Glastonbury, Glastonbury: The Threasory of the Carcasses of so famous, and so many rare Persons ... How Lamentable, is thy case, now? How hath Hypocrisie and Pride, wrought thy Desolation? Though I omit [here] the names of very many other, both excellent holy Men, and Mighty Princes (whose Carcasses are committed to thy Custody,) yet that Apostlelike

Ioseph, That Triumphant BRYTISH ARTHUR, And now, this Peaceable, and Prouident SAXON, King Edgar, do force me, with a certayn sorrowfull Reuerence, here, to Celebrate thy Memory.[1]

To the next generation Glastonbury became almost a *memento mori*, a sad but romantic reminder that even the most noble and durable of monuments must at last fall. Michael Drayton's comprehensive topographical poem, the *Poly-Olbion* (completed in 1622), powerfully captures this feeling of wistful nostalgia:

> O three times famous Ile, where is that place that might
> Be with thy self compar'd for glorie and delight,
> Whilst *Glastenbury* stood? exalted to that pride
> Whose Monasterie seem'd all other to deride?
> O who thy ruine sees, whom wonder doth not fill
> With our great fathers pompe, devotion, and their skill?
> … What? Did so many kings do honor to that place,
> For Avarice at last so vilely to deface?
> For rev'rence, to that seat which hath ascribed beene,
> Trees yet in winter bloome, and beare their Summers greene.[2]

The actual process of natural decay from Drayton's time up to the twentieth century has been considerably assisted by human agency. After his father's death in 1547, King Edward VI granted the ruins and considerable grounds – valuables removed, roofs stripped of lead, dressed stones hauled away – to Edward Seymour, Duke of Somerset, who brought over a colony of Protestant Dutch weavers and established them on the site c.1550. When the Duke of Somerset was attainted in 1551, the property reverted to the Crown, but the colony struggled on. Within the monastery enclosure itself the Dutch built two dye houses, a brew house and a bake house. Ultimately they were naturalized and by incorporation became an English guild. After Mary Tudor ascended to the throne in 1553, however, the period of toleration ended and the Dutch fled to Frankfurt, although the tradition of cloth trade which they had established did continue in a minor way in the area for a number of generations.

During Mary's brief reign of five years four of the former monks – John Phagon, John Neot, William Athelwold and William Kentwyne – petitioned for a restoration of the monastery:

---

[1] *General and Rare Memorials Pertaining to The Perfect Arte of Navigation* (1577; rpt. Amsterdam, 1968), p.56. Julian Roberts, Keeper of Printed Books, Bodleian Library, Oxford, first pointed this allusion out to me.

[2] *The Poly-Olbion. A chorographical Description of Great Britain*, in J. William Hebel *et al.*, eds., *The Works of Michael Drayton*, 5 vols. (Oxford, 1961), 4.56.

... if there have been any flagitiouse deed since the creation of the world punyshed with the plague of God, in our opinion the overthrow of Glassenbury may be compared to the same, not surrendred as other, but extorted, the Abbot preostly putt to dethe. ... Wee aske nothing in gift to the foundation, but only the house and scite, the residue for the accustomed rent, in that with our labour and husbandrye we may live here a few of us in our religious habbitts, till the charitie of good people may suffice a greater number.[3]

The death of Queen Mary, of course, put an end to any of these plans for a return to the old monasticism. In June 1559, the new queen, Elizabeth I – a Protestant like her father – granted the site to Sir Peter Carew and it thereafter remained in private hands up to the beginning of the twentieth century. The time for Melkin's prophecy of renewal and miracle to be fulfilled, it appears, was not ripe.

Over the generations the ruins served as a quarry, providing dressed stones to be used in the construction of cottages and even roadways. During the reign of Queen Anne the remaining fragments of the refectory were at last demolished and at some time prior to 1710 the masonry of the vault beneath it was used in the building of a Market Hall. By the early eighteenth century, then, when the antiquary Samuel Gale saw the 'bare ruined quires', much of the original fabric had disappeared:

Upon the Dissolution in 1540, this noble Monastery fell to decay, nothing being now left but vast Ruins, discovering its former Grandeur. Of the great Church of the Abbey there remains yet standing one side Wall of the West Nave, one Arch of the North, and about three Arches of the South Cross or *Transeptum*, and two great Pillars of the Arch that supported the East side of the great square Tower in the middle of the Fabrick. Both the Walls and the side Isles by the Choir remain, containing eight Windows in each; and the Wall at the East end for about three Foot high, is yet seen above the Rubbish. A little Westward from the great Church stands the Chapel of St *Joseph of Arimathea*, which hath somewhat better escaped. The Fabrick being still entire, excepting the Roof, and the great Arch, which seperated the Chapel from the spatious Portico that led to it, which are broke down, as well as the Pavement, quite into the Vault underneath. 'Tis an Oblong curiously wrought and painted after the *Gothick* Style; at each Angle was a Tower, terminating in a lofty Pyramid of Stone, having a Staircase within. One of them is fallen down as far as the Roof of the Chapel.[4]

[3] Quoted by T.B.Snow, 'Glastonbury', *The Downside Review* 9 (1890), 203. For other references to the petition see *The Victoria County History of Somerset* 2.96.
[4] Quoted by Browne Willis, *A history of the mitred parliamentary Abbies* ..., 2 vols. (London, 1718–19), 2.197–98.

Not long afterwards, even St Joseph's Chapel went. As William Stukeley sadly laments in his *Itinerary* of 1723:

> within a lustrum of years, a presbyterian tenant has made more barbarous havock there, than has been since the Dissolution; for every week a pillar, a buttress, a window-jamb, or a angle of fine hewn stone, is sold to the best bidder: whilst I was there they were excoriating St. Joseph's chapel for that purpose, and the squared stones were laid up by lots in the abbot's kitchen: the rest goes to paving yards and stalls for cattle, or the highway. I observed frequent instances of the townsmen being generally afraid to make such purchase, as thinking an unlucky fate attends the family where these materials are used; and they told me many stories and particular instances of it: others, that are but half religious, will venture to build stables and outhouses therewith, but by no means any part of the dwelling-house.[5]

Stukeley's description of St Mary's Chapel is even more poignant: 'the roof beat down by violence, and a sorry wooden one in its place, thatched with stubble to make it serve as a stable: the manger lies upon the altar and niche where they put the holy water.'

By the time Stukeley arrived, the abbot's lodging had recently been demolished and Stukeley had to content himself with a drawing of it made by his friend Mr Strachey. Charles Eyston, who wrote a history of the monastery under the encouragement of the antiquary Thomas Hearne, did arrive just in time to record a description of this building:

> Some part of it was standing when I first went to Glastonbury in September 1712 ... It stood ... south of the great hall, and the main of the Building ran North and South. The front of it was towards the West, and was built almost in the Form of a Great Roman E, only at the North and South End of it, it jutted out some yards at each End. It was only three Stories high, and, as near as I can remember, had ten large Stone Windows on each Floor in the Front. To come into this Apartment you mounted half a dozen or more handsome Stone Steps, which let you into several Stately Rooms, which, for the most part, were all wainscotted with Oak, the Ceilings as well as the Sides of the rooms. In divers Pannels of the Wainscot ... there were neatly carved the Arms of England, quarterly France and England, and the Coat of Arms of the Abbey, which was Vert, a cross, Bottone Argent; in the first quarter our Blessed Lady, with our Saviour in her right arm and a Scepter in her left, all Or, being the Coat of Arms, that was born by our famous Brittish King Arthur ... Up one Pair of Stairs at the

[5] *Itinerarium Curiosum: Or, an Account of the Antiquities, and Remarkable Curiosities in Nature or Art, Observed in Travels Through Great Britain* (London, 1776), p. 152.

Southeastern end of the Building, stood, as is, I was told, the Abbat's Bedchamber. It was, as neer as I can guess, about eighteen foot in Length, and about fourteen in Breadth. It had in it an old Bedstead without Tester or Posts, was boarded at Bottom, and had a Board nailed shelving at the Head. This Bedstead, according to the Tradition of the Place, was the same that Abbat Whiting laid on, and I was desired to observe it as a Curiosity. This Apartment was much out of Repair, when I saw it. It rained in in many Places, by the Roof's being faulty in many Places. ... The windows were much broken, and some of them were unglazed. I inquired how it came to lay so neglected, and was answered, that it laid for some Years empty, no body caring to live there, it having been observed, that never any body, that had dwelt there, had ever thrived. Nay, I was then and there told, That the Inclosure there had never continued in one Family thirty Years together, since the Abbey was dissolved. To this Apartment belonged a Garden and two Stables, one for the Abbot's Saddle Naggs and Geldings, and the other for Mules and Horses for his Horse Litter.[6]

When the abbot's hall did at last come down, many of the stones were used in the construction of a still extant building on Magdalene Street.

The only building to survive intact up to the eighteenth century was the abbot's kitchen, which owes its survival in part to the fact that it served as a Quaker meeting house for many years. It is more or less the same now, too, as it was when Stukeley wrote admiringly about it:

a judicious piece of architecture: it is formed from an octagon included in a square; four fire-places fill the four angles, having chimneys over them: in the flat part of the roof, between these, rises the arched octagonal pyramid, crowned with a double lantern, one within another: there are eight curved ribs within, which support this vault, and eight funnels for letting out the steam through windows; within which, in a lesser pyramid, hung the bell to call the poor people to the adjacent almery, whose ruins are on the north side of the kitchen: the stones of the pyramid are all cut slaunting with the same bevil to throw off the rain. They have a report in the town, that king Henry VIII, quarrelling with the abbot, threatened to fire his kitchen: to which he returned answer, That he would build such a one as all the timber in his forest should not burn.[7]

The last period of real destruction occurred at the end of the eighteenth and beginning of the nineteenth century during the tenancy of another Puritan, one John Down, mayor of Glastonbury and a local brickmaker, who used gunpowder to dislodge stones and turn the site into a quarry. The essential

[6] *The History and Antiquities of Glastonbury* (Oxford, 1722), pp. 73–75.
[7] *Itinerarium Curiosum*, p. 152.

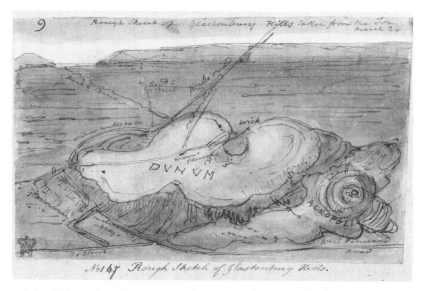

John Skinner's early nineteenth-century drawing of Glastonbury as a Roman fort. BL, MS 33681, fol.238.

structure was so formidable, however, that even this assault could not fully level it. Fortunately, subsequent owners – beginning with John Fry Reeves in 1825 – showed themselves more sympathetic to the ruins, more antiquarian and less utilitarian in their orientation, although in 1882, after the passage of the first Ancient Monuments Preservation Act, the then owner is said to have retorted to criticism about his neglect of the buildings: 'Well, they are ruins now, and if they fall down they will be ruins still, won't they? What do you want more?' Public opinion, too, began to change and this was a factor encouraging preservation. During the nineteenth century there was a renewal of interest in all things medieval: 'gothic' was no longer a term of opprobrium. On the literary and artistic side came the great flowering of chivalric and specifically Arthurian works. Later in the century, for example, when Alfred, Lord Tennyson, came to describe Glastonbury in his Arthuriad as the final destination of the Holy Grail, it is no wonder that his readers – including Gerard Manley Hopkins – would direct themselves to the ruined abbey and pause in reverent wonder.

On a more practical level, the nineteenth century saw the first serious historical/archaeological surveys. In 1826 Richard Warner published a major study, *A History of the Abbey of Glaston*, remarkable for the comprehensive use of source material as well as for the copiousness and elegance of the illustrations. Later in the century, in 1866, Robert Willis wrote *An Architectural History of Glastonbury Abbey*. Willis was a superb scholar with a detailed knowledge of ecclesiastical sites

Glastonbury Abbey from sepia print, c.1860.

and his book, which remains an indispensible aid, made great strides in drawing together the evidence of the medieval texts and linking it with the specific remains.

The final rescue of the site from the vagaries of private ownership occurred in 1907 when Stanley Austin let it be known that he would put the property up for auction on 6 June, 1907. As in all aspects of Glastonbury history there were some dramatic elements and a certain number of complications. The successful bidder on the great day was Ernest Jardine, a wealthy industrialist, who obtained the site for £30,000. His chief opponent was an equally prosperous American woman who – as subsequent tradition has it – wished to establish a 'School of Chivalry' at Glastonbury and who was thwarted in her plans only because she missed a train connection en route to the auction. Be this as it may, Jardine himself was acting as a holding agent for the Church of England and by 1908 Dr George Kennion, bishop of Bath and Wells, had raised sufficient funds to buy the site from Jardine and ownership was henceforth vested in the Bath and Wells Diocesan Trust.

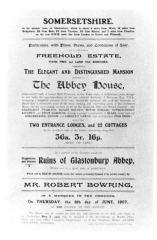

Catalogue announcing sale of Abbey House and ruins in its grounds.

Their authority secure, the trustees almost immediately approved the appointment of a professional to oversee excavation. The choice fell upon Frederick Bligh Bond, a practicing Bristol architect and expert on ecclesiastical architecture, who was just completing a book on roodscreens and roodlofts. Bond had a passion for Glastonbury and immediately got to work. His digs, extending over a decade, brought to light quantities of fascinating remains and led to valuable conclusions: he located the two western towers, the great north porch, the form of the transepts and much of the layout of the monastic buildings. Ultimately he published ten detailed reports in the *Proceedings of the Somerset Archaeological and Natural History Society*.[8] Bond's own chief interest centred on the Edgar Chapel, added by Abbot Beere to the end of the church, east of the High Altar. By Bond's calculations, his discovery of the remains of this chapel with apse brought the length of the whole church to approximately 594 feet (an internal measurement of 581 feet) and made it therefore the longest church in England.

By Bond's reckoning there was an occult significance to the length of the building and the manner in which it aligned with other aspects of the whole site. As Bond saw it, the great medieval ecclesiastical structures, of which Glastonbury was England's most spectacular example, were designed in terms of the science of gematria – that is, there was an overriding principle of geometrical and numerical perfection. The tran-

[8] Bond also published *An Architectural Handbook of Glastonbury Abbey* in 1909; this has been re-issued by Research Into Lost Knowledge Organization (1981).

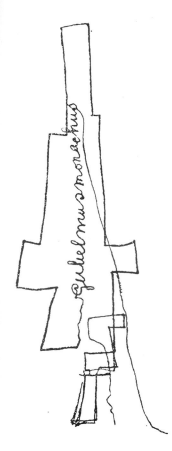

The plan of the abbey church with the Edgar chapel to the east, as revealed to Bligh Bond by the monks through automatic writing.

scendent plan in the construction of the church was the reproduction of the form of the rhombus of two equilateral triangles.

Like his more celebrated contemporaries, such as W. B. Yeats, moreover, Bond believed in a kind of universal mind, similar to the collective unconscious about to be popularized by C. G. Jung. This *spiritus mundi*, Bond speculated, could occasionally be tapped and certain individuals could thus break through the barriers of time and space. His own spirit guides, according to *The Gate of Remembrance* (first published in 1918) were the medieval monks themselves. In particular, he was led by Johannes Bryant (1497–1533) – 'a simple child of nature', not really suited for his monastic profession:

> He ever loved the woods and the pleasant places which lie without our house. It was good, for he learnt in the temple of nature much that he would never hear in choro. His herte was of the country and he heard it calling without the walls and the Abbot winked at it for he knew full well that it was good for him. He went a-fishing, did Johannes, and tarried oft in lanes to listen to the birds and to watch the shadows lengthening over all the woods of Mere.[9]

Johannes, in fact, bears many resemblances to an actual Glastonbury monk of his supposed period, John Neot, a close friend of Robert Joseph, the famous literary monk of Evesham, about whom David Knowles has written most engagingly (subsequently, it should be noted, to the publication of Bond's

Bligh Bond's view from the choir, showing his conjectural reconstruction of the nave.

[9] *The Gate of Remembrance*, 4th edn. (Oxford, 1921), p. 86.

book). In one surviving letter, for example, Robert Joseph sends the following exhortation to young Neot:

> See, the air is mild, and the breeze light from the west; the thickets ring with bird song and are merry with the sight and scent of blossom. Up then! Drop Scotus, take up your bowls and be off to the green; you will bring back a bushel of health as well as a sixpence or two. If you don't feel like bowls, go fishing.[10]

Not surprisingly, Johannes' charm did not make *The Gate of Remembrance* and its thesis any more palatable to the orthodox establishment. In particular, the Dean of Wells, Joseph Armitage Robinson – himself a considerable scholar and the man who would subsequently write the single most authoritative book on Glastonbury and the Arthurian legends – was appalled. For his part, Bond was unwilling to compromise with his detractors: on the contrary, he became more and more high-handed in his stance and possessive of the site as criticism mounted. His growing paranoia was accompanied by a slackening of rigour in his use of up-to-date archaeological techniques. By the early 1920s the situation was intolerable and resolved itself only with Bond's dismissal in 1922 – a blow from which he never fully recovered.[11]

Subsequent excavations were carried on under the auspices of a variety of archaeologists, and in the 1950s Dr C. A. Ralegh Radford took over.[12] As it happens, Radford had first visited Glastonbury as a boy and had met Bond *in situ*. By his own testimony, too, from 1925 onwards he visited the site every year that excavations were in progress. Although his own digs took place only between 1951 and 1964, then, his intimate association with the ruins stretches over the whole period that it has been professionally excavated. Radford's full reports have not yet been issued, but in his preliminary publications he has given a general outline of his findings.[13] In his analysis of the earliest church, in particular, Radford has taken a somewhat unorthodox, even radical, stance. He is willing, for example, to postulate the existence of a Christian community at Glastonbury in Celtic times and he considers this community in the context of the whole of the Island of Avalon. He also speculates that the substantial earthen bank just past Edgarley

10 See *Bare Ruined Choirs*, p. 24.
11 On Bond see the biography by William W. Kenawall, *The Quest at Glastonbury* (New York, 1962); also Marshall McKusick, 'Psychic Archaeology: Theory, Method and Mythology', *Journal of Field Archaeology* 9 (1982), 101–06.
12 For full references to the excavations of the site see M. Aston and R. Leech, *Historic Towns in Somerset* (Bristol, 1977), pp. 57–62.
13 'Glastonbury Abbey before 1184: Interim Report on the Excavations, 1908–64', *Medieval Art and Architecture at Wells and Glastonbury* (British Archaeological Association, 1981), pp. 110–134.

William Camden's rendering of the lettering on the leaden cross. Found on p. 166 of the 1607 edition of the Britannia.

Twelfth-century tympanum on north door of St Mary's church at Stoke-sub-Hamdon, about one mile from Montacute. The lettering identifying 'Sagitarius' is almost identical to that on the leaden cross.

on the Shepton Mallet road, known locally as Ponter's Ball, forms the remains of an even earlier enclosure, marking the limits of a pagan Celtic sanctuary.

Much of Radford's field work has concentrated on the ancient cemetery, within which he has found the traces of post holes; from these he has postulated the existence of at least four wattled oratories dating from the Celtic period. By Radford's calculations there were also two large hypogea which may well have housed the remains later attributed to St Indract and St Patrick. Within the cemetery enclosure Radford also uncovered the foundation of the two famous pyramids described by William of Malmesbury, between which King Arthur was supposedly buried. Examining this specific area, Radford found evidence of a large irregular hole, at the bottom of which could be seen the remnants of several very ancient slab-lined graves, one in a position of particular prominence. In sum, Radford is willing to concede that

> The foundation of the Christian sanctuary at Glastonbury can be traced back into the period of British rule before the Saxon conquest of Somerset in the middle of the seventh century. Christian inscriptions in Wales show that for laymen, mainly chieftains, burial within the monastic cemeteries gradually replaced the older use of small family burial grounds in the course of the sixth century. A man such as Arthur, if resident in mid-Somerset in the sixth century, would probably have been buried at Glastonbury, and a warrior of his fame might be expected to be found buried alongside the mausoleum of the saint. By analogy with custom in other British lands, one would expect his tomb to have been marked by a monolith recording in Latin his name and patronymic and possibly with a simple epitaph. The raising of the level in the tenth century would have buried this monolith even if it were not removed. It is at this stage that the replacement of the monolith by the leaden cross would be appropriate, and the lettering of the cross as engraved by Camden is more likely to be of the tenth than of the late twelfth century.[14]

[14] See also *Avalonian Quest*, pp. 68–73. Other scholars, nevertheless, have brought forward strong arguments for assigning the cross itself to the twelfth century. For example, in 'King Arthur's Leaden Cross' (*Somerset and Dorset Notes and Queries* 31 [1984], 366–67) Stephen Morland observes that the epithet 'inclitus' is not known to have been applied to Arthur until after Geoffrey of Monmouth started his vogue for Arthurian matters. Aelred Watkin has pointed out, moreover, that there is late twelfth-century carving over the doorway of the church in Stoke-sub-Hamdon whose lettering is identical in form to that found on the cross. Although the actual cross has long since disappeared, there have been various rumours over the years concerning its whereabouts. The last fully reliable account, however, is found in a late seventeenth-century manuscript – Bodleian Rawlinson B.416A, fol. 10v – where it is reported that 'the plate of lead in the underside of the cover of his [Arthur's] coffin at the dissolution of the Abbey happened to be preserved and was within this 100 years in the Reverstry of the parish church of St Johns in Glaston but is now lost.'

View of the exterior of the Lady Chapel by Rev. D. T. Powell. BL, MS Addit. 17463, fol.135.

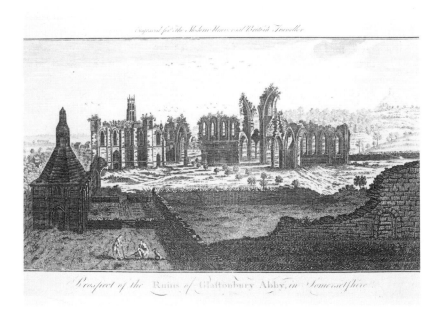

Engraving of the ruins. From The Modern Universal British Traveller *(London, 1779).*

We have come, so it seems, full circle from the contemptuous dismissal of all early Glastonbury history as monkish imposture by the more rigorous of the nineteenth-century historians. Radford's view clearly stands as a kind of antithesis to Ferdinand Lot's shrugging appellation of Glastonbury Abbey as nothing more than a medieval *officine de faux*.

EPILOGUE

I

No account of Glastonbury Abbey can be fully satisfactory without at least a passing reference to the flowering thorn or to the tradition that Our Lord himself came to Glastonbury.

Towards the end of the fifteenth century Abbot Richard Beere adopted a new shield for himself and for the monastery: 'a green cross raguly with blood drops and two cruets'. In this device we have most obviously a pictorial allusion to the Holy Blood which Joseph of Arimathea caught from the wounds of the crucified Christ and which he subsequently brought to England. Why, however, is the cross green and why is it sprouting new shoots? Beere's reference here, in fact, may constitute one of the first known allusions to what has become Glastonbury's most popular relic: the Holy Thorn, shoots of which still thrive at Glastonbury itself and throughout the English-speaking world.

Beere's shield as shown in fifteenth-century glass at St John's, Glastonbury.

The early sixteenth-century *Lyfe* of St Joseph specifically mentions this miraculous freak of nature, although it does not in fact associate the thorn with Joseph's mission:

> Thre hawthornes also, that groweth in Werall
> Do burge and bere grene leaves at Christmas
> As fresshe as other in May, whan the nihtyngale
> Wrestes out her notes musycall as pure as glas;
> Of all wodes and forestes she is the chefe chauntres.

In the 1530s King Henry VIII's agent, the sceptical Dr Layton, refers to the thorn in one of his letters concerning the contents of monastic houses:

> By this bringer my servant I send you reliquaries; first, two flowers wrapped in white and black sarcenet that on Christmas eve, *hora ipsa qua Christus natus fuerat*, will spring, and burgeon, and bare blossoms ... Ye shall also receive a bag of relics, wherein ye shall see strange things ... as God's coat ...[1]

When William Turner, Dean of Wells, 1551–54, 1560–68,

---

[1] Quoted in G.H. Cook, *Letters to Cromwell and others on the Suppression of the Monasteries* (London, 1969), pp.39–40.

A page from the Herbal of William Turner, Dean of Wells. Ten lines from the bottom he refers to the Glastonbury thorn.

composed his comprehensive *Herbal* he made the following note in his chapter 'Of Oxyacantha':

> In Summerset shyre about six myles from Welles in the parke of Gassenberry there is an hawthorne which is grene all the wynter as all they that dwell there about do stedfastly holde.

During the reign of Queen Elizabeth a rabid Puritan tried to chop down the thorn, which he apparently viewed as a heathen icon. On his first try, his axe was miraculously deflected from the tree and cut into his leg; on the second attempt, a chip flew into his eye and partially blinded him. Its assailant suitably punished for his blasphemy, the thorn continued to bear witness to its miraculous origin and survived into the seventeenth century, when it was finally hacked down by a Roundhead soldier. Fortunately, numerous shoots had been taken from the original thorn and these were successfully propagated at Glastonbury and elsewhere.

At some point after the Dissolution the story of the Holy Thorn as we now know it evolved, and it was asserted that Joseph fashioned himself a staff from a flowering hawthorn before he left the Holy Land on his journey west.[2] This staff he carried with him as he travelled to France and thence to North Wales. Finally he crossed the sea moors by ship and, exhausted from travel, disembarked on the side of a hill near to his final destination at the Isle of Avalon. At this location, where he and his companions showed themselves to be 'weary all', he thrust his staff into the ground and it miraculously rooted. Ever since, first the staff and then its descendants have produced flowers on Christmas Day in memory of Our Lord's birth and of St Joseph's mission to the English.

When King Charles I was given a sprig of the thorn he cannily observed that the Holy Thorn appeared to follow the Old Style Calendar – retained in Protestant England even after Pope Gregory XIII's calendarial reform of 1582. In 1752 when at last the English year was brought into line with European practice and eleven days dropped, the Thorn was consulted somewhat in the manner of an oracle. In January 1753, the *Somerset Evening Post* reports, 'A vast concourse of people attended the noted Thorn on Christmas Day, New Style, but to their great disappointment there was no appearance of its blowing, which made them watch it narrowly the 6th January, the Christmas Day, Old Style, when it blowed as usual.' And so it has continued faithfully to do up to modern times, although especially mild weather can occasionally coax an earlier blossom.

[2] As early as 1677 Dr Plot refers to the tradition that Joseph of Arimathea brought the Holy Thorn to Glastonbury. In 1715 Eyston gives the story in the form it is still generally preserved: his source was a local innkeeper.

According to the nineteenth-century antiquary John Clark, the stump of the earlier tree on the eastern eminence of the hill could be seen up to the mid-eighteenth century. Clark himself placed a memorial stone with the inscription I A XXXI [in memory of Joseph of Arimathea's arrival at Glastonbury] at what he considered to be the correct site. A much earlier engraving by Wenceslaus Hollar, however, seems to indicate that the original thorn was planted just to the right of the present Roman Way about half a mile from the town, and it is here that a commemorative shoot was officially planted in the autumn of 1985.

Even if the scientifically minded modern sceptic can point out that the thorn is a perfectly well attested Levantine species – it is designated *Cratagus Oxyacantha Praecox* – presumably brought home by a medieval pilgrim, the image of the winter blossoming of the Holy Thorn is a particularly resonant symbol, one which has appealed to generations of pilgrims and writers alike. The Restoration writer Charles Sedley gallantly suggests that his Cornelia 'Blooms in the winter of her days, / Like Glastonbury Thorn.' In his Hymn 32, the eighteenth-century poet Christopher Smart observes with wonder that 'Winter blossoms burst untimely / On the blest Mosaic thorn'. Jonathan Swift, on the other hand, thunders out that for Ireland to flourish would 'be against every Law of Nature and Reason; like the Thorn at Glassenbury, that blossoms in the Midst of Winter.' Tennyson's *Idylls of the King* is especially lyrical:

> This [the Grail] ... the good saint
> Arimathean Joseph, journeying brought
> To Glastonbury, where the winter thorn
> Blossoms at Christmas, mindful of our Lord.

Marie-Louise von Franz, the most important of the disciples of the pioneering psychoanalyst C. G. Jung, believes that there is a psychological explanation for the power of this image in its Arthurian/Glastonbury context. She notes that in the mythology of ancient Greece the hawthorn served as a decoration on the bride's nuptial bed and the altars of Hymen were lit by torches made of its wood. In European culture the hawthorn has traditionally been used to exorcise witches and other evil spirits. This salutary aspect of the hawthorn in its Christmas flowering seems to suggest that love can overcome magic, that 'Merlin's eternal conjunction with Morgana is thus an image of the hierosgamous, the supreme union of opposites.'[3]

The modern custom of sending a sprig of the flowering

---

[3] See 'Antichrist or Merlin: A Problem Inherited from the Middle Ages' in James Carley, ed., 'The Medieval and the Modern', *Book Forum* 5.2 (1980), 234–43, at 240.

thorn to the reigning monarch at Christmas, still faithfully observed each year, originated in 1929 during the reign of George V.[4]

II

Even in the middle ages, there are some hints of a tradition that Jesus himself came to Glastonbury. The earliest *Life* of St Dunstan (c.1000) states that the Old Church was built by no human agency and that it was dedicated by Our Lord himself to the memory of his Virgin Mother. In the twelfth century William of Malmesbury attests that when St David attempted to rededicate the church in the sixth century, he was visited by Jesus in a dream and told that this act would be a profanity since Jesus himself had already performed the dedication. Remarkable as they are, nevertheless, these medieval stories seem to indicate a belief that Jesus visited Glastonbury in a spiritual rather than in an earthly form. At some much later point, long after the Dissolution, another set of legends came into being, elaborating and transforming the medieval traditions. The rich merchant Joseph of Arimathea, so this line of reasoning affirms, came to England. Why? Could it be because he had business dealings in Britain, which was famous throughout the ancient world for its tin. Might Joseph have not been an importer of British tin to the Holy Land? And why did Joseph take such an interest in Jesus in any case? Might he not have been a relation? What, moreover, did Jesus do during the hidden years before his public mission began? Could he not have travelled to Britain with his uncle? Sabine Baring-Gould, the nineteenth-century collector of English oral traditions concerning the saints, tells us that

> Another Cornish story is to the effect that Joseph of Arimathea came in a boat to Cornwall and brought the child Jesus with him, and the latter taught him how to extract tin and purge it of its wolfram. When the tin is flashed then the tinner shouts 'Joseph was in the tin trade.'

William Blake seems to be dealing with similar traditions when he portrays 'Joseph of Arimathea Among the Rocks of Albion' and when he asks

> And did those feet in ancient time
> Walk upon England's mountains green?

William Blake: Joseph of Arimathea among the Rocks of Albion.

[4] Apparently James Montague, bishop of Bath and Wells, sent an annual gift of blossoms to Queen Anne, wife of James I.

184

And was the holy Lamb of God
On England's pleasant pastures seen?[5]

For many who in modern times make the annual pilgrimage to Glastonbury on the last Saturday in June, then, the green expanse of lawn and weathered stone offers much more than a nostalgic reminder of late medieval piety. The pilgrimage comes as a powerful affirmation of a living belief that this is indeed 'the holyest erthe', one of the cradles of Christianity in the West. For a variety of casual visitors to this annual celebration, too, the reaction must be the same as that of the worldly sophisticates who chanced upon the humble church in Oliver Goldsmith's 'Deserted Village': 'fools, who came to scoff, remain'd to pray.'

Annual pilgrimage, June 1985.

[5] For those who are tempted to make much of these lines, however, it is worth pointing out that in 'Milton' Blake also situates Calvary between South Molton Street and Stratford Place.

SOURCES OF ILLUSTRATIONS AND ACKNOWLEDGEMENTS

The author and publishers are grateful to be the following for providing photographs and for permission to reproduce the illustrations.

BBC Hulton Picture Library 23, 32, 51, 61, 69, 94, 124, 174, 179
Birmingham Museum and Art Gallery 91
Bodleian Library, Oxford 10, 115, 132, 134, 140, 155
British Library, London 3, 71, 118, 124, 153, 165, 168, 174, 179
British Museum. (Reproduced by courtesy of the Trustees) 18, 184
Giraudon xxviii
Longleat House, Warminster, Wiltshire. (Reproduced by permission of the Marquess of Bath) 137
Trinity College, Cambridge. (Reproduced by permission of the Master and Fellows) 21, 115, 126
National Galleries of Scotland 148
Redpath Communications vi, 26, 27, 28, 29, 30, 37, 42, 43, 60, 62, 63, 64, 68, 72, 75, 77, 107, 109, 111, 178, 181, 185
Royal Commission on the Historical Monuments of Englnad 86
Somerset Archaeological and Natural History Society 41
Stanbrook Abbey. (Reproduced by permission of the nuns) 130
Society of Antiquaries 34, 35, 113
The University of Victoria Archives, McPherson Library, University of Victoria viii
Wells Cathedral (By permission of the Dean and Chapter) 90, 137, 182

Title page illustrations: Glastonbury Tor, aerial photograph from Marilyn Bridges' *Markings: Aerial Views of Sacred Landscapes* (Phaidon, 1986)

Half title: Angel from north doorway of Lady Chapel

INDEX

(The index covers the main topics discussed in this book, but it is not comprehensive and does not include references to individual relics or books in the library, every location listed in charters, or various other *minutiae*.)

Reverendis.Dno.Dno.Willo.Wake Archiep.Cant &c &c Tab.votiua.

iophs chappel B. *The Abby Church.* C. *St Marys chappel* D. *Edgars chappel.* E. *The high Alta*